Dominican Sisters *of* Mary
Mother *of the* Eucharist

And

Mary's

Yes

Continues

RELIGIOUS VOCATIONS IN THE NEW MILLENNIUM

Published by Lumen Ecclesiae Press
  4101 East Joy Road
  Ann Arbor, Michigan 48105

Cover Artwork: *The Mystical Marriage of Saint Catherine,* Bartolomeo Neroni

General Editor: Sister Joseph Andrew Bogdanowicz, O.P.
Copy Editors: Claudia Volkman and Sara Rennekamp
Book Design Layout: Linda Kelly
Cover Design: Amy Beers
Copyright: Sally Wagner

ISBN 978-0-9982607-2-3 (soft cover)
  978-0-9982607-4-7 (hard cover)

First Printing
Printed in the United States of America

Dedication

In the evening of life, the Virgin of the Salve has come for 800 years to draw all faithful Dominican men and women under her mantle. In both the dawning and the evening of the writing of this book, the Dominican Sisters of Mary, Mother of the Eucharist wish to dedicate it to Mary, Mother of all vocations, under those protection the Sisters were able, by gift of their Dominican vocation, to consecrate all the days of their lives to Jesus through Mary.

Witness of God's Love

I'm delighted to recommend this dynamic work of the Dominican Sisters of Mary, Mother of the Eucharist to women in discernment of religious life as well as those who wish to better understand its theological roots through personal witness. This book portrays a healthy blend of theology along with personal testimony of various Dominican Sisters in their community. It seems especially important for any woman discerning the Dominican charism in particular to prayerfully read this book. It is unique of its kind and filled with the real–life joys and challenges of recognizing and living the call to religious life.

It's an inspiration to see women like these respond to God's invitation to witness His love for them and their love for Him to a world so desperate for love, desperate for God. They witness to Pope Francis' bidding to Religious to "wake up the world" and evangelize by their lives of joy, lived for Christ! They also are living proof that God is real, and they are staking their lives on this truth.

In thanksgiving for you, women who are living the call to religious life, as well as those reading this book in discernment of God's will for your lives, I pray God's blessings accompany you.

Your brother in Christ and in consecration to Him and His service,
His Excellency, Bishop Earl Boyea,
Bishop of the Diocese of Lansing, Michigan

Contents

Part 1: Foundations

i

Part 3: From the Heart of the Church

Foreword

"How did you know you were going to be a Sister?"

This is a question we often receive as women Religious from people in all walks of life. Indeed, a Religious vocation comes from a mysterious calling, an intimate encounter with the Lord in the depths of one's heart and soul. Vocational discernment occurs in His timing and in His ways; it is as unique as each soul He has created to be His own.

A young woman who enters Religious Life has not so much *decided* to be a Sister as prayerfully *discovered* the treasure of her vocation. Each person receives at his or her Baptism the promise of all the graces needed to journey securely through this life to Eternal Blessedness. Thus, the vocational discernment process is one of gradually unwrapping the gift God has given to discover what lies hidden. Not to be open to considering God's will for one's vocation would be akin to refusing to open a priceless gift and remaining content to admire the wrapping paper. But actively to seek God's will for one's life is to search for the pearl of great price or the treasure buried in the field (Mt. 13:44-46).

Ultimately, God desires happiness for all those He has made. Whatever one's vocation may be—whether married life, single life, priesthood, or consecrated life—it is the means through which one will find true and lasting happiness and peace in God. In his inaugural Mass as the Holy Father, Pope Emeritus Benedict XVI, referring to his predecessor Pope St. John Paul II's first homily as Pope, said:

> Are we not perhaps afraid to give up something significant, something unique, something that makes life so

beautiful? Do we not then risk ending up diminished and deprived of our freedom? And once again the Pope said: No! If we let Christ into our lives, we lose nothing, nothing, absolutely nothing of what makes life free, beautiful and great. ...Do not be afraid of Christ! He takes nothing away, and he gives you everything. When we give ourselves to him, we receive a hundredfold in return.

Once we have encountered Christ in such a way that we know we can completely trust Him, nothing else will fill our lives with purpose or joy except to follow wherever and however He might lead.

This discipleship will necessarily entail sacrifices and the Cross, since that is the way He Himself lived on earth. However, the reward He gives to us is His very self. If after encountering Christ as His disciple, one experiences a call to belong more radically to Him, He alone becomes enough for that soul. He alone can fill the deepest longing of the heart to whom He wills to espouse Himself.

This book, containing reflections and articles written by the Dominican Sisters of Mary, Mother of the Eucharist, seeks to answer the questions of those who are considering a Religious vocation for their own lives, as well as those who love and support someone considering the vocation of consecrated life. It is our hope that its pages will contain information and insights that will aid those of you who are wrestling with God's call for yourself or your loved ones. "Commit your way to the Lord; trust in Him, and He will act" (Ps. 37:5). If you are living your life in an authentic search for Christ each day, He will reveal Himself and His will for you, for He desires your happiness and the happiness of those you love, even more than you could ever desire it yourself!

Mother Assumpta Long, O.P.

Introduction

Growing up in a beautiful Catholic family, this very inquisitive child was always asking questions! I wanted to know everything—and I wanted to know it immediately. My dear parents continued to claim me as their child...even when my mind and mouth would never stop! But when I reached the tender age of five-and-a-half, they were finally able to share me with the Sisters as I began first grade in our St. Mary's Catholic School. It didn't take long for the Sisters to realize that this second Bogdanowicz daughter had a mouth that wouldn't stop. Though I was oftentimes corrected, I never lost my zeal to know truth, and questions never ceased captivating my thoughts. So, with the addition of "Sister" in my life, I had another reservoir in whom to entrust my questions.

Our family's evening dinners were replete with conversation trying to answer such questions as "Why this?" "What's that?" "Could you please explain...?" It wasn't uncommon that my questions would involve God and our Catholic religion, and when my parents might grow weary or their efforts did not succeed in an explanation I could own, they'd prompt me to "Ask Sister!" and believe me, I did! For in the first instant I saw her, everything about Sister had renewed my inquisitiveness—the habit, her daily schedule, how did she pray, what did she say to Jesus when she received Him in Holy Communion, and how many Sisters were there in the world anyway?

Twelve years later, I stood with my Catholic high school class and gladly accepted my signed diploma. My early mind had expanded with more penetrating questions over my entire Catholic education years and, though it was most difficult for my mother in particular, her second and only other daughter would be following her first one into the convent in August. The diploma was like a key I needed to possess; the real treasures I already had: my beautiful family, my Catholic Faith, and my acceptance letter to enter the Dominican Sisters in August! Finally, I thought, all my questions will be answered. If one Sister did not know something, at least one of the other one hundred would—after all, Dominicans are teachers! But the topic most burning in my heart at that time and for which I had become impatient concerned how I could best live the rest of my life as a consecrated spouse of Christ. Though none of my friends accompanied me into the convent or went to a seminary, I knew even then that I would do everything possible to help others follow God's particular will for them to find their way to Heaven. I wanted everyone to possess this Union, this Happiness.

Now, decades later, I find my heart filled with immense gratitude for all the years I have been able to work as a Vocation Director in my Community. If it is true that we are born for a particular purpose, this has to be it for me! I thrill when anyone finds his/her vocation, but my heart jumps spiritual leaps of joy when a young woman enters a convent or a young man finds his way to the priesthood! The Church needs wise and loving moms and dads...those living good lives as consecrated Religious just as much as those living good family lives!

While this task has been challenging and somewhat natural to me, it has certainly given me an abundance of joys and sorrows. Joys abound when young people are knowledgeable and open to the Holy Spirit's promptings. But a deep sorrow (which also morphs into an intense challenge) has been the fact that for decades now, young people have not known many Religious Sisters...if any. When a young woman comes to me and expresses a passionate desire to give God "more," I ask if she is aware of the Consecrated Life. Frequently, she thought it had ended with the death of St. Thérèse of the Child Jesus. Then she met me or my Sisters or other Religious women! How sad was her previous ignorance—an ignorance for which she bore no fault but, too often, does bear the consequences. If my time with this young woman is short, I will hug her and give her a card about our Vocational Discernment Retreats while encouraging her to make such a retreat and simply be open to God's beautiful will for her. I promise my prayers and my emailed responses.

Over the years it has become strikingly clearly that I grew up in truly great times—not perfect, but promising times. I ask myself how many families today gather each evening for dinner, conversation, and prayers together. Are children's questions being patiently answered and, as they grow into maturity, are their innate spiritual desires being understood and nourished? Are teens gifted with the exciting challenge to become and give their best? And should a young person experience a deep desire to "love more," would anyone be around to ardently listen to them and to assist with answers...or, at the very least, to suggest books from which their answers might be gleaned?

This last thought reveals a serious contemporary problem. Where are contemporary books that show the beauty of Religious Life? For young women, I often suggest reading the lives of the saints and other excellent Catholic writings. But to answer questions regarding the evangelical counsels, a personal presence is oftentimes necessary today, and too few Religious Sisters and priests are readily available or can be found in Catholic institutions. Therefore, the imminent need is to write and publish interesting and thought-worthy books that will answer the questions young people have about Religious vocations. But not only young people! I receive so many questions from parents and even from wonderful priests, who live their sacramental Ordination with great devotion but who have never known or been around Religious enough to understand the mysterious beauty of our total dedication to Christ.

To hold a book—the right book—is to hold a whole world of answers to burning questions and of possible dreams that the Holy Spirit just might bring into fruition in an open heart! A paraphrase of the great St. Augustine— whose Rule we Dominicans hear read in the refectory every week and by which we live—goes like this: "The Holy Scriptures are our letters from home" (Exposition of Psalm 90, Sermon 2). Trusting the wisdom of this great Doctor of the Church, such a sentiment fits nicely inside my heart, and I hope it does the same within yours. If so, this book—*And Mary's Yes Continues*—should find a home in your heart, as it was written by a variety of young women who left their homes to follow Christ and who wish to share their letters with you.

From our home to yours—whether you are a priest, a parent, a candidate, or a young and inquisitive child—my Sisters and I pray that something in this book will open your intellect and heart to a fuller embrace of God's astonishing challenges toward your unique holiness and holy completion!

I prayed for this book at the site in Siena where Catherine had an exchange of hearts with the Lord. In the words of Pope St. John Paul II, "Be not afraid to open your heart to Christ."

Sister Joseph Andrew Bogdanowicz, O.P.

Lord, Increase the Harvest

To see a consecrated woman is to see the love of God for His people, to see the Church; to remind myself once again, "Yes, God's love for us is superabundant." When I see a Sister, I think to myself: "Here is a young woman who has freely chosen to forego the good of husband and children. She has known in her life the love of Jesus Christ the Bridegroom." As a priest, my own vocation is strengthened.
—Fr. Benedict Croell, O.P., Vocations Director, Dominican Province of St. Joseph

Who incarnates the priesthood of God but his Blessed Mother? For in her "yes," the eternal Son is given the hands for offering sacrifice and the human heart that is now beating in loving unison with sinners. In her vows a consecrated woman echoes this fiat of Mary, and in so doing continues to incarnate the Mystical Body in a profound and priestly way. That is why priests—us "other Christs"—look to and draw so much strength from the consecration and the challenges of these "other Marys!"
—Fr. David Meconi, S.J., Associate Professor of Theological Studies at Saint Louis University and Augustinian Scholar

"Speak Lord for your servant is listening" (1 Sam. 3:10). Too often we ask God to speak to our hearts, but when He does, we tend to tremble and try to ignore Him. Mary's "yes" trusted that God would always walk with her; we see this same "yes" lived out in the lives of Sisters, who are relentless in their witness of joy, hope, and trust of and in Jesus Christ. Perhaps God is calling you or someone close to you to Religious Life. Take some time to read and reflect on the message of this book. Trust in Jesus and respond: "Speak Lord for your servant is listening."
—Rosemary C. Sullivan; Executive Director of National Conference of Diocesan Vocation Directors

The Church needs more Sisters because they bear witness that the love of God is real and fulfills the deepest desires of the human heart. They confound the wisdom of the world that says you can't be happy without sex, money, and total freedom from any constraint. By the smiles on their faces and their compassionate hearts, Sisters radiate God's love and show that their Bridegroom, Jesus, is truly present and active in the world.

—Dr. Mary Healy, author and Professor of Sacred Scripture at Sacred Heart Major Seminary

Sisters stay busy pursuing a life of perfection by responding well to the responsibilities of Religious Life. The pursuit of holiness involves a demanding prayer life and charity within Community and the freedom to serve, without the responsibilities of the married life. We need more Sisters today because the battle for souls is greater.

—Mother Mary Gabriel, S.S.E.W., Foundress and Superior General of the Sister Servants of the Eternal Word in Birmingham, AL

Other than God Himself, the world needs nothing more than men and women who live totally committed to Him. This radical response to God needs to be lived in every way of life. But in our day the beautiful witness of consecrated women is desperately needed. God is invisible, but His truth, goodness and beauty are made visible most clearly in the lives of those women who leave all to follow Him. The world longs to see the love of God manifested in the joy-filled eyes of women who live in union with Him. Today we need wonderful teachers, but even more, we need authentic witnesses of God's love and mercy. More than any other way of life, consecrated women are an icon of the Church, who is loved by her God and rejoices in His goodness. Their testimony is the good news that God did not send His Son into the world to condemn it, but that we might be saved through Him (see Jn. 3:17).

—Curtis A. Martin, founder and CEO of the Fellowship of Catholic University Students (FOCUS)

From World Youth Days to concerts, I have often had the opportunity to work with and meet Religious Sisters. Their grace-filled joy reminds us of the heavenly life we are all called to; by being a Bride of Christ, they show us what we all are made for! The visible witness of the habit and their life of order and prayer encourages us all to be visible signs of the God's love and mercy in the world! We truly depend on the prayers of Religious Sisters, and they remind us to keep our eyes fixed on Christ!
—Matt Maher, singer and songwriter

When John Cardinal O'Connor first met Mother Teresa, she looked into his eyes and said, "Give God permission." Isn't that each Christian's desire? That God allows us to be part of His plan of salvation is astounding. We are invited by St. Paul to "make up what is lacking in Christ's sufferings," and in the great mystery of the Church, Christ invites each of us to a unique role in the Mystical Body of Christ. Some bring Christ's love in a radical way through the evangelical counsels of poverty, chastity and obedience, to a world where many have been ravaged by the culture of death. God invites these souls to live a spousal union with Him on this side of Heaven. Pouring out His love as balm, they prolong His Incarnation as His hands and feet, ears and eyes. If God calls you to live out this love; if this is how He has created your heart, be not afraid to "give God permission." Love with freedom, joy, and reckless abandon. The Church not only needs these heroic souls, but in responding to this sublime invitation, they find fulfillment of the deepest desires of their hearts.
—Mother Agnes Mary, S.V., Superior General of the Sisters of Life

Part 1: Foundations

Chapter One

That Nagging Feeling...
Religious Vocations in the Third Millennium
—Sr. Joseph Andrew Bogdanowicz, O.P.

I've felt an inclination toward Religious Life since high school, but I did my best to try to bury that idea while I was away at college hoping that it might just go away so I could proceed with the "normal life" that my friends and family insisted should satisfy me. In an effort to find that satisfaction, I returned to school to study law... I don't think that I am suffering from any lack of courage, but I am lacking someplace to test that courage. I think my greatest fear is in saying no to what may be an invitation from God to come and see. I don't want to get down the road, into my forties or fifties and then begin to wonder "what if." What if I had accepted that invitation? Could spending my life for God in the service of others be that missing something which I can't quite find now? I really need to find out.

I smiled one cold November morning in 2001 upon opening my mail and reading the above words. Written by a twenty-seven-year-old practicing law in her father's firm in upstate New York, the letter reminded me strongly of the question posed almost two thousand years ago by the young man of the Gospel to Our Lord: what "more" could he do for God? (see Mt. 19:16–30). For within the hearts of all young people is the desire for greatness. Once a heart turns toward God, no one can guess the height and depth and breadth of its magnanimity.

As I continued reading this lawyer's letter, I began to chuckle aloud as she described a memorable exchange with her father. She had approached him to explain that she had found a relentless lover who had been pursuing her for quite some time. "A heavy date last night, eh?" questioned her solicitous but clever father as he studied his red-eyed daughter. Equal to the match, the young woman replied, "You can certainly say that, Dad, and he is not anyone you would suspect. But you need to know, Dad, that marrying him is going to necessitate for me a change of employment."[1]

This vocational letter was not atypical of the times. The beginning of the new millennium proved exciting for our then only three-year-old Community bursting with vocations, and for me as the Vocation Directress of this growing Community with many years' experience in that role. The growth of Communities like ours appeared to be turning back the tide of disappearing women Religious and decreasing priestly vocations. Pope St. John Paul II's call for the New Evangelization, his summons to "open wide the doors to Christ," and the energy sparked across the globe through each World Youth Day, inspired young people to plunge into an authentic search for their vocations, impelled by a burning desire to fulfill the Divine Will. There seemed to be no barriers of age, education, talents, or family background that could hold them back.

My own theory for this explosive renewal concerning Religious vocations was that the depletion of Religious and priests in the 1960s, 1970s, and 1980s had left immense voids in vitally important areas of both contemplative and apostolic Religious Life. The "springtime" predicted by Pope St. John Paul II, and largely planted and watered by his encouragement, had begun to fill these voids with priestly and Religious vocations whose narratives expanded the vocational categories of previous eras.[2]

While much of this graced spirit remains today, almost twenty years later, it can be hard–pressed by modern radical societal and cultural changes. Yet, no matter the historical period, two truths will always remain. First, in every era God chooses some whose path to sanctity involves a radical witness to the primacy of spiritual goods over worldly goods. Second, discovering her unique talents and, ultimately, her vocation, is always the challenge and joy of a woman's young adulthood.

My brief experience has solidified the conviction that we will not see an increase of priestly vocations if we do not have a resurgence of women in consecrated life. The complementarity of men and women seeking radical discipleship cannot be ignored in Scripture, in the history of the Church, or in our contemporary times. As a Vocation Director and seminary Formator, I have encountered many priestly candidates who could point to the prompting and inspiration of women Religious. From those who taught me in grade school to those I encountered in graduate school, women Religious invariably incite new depths of self-knowledge, self-possession, and self-gift in the heart of a man attentive to God's love.
—Fr. Paul Hoesing, Dean of Seminarians at Kenrick-Glenon Seminary and President of the National Conference of Diocesan Vocation Directors

What are some of the differences between today's world and the one which first crossed into the third millennium, and how might these affect authentic vocational discernment?

$\mathcal{M}$ILLENNIAL MUSINGS

Amanda just graduated *summa cum laude* from an Ivy League university. Laurie, a successful businesswoman, is living in a classy condominium in a big city and working hard to pay off student debts. Maria is a nurse but has never felt fully satisfied with her work and can't understand why. Caroline, a senior in high school, is passionate about life and certain God has a plan for her future. What do they all have in common? Each of these young women is planning to join a Religious Community and eventually make vows of poverty, chastity, and obedience for the rest of their lives.

What is unique about this contemporary generation of Sisters? Where do they come from? What challenges do they face as they strive to give themselves more fully to God?

On April 25, 2016, the total population of millennials (those born after 1980) officially surpassed the previous largest generation of Americans, the baby boomers (born from 1946 to 1964). Comparing these two generations and what they brought to their vocational quests proves fascinating.

Baby boomers filled their roles in society as loyal members of political parties, proud members and supporters of the military, defenders of traditional marriage, and active participants in churches. In contrast, today's millennials are wary of authority; they distance themselves from established institutions, both religious and secular. They also seem to mature more slowly and fear making a life-long commitment. For many young adults, career options seem limitless; narrowing the possibilities to a single vocation proves daunting. When a young woman in her thirties today is asked to describe her plans for the future, she often replies with a vague and unconcerned, "I don't know. Maybe I will get another degree."

Settling down and giving one's heart fully to another is not a priority. Statistics confirm this: 68 percent of millennials have never been married, and those who do marry tend to wait until later in life. In the 1960s, for example, the average American woman married at age twenty-one and the average man at age twenty-three. Today, the average woman marries at age twenty-seven and the average man at age twenty-nine.[3] Among the baby boomers, only 7 percent of women completed an undergraduate degree as a young adult, while today more millennial women earn higher education degrees than their male counterparts. In the 1960s the majority of women were not in the labor force; today that statistic has reversed and, among the women not working, 22 percent cite school as their main reason for not holding a job.[4] Delayed vocational choices mean challenges foreign to earlier generations of prospective Religious, including heavy college debt and few resources to pay it.

The decades since the 1960s have seen a marked decline in the Catholic culture within the United States that emphasized thorough catechesis and the beauty of Religious and priestly vocations. In the past, a novice mistress could assume her charges knew the faith and came from homes where it was practiced. Today young women often need a full course in basic catechesis. Their knowledge of essential doctrines and love for the Church begin to take firm root after they have entered a Religious Community.

The erosion of a strong Catholic culture also means that young women who do consider a vocation to Religious Life are often seen as unusual by their peers. It can take heroic courage to announce their plans to join a Religious Community. Many face opposition from those closest to them—including their family—rather than the support for God's gift of a "vocation in the family" that was the typical response in the past.

Another difference: technology. An earlier world of typewriters, card catalogs, and newspapers has disappeared under a continuously changing tidal wave of technology, which frightens baby boomers but excites millennials.

Technology has transformed the vocational landscape in positive ways by allowing young people to discover, through the Internet, various Religious Communities and charisms that they might never have known. Technology and new media also allow cloistered Communities to share their lives through websites and videos. With these new avenues of encounter, serious challenges also emerge. Technology seems to contribute to a growing phenomenon of apathy among young people while also impeding their development of authentic interpersonal relationships. One main reason for this has been labeled "acedia."

Acedia

In his book *The Seven Deadly Sins Today*, Henry Fairlie describes *acedia* as "a morbid inertia" that can shut down a person's life by blinding him to the transcendent more for which he was created.[5] In the mid–1940s, renowned English writer Evelyn Waugh suggested that acedia might be the "besetting sin of our age." Had he lived to see the age of the smart phone, he would have declared it with certainty.

Acedia, which stems etymologically from the Greek word for "carelessness" or "indifference," was termed the "noonday devil" by Christianity's early ascetics of the desert. Man has always been tempted, and always had the means, to distract himself from what really matters in life. But the prevalence of technology in today's world heightens this temptation and multiplies exponentially the means of yielding to it. Because we are entertained, we oftentimes fail to realize how empty our lives are becoming. When such an inkling inevitably begins to dawn, we quickly fill the void with the latest gadget or app.

Kathleen Norris, a poet and nonfiction author, diagnoses the situation: "The one sin of acedia is responsible for many of the ills of our high–tech, breakneck-paced, yet apathetic, contemporary world... In other words the couch potato and the overachiever may be suffering from the same problem, which ultimately boils down to the refusal to engage fully with life in the present moment."[6] How so? Both couch potatoes and overachievers are compensating, by different means, for the same interior emptiness.

Acedia is particularly damaging to potential Religious vocations, since the kernel of a vocation is the realization that something—Someone—exists of such consummate goodness that He demands one's utmost devotion and the complete gift of one's life. This is the pearl of great price, the treasure hidden in a field "which a person finds and

as an intermediary. Young women who have learned to re-solve conflicts at a distance will encounter a steep learning curve in Religious Life, as the mediating cushion of technology will be, in many cases, removed. In the end, forming relationships based on charity will always require attentiveness and patience, virtues compromised by the immediacy of technology.

Over half of today's students from ages eight to eighteen use the Internet, watch TV, or use some other form of media either "most" (31 percent) or "some" (25 percent) of the time while they are doing homework.[9] Technology also, in many cases, slowly erodes a young person's ability to focus entirely on a task at hand. In a 2010 *New York Times* article, Matthew Richtel, who won a Pulitzer Prize for his series on distracted driving, coined a memorable phrase: "wired for distraction." He cited the example of a young, intelligent man entering his senior year of high school without having completed his summer reading assignment due to tech-re-lated distractions. The young man's explanation? "On YouTube, you can get a whole story in six minutes... A book takes so long. I prefer immediate gratification."[10]

This learned appetite for immediate gratification can severely compromise a young Religious' ability to forge deep relationships within her new Community as well as with Christ in prayer. The communal life of a Religious vocation, built upon intricate personal relations, does not materialize immediately; it involves self–sacrifice more often than self-gratification. In this same vein, it also takes patience and dedication to develop the prayer life necessary to sustain her personal relationship with Christ, the Spouse of every Religious.

Finally, a growing concern of the digital world is the creation, through social networking sites and personal websites, of public and ineffaceable repositories holding personal information and confidences. In an earlier time, such confidences were shared via letters or conversations with mentors and friends. Today these public entrustments can prove damaging when a person later seeks entrance into the novitiate, seminary, or workplace.

$\mathcal{M}$OVING FORWARD WITH HOPE...

In the midst of the contemporary collapse of many traditions and the escalation of cyberspace dependency, some young people still choose to base their lives on the love of God. Such a decision brings to mind a quote of St. Bernard from his treatise *De Amore Dei*, "The measure with which to love God is to love without measure."[11] Similarly, Pope Benedict XVI wrote, "To live no longer for ourselves but for Christ: this is what gives full meaning to the life of those who let themselves be conquered by him."[12] The goal of priestly and Religious Life is to reach the virtuous state of interior flexibility before the Divine Will. Because of this, seminaries and convents remain God's citadels, strongholds where all people may find him more easily, where the heart of Jesus tenderly keeps watch.

Such truths are most appealing to young people who, by nature and by God's mercy, are idealistic and desirous of greatness. Witness the more than thirty-year-old phenomenon of World Youth Days! Millions of youth have chosen to brave monumental challenges, live through sacrificial pilgrimages, and sleep on wet, miry grounds surrounded by millions of other young people from around the world, all in hope of catching a quick glimpse of the Holy Father and of hearing a message that stretches their hearts in heroic dimensions! At the 2016 World Youth Day in Poland, Pope Francis slipped in a warm greeting to the people of Brazil, who were preparing for the Olympics, as he proclaimed to the 3.6 million pilgrims in Błonia Park: "I hope that this will be an opportunity to overcome difficult moments and commit...to working as a team to build a more just and safe country, betting all on a future full of hope and joy."[13]

Although the sighting of the Holy Father at World Youth Days may be fleeting, the effects of his presence and message endure; stories attest that World Youth Day experiences successfully claim a permanent place in the hearts of the youth. Why? Because young people are made to take risks, to have courage, to nurture improvement in the world—and all this in the name of the virtue which belongs foremost to youth—hope![14] Perhaps the best manner to express this hope today is precisely by reversing the challenges outlined above with their positive counterparts!

ℛEORDERING ACEDIA

"May the God of hope fill you with all joy and peace in believing, so that you may abound in hope by the power of the Holy Spirit" (Rom. 15:13).

The Dominican Doctor of the Church, St. Thomas Aquinas, contrasts acedia with "spiritual joy,"[15] a gift of charity to which acedia is directly opposed.[16] He further explains, "One opposite is known through the other, as darkness through light. Hence also what evil is must be known from the nature of good."[17] Oftentimes, a person recognizes the value of a good only when he or she understands what sadness would result from its absence.

Young people are seeking joy—they are made for it; we all are. Young women will notice Religious Sisters who smile, whose laughter can be heard echoing through the halls of the schools or across the volleyball court during their students' competitions. Might this joy be the antidote to hiding from the difficulties of life behind phones and video games? Experiential knowledge of this joy is essential before any young woman will begin serious consideration of a possible Religious Vocation. She must come to realize that this joy is the result of a life completely given in loving response to the invitation of Love Himself.

Friendship with Christ always leads to the joy that is the fundamental activity of the beatific vision. This is a friendship initiated by God, who took the first step in sending His Son to us in the Incarnation, and who also takes the first step in calling young  women to Religious Life. Without the beckoning hand of God, both eternal beatitude and the Religious Life that is its sign and foretaste here below would seem impossible:

> It could seem to someone that man can never attain to this state of beatitude (*and one could add, Religious Life*) because of the immense distance of his and God's

this message had been sent by a young woman who quite possibly had a Religious vocation, because she already possessed self-knowledge, honesty, an active sacramental life, a great sense of humor, gratitude in prayer, and an esteem for the Church and Religious Life. The theme of her "nagging feeling" is a common refrain among young women called to this vocation and responding to grace. The "Hound of Heaven" gently yet relentlessly does pursue us! After all, how many young people today are frequenting Confession and Eucharistic adoration and "struggling" to get their relationship with Mary back on track? Hopefully, far more than we might realize!

In our three annual vocational discernment retreats, we welcome young women who come from around the world, sleeping bags in hand—for we have no beds in our school, which is the only place spacious enough to house the average 150 women who attend. In those twenty-four hours, including all-night Eucharistic adoration, young ladies lay their lives on the line for Christ—and His goodness does not leave them disappointed! Whatever their vocation is, they begin to lean into it spiritually. If it is Religious Life, they prayerfully discern a particular spirituality, charism, and thus a Religious Community. This most important "first step" needs to be followed by many  more steps in completing the detailed application process of the particular Community. For our Ann Arbor, Michigan,

Dominican Community, the process will include more one-on-one time with the Vocation Directress; the completion of psychological and physical examinations; obtaining reputable recommendations, high school and/or college transcripts; a lengthy personal questionnaire; and other portions of the official application. A pre-postulancy week spent at the Motherhouse leads to the final consideration of official acceptance for entrance.

The author of the above letter clearly expresses that she has a heart for helping others know and live their faith as seen, for example, in her reference to National Evangelization Team ministry work. She already knows that it is only in giving herself away that she will eventually come to find herself. *Gaudium et Spes* expresses this truth, stating that "Man, who is the only creature on earth which God willed for itself, cannot fully find himself except through a sincere gift of himself."[21] And, with that sincere self-gift, the Holy Spirit leads the young woman out of her comfort zone into a moment of great courage: a vocational decision.

THE KEY TO DISCERNMENT: MARIAN DEVOTION

A young lady who is in the process of discerning her vocation should consider the fact that any woman—regardless of her particular vocation—who does not have, nor wish to have, a personal devotion to the Mother of God would rarely even begin to understand Religious Life. This vocation would find her married to Mary's Son, and she should certainly desire a good relationship with her mother-in-law! As our Sisters frequently say, a Sister is an icon of Mother Mary in the world today, and thus her virtues must be infused with a Marian receptivity to grace. This readies her heart for the important role of spiritual maternity to all people.

In quick summation, young women today generally have:

- solid educations and experiences with the world,
- zeal to lead peers in their personal encounters with Christ,
- a deep longing for community found both in the Church and in one's vocation,
- radical determination as they often enter Religious Life in the face of great opposition from family and friends,
- a natural ability to use media to evangelize, and
- hearts on fire with a desire to live good lives and to leave the world a better place for their presence in it.

And so we return to the two truths with which we began this chapter: In every age, including our own, God chooses persons to witness to and live the exclusive, joyful relationship with Him that will constitute our heavenly beatitude. And young people today, as ever, are embracing the challenge of recognizing this call. Consider this blog post from a Harvard alum of 2010, now a Dominican friar:

> It is easy to succumb to a false view in which our commitments trap us and hold back our freedom. The reason we need vows is to help us through these crises of a divided heart. By faithfulness to vows, we are able to make the sacrifices that free us from undue attachments [to] lesser goods. Without the strength of the vow to hold us in place during these struggles, we would surely fall off the road long before developing the love we are capable of. So the next time that we feel frustrated by confining commitments, we can pray

for truer vision. Seen aright, the shackles of love are not shackles at all, but the sweet bonds of communion with God and neighbor.

These are fighting words from a young man whose generation usually selects "maybe" on Facebook invitations and texts a change of plans within minutes of a scheduled meeting. This Brother has discovered that a commitment to one avenue, a loss of "options," leads in fact to freedom to love, an expansive and limitless freedom.[23]

In closing, allow me to share two quotes which well express Religious Life and the joyful manner in which the Church asks us to live it, as a spousal relationship with Christ. This joy becomes a witness to a world oftentimes gone astray but still retaining a deeper longing for holiness. Pope Francis speaks of this joy so appealing to youth:

> [Where] there are consecrated people, seminarians, men and women religious, young people, there is joy, there is always joy! It is the joy of freshness, the joy of following Jesus; the joy that the Holy Spirit gives us, not the joy of the world. There is joy! But where is joy born? Joy is born from the gratuitousness of an encounter! It is hearing someone say, but not necessarily with words: "You are important to me." This is beautiful... And it is these very words that God makes us understand. In calling you God says to you: "You are important to me, I love you, I am counting on you." Jesus says this to each one of us! Joy is born from that! The joy of the moment in which Jesus looked at me. Understanding and hearing this is the secret of our joy.[24]

And finally, even our youngest postulant can be a source of great wisdom through her joyful purity of heart: "I am so grateful to be here. Every day is a new adventure! But best of all, I am all His and He is mine. Nothing else could ever make me so completely happy!"

Nothing but our vocational completion in Christ will fill our hearts and thus make our time here on Earth a taste of the eternal beatitude to come.

Endnotes

[1] For more on the story, see Sr. Joseph Andrew Bogdanowicz, OP, "Religious Vocations for a New Millennium," Lay *Witness* Magazine – Catholics United for the Faith, 2001, 36-37. Reprinted with permission from the publisher.

[2] Ibid.

[3] Eileen Patten and Richard Fry, "How Millennials Today Compare with Their Grandparents 50 Years Ago," Pew Research Center Integrated Public Use, last modified March 19, 2015, http://www.pewresearch.org/fact-tank/2015/03/19/how-millennials-compare-with-their-grandparents/.

[4] Ibid.

[5] Henry Fairlie, *The Seven Deadly Sins Today* (Notre Dame, Indiana: University of Notre Dame Press, 1978), 113.

[6] Carissa Smith. "Acedia: The Forgotten Sin," Christ & Pop Culture. Last modified October 8, 2008, http://christandpopculture.com/acedia-the-forgotten-sin/.

[7] For more information, see Sr. Catherine Thomas Brennan, OP, "Happiness in Accord with Virtue: The Philosophy of Religious Life," in this book.

[8] Katherine Bindley, "When Children Text All Day, What Happens To Their Social Skills?" *The Huffington Post*, last modified December 10, 2011, http://www.huffingtonpost. com/2011/12/09/children-texting-technologysocial-skills_n_1137570.html.

[9] "Daily Media Use among Children and Teens up Dramatically from Five Years Ago," The Henry J. Kaiser Family Foundation, last modified January 20, 2010, http://kff.org/disparities-policy/press-release/daily-mediause-among-children-and-teens-up-dramatically-from-five-years-ago/.

[10] Matt Richtel, "Growing Up Digital, Wired for Distraction," *The New York Times*, last modified November 21, 2010, http://www.nytimes.com/2010/11/21/technology/21brain.html.

[11] Bernard of Clairvaux, *On Loving God: De Diligendo Deo* (Vancouver, BC: Eremitical Press, 2010).

[12] Benedict XVI, "Celebration of Second Vespers of the Ascension with the Benedictine Abbots and Communities of Monks and Nuns, Homily at Monte Cassino," Vatican, May 24, 2009, https://w2.vatican.va/content/benedict-xvi/en/homilies/2009/documents/hf_ben-xvi_hom_20090524_vesprimontecassino.html.

[13] "Pope on World Youth Day: Poland Reminds Us of Christian Vision and Message of Mercy," *National Catholic Register*, last modified August 3, 2016, http://www.ncregister.com/daily-news/pope-on-world-youthday-poland-reminds-us-of-christian-vision-and-message-o.

[14] "In you young people there is hope, for you belong to the future, as the future belongs to you. To you belongs responsibility for what will one day become reality together with yourselves. In this regard, the first and principal wish of the Church is that you should 'always be prepared to make a defense to anyone who calls you to account for the hope that is in you.'" John Paul II, Dilecti Amici: Apostolic letter to the youth of the world on the occasion of International Youth Year, Vatican, March 31, 1985, https://w2.vatican.va/content/john-paulii/en/apost_letters/1985/documents/hf_jp-ii_apl_31031985_dilecti-amici.html.

[15] Thomas Aquinas, *Summa Theologiae*, II-II q. 23 art. 2, ad 1; II-II q. 35 art. 2 and 3.

[16] Even more than envy (the vice mentioned immediately after acedia, in *Summa Theologiae* II-II q. 36). Acedia sorrows over the divine good *(the first precept of charity: Love God), while envy sorrows over a neighbor's good (the second precept of charity: Love your neighbor).* Further, envy sorrows over a neighbor's good as excelling my own (so its object is neither something my own, nor something shared by me). It does not sorrow (at least directly) over the spiritual good of friendship itself, as sloth does, much less friendship with God. For a defense of the priority of loving God, see: *Summa Theologiae* II-II q. 23 art. 5, ad 1: "God is the principal object of charity, while our neighbor is loved out of charity for God's sake."

[17] Thomas Aquinas, *Summa Theologiae*, I q. 48 art. 1, ad 1. Dominican House of Studies, http://dhspriory.org/thomas/summa/FP/FP048.html#FPQ48OUTP1.

[18] Thomas Aquinas, *Summa contra gentiles* IV, chap. 54. Translation by the author, parenthetical expression is the author's own emphasis.

[19] *Catechism of the Catholic Church*, 2nd ed., (Huntington, IN: Our Sunday Visitor, 1997), 2705.

[20] John Paul II, "12th World Youth Day, Baptismal Vigil with Young People," Vatican, August 23, 1997, https://w2.vatican.va/content/john-paul-ii/en/travels/1997/documents/hf_jp-ii_spe_23081997_vigil.html.

[21] Second Vatican Council, *Gaudium et Spes: Pastoral Constitution on the Church in the Modern World*, 24. Vatican, December 7, 1965, http://www.vatican.va/archive/hist_councils/ii_vatican_council/documents/vatii_const_19651207_gaudium-et-spes-en.html.

[22] Edith Stein, *Woman* (Washington, D.C.: ICS Publications), 132ff.

[23] Norbert Keliher, OP, "The Shackles of Love," *Dominicana Journal*, October 13, 2016, http://www.dominicanajournal.org/the-shackles-of-love/.

[24] Francis, "Address for Meeting with Seminarians and Novices," Vatican, July 6, 2013 https://w2.vatican.va/content/francesco/en/speeches/ 2013/july/documents/papa-francesco_20130706_incontroseminaristi.html.

Chapter 2

Staking One's Life on the Reality of God...
Theology of Religious Life
—*Sr. Albert Marie Surmanski, O.P.*

A Religious vocation is rooted in the mystery of God made Man. When the Word of God took on human nature and died on the cross, He offered a sacrificial love able to captivate totally the human heart. The call to Religious Life flows out of this love.

WITHIN THE MYSTICAL BODY

Jesus offers His saving love to everyone. He died on the cross to save all of humanity. This does not mean, though, that He calls everyone to follow Him in exactly the same way. Even during His earthly life, Jesus interacted with different people according to the unique plans He had for each one of them. Jesus was born to Mary, the only woman ever chosen to be the Mother of God. St. Joseph guarded Christ during His childhood as a foster-father but disappears from the Gospels before the crucifixion. Jesus preached the Kingdom of God to the multitudes. He healed many who came to Him. Out of those who responded to His preaching, He chose twelve men to be His Apostles and carry His message to the ends of the earth as the first bishops of the Church. He often visited the family home of Mary, Martha, and Lazarus, and was grateful for their hospitality. He told a rich and honest young man to sell all of his possessions and follow Him (see Mt. 19:21). In contrast, when the dishonest tax-collector Zacchaeus converted, Jesus was satisfied that he restored what he had stolen and gave half of his wealth to the poor (see Lk. 19:8).

Within the Church, the Mystical Body of Christ, there are many different but complementary roles, just as there are many different but compatible parts to the human body. All of the members of the Mystical Body share the same supernatural life. They are all united to Christ the Head, yet they live their friendship with Christ in different ways. In his First Letter to the Corinthians, St. Paul says, "There are different kinds of spiritual gifts but the same Spirit; there are different forms of service but the same Lord... As a body is one though it has many parts, and all the parts of the body, though many, are one body, so also with Christ" (1 Cor. 12:4-5, 12). To follow Christ as a Religious Sister is one way of living out the Christian vocation as a member of the Church. It is a role vital to the health of the Mystical Body.

THE CALL

The desire to follow Jesus as a Religious Sister is a response to Jesus' call. It is He who chooses us. Even though the decision to follow Him is a free, personal choice, He is the source of the strength to say "yes." The Church document *Essential Elements* describes this call as an invitation to enter into a life-giving relationship with God:

> God calls a person whom He sets apart for a particular dedication to Himself. At the same time, He offers the grace to respond so that consecration is expressed on the human side by a profound and free self-surrender.

The resulting relationship is pure gift. It is a covenant of mutual love and fidelity, of communion and mission, established for God's glory, the joy of the person consecrated, and the salvation of the world.[1]

How is the call to Religious Life experienced? Some may literally hear Jesus speaking to them, but this is rare. Most often, Jesus begins to "speak to her heart" (Hos. 2:16) by quietly and gently drawing her to Himself. His call may be felt in the peace of silent prayer before the Blessed Sacrament. It can come through seeing the joy in the faces of those who have consecrated their lives to God. It can stir as a movement of compassion toward those in need and the desire to open a motherly heart to the suffering.

I think the first echo of a Religious vocation came to me when attending a Catholic elementary school where the faith was taught poorly. I remember feeling sad that so many of my classmates did not seem to recognize Jesus in the Eucharist. I first recognized the desire for Religious Life one day after Mass when I was fourteen years old. I was suddenly transfixed with the realization that the greatest joy in life was going to be found in knowing God. Whatever I did, He would be with me, giving light and meaning to my life. This was followed by a sense that Christ was inviting me to become a Religious Sister. What was most important was not the intensity of this experience but the fact that the desire stayed in my heart. During the process of preparing to enter the convent and my formation as a Dominican, Jesus supported me and enabled me to take each step forward. This support of divine grace and the acceptance of my vocation by my Community is what let me know that my call was genuine.

In our time, we hear of reports of an increasing number of people who no longer place an importance on religion, or profess to no longer believe in God at all. Many have lost true hope. The Church and our world needs more witnesses—and credible witnesses! It could be argued that Religious Sisters are needed in our era of history more than any other, precisely because they are such credible witnesses to the love and mercy of God in Jesus Christ. They witness not with words alone, but with the whole of their lives, and so it is a witness that must be taken seriously.
—Most Reverend James V. Johnston, Jr., Bishop of Kansas City-St. Joseph

In IMITATION OF CHRIST

Religious Life is a way of drawing near to Christ through imitating His way of life. Christ lived a life of simplicity. He traveled from place to place with "nowhere to rest His head" (Lk. 9:58). He never married, staying totally available for his work of proclaiming the Kingdom. During His life, Jesus would often "depart to the mountain to pray" and spend all night there (Lk. 6:12). In this prayer, He found His refreshment in the overflowing Trinitarian love. His communion with the Father and the Holy Spirit sustained Him in His mission. Jesus also lived a life of obedience to the Father. He described His purpose on earth as the fulfillment of the Father's will. He said, "I came down from heaven not to do my own will but the will of the one who sent me" (Jn. 6:38). A Religious Sister shares in these three aspects of Christ's life through her vows of poverty, chastity and obedience. By the vows she is consecrated to God and set apart for His service in a unique way.

THE EVANGELICAL COUNSELS

These three vows are known as the "evangelical counsels." They are "evangelical" because they come from the Gospel. They are "counsels" because the vows are not necessary to the Christian life. They are "suggestions" or "advice" lived by some but not by all. These counsels differ from the commandments in that commandments are given to all. They either forbid absolute evils or enjoin necessary goods. For example, the first commandment tells us that we must worship the true God, not idols. Everyone must do this. In the same way, the fifth commandment forbids murder. To take human life unjustly is always wrong.

The evangelical counsels are not directly about avoiding evils. They are about setting aside lesser goods for the sake of focusing on the highest good of all: God. Their purpose is to foster virtue. They point the way down a particular path toward holiness. If the human race were not fallen, there would be no reason for the evangelical counsels. Every contact with anything God had created would lead us closer to Him. But our hearts are easily distracted. Even good things can tempt us away from God. No one who looks at today's world with any degree of honesty can deny that it is all too easy to become enslaved by material things, pleasures, and power. When a Religious makes her vows, she does not deny that material things, pleasures, and power are good when used rightly. By her life, however, she testifies that they are not the highest good. When a Religious says "no" through the three vows, she is really saying "yes" to the highest good: God!

THE VOW OF POVERTY

By the vow of poverty, a Religious Sister gives up the ownership of personal possessions. She will hold all things in common with the other members of her Community. She will live simply, using the things of this world without owning them. In doing this, she expresses her trusting dependence on God to provide for her. She also enters a way of life in which she must live closely with the other members of her Community, relying on them and having them rely on her. Having many possessions can be a distraction from God, either because the heart clings to them, wanting more and more, or simply because taking care of them can involve a lot of work. By setting aside personal possessions, the Sister's life is made simpler so she can focus on God more intensely. She testifies that God is her greatest treasure.

THE VOW OF CHASTITY

A Religious Sister promises to abstain from marriage and sexual activity by her vow of chastity. She does not do this because marriage and children are bad things. Marriage is a holy Sacrament, and children are one of the greatest blessings in this life. The consecrated Religious gives up marriage and children in order to have a heart free to love God in an undivided way. Her vow makes her available to love in a sisterly or motherly way those whom God puts in her life. The life of celibate dedication to God began to emerge even in the early Church. In one of his letters, St. Paul gives advice to the Christians of Corinth, reminding them that "An unmarried woman or a virgin is anxious about the things of the Lord, so that she may be holy in both body and spirit. A married woman, on the other hand, is anxious about the things of the world, how she may please her husband" (1 Cor. 7:34). By their teaching, prayer, and witness, Religious women should support families who take on the cares of raising children.

When I was considering Religious Life, it was the vow of chastity that appealed to me the most. I came from a beautiful Christian home and liked the idea of marriage and children. But as I prayed about my direction in life, I felt that Christ was making such a strong claim on my heart that I could not give it to another man. Through the vow of chastity, a Religious Sister is a bride. Her heart, her life, and her service belong exclusively to Christ. Given to Christ, then, she is poured out on those to whom He sends her. Although the Religious Sister will not physically give birth to any children, this does not mean that her life will not be fruitful. Her union with Christ will help bring spiritual life to many. She is still a woman and will love with a woman's heart. As Dominicans, we experience this "spiritual motherhood" in a variety of ways—first and most importantly through our life of prayer. We also experience it through our apostolate of teaching, in which we help our students receive and cherish the truth of Christ and so grow up into the men and women they are called to be.

THE VOW OF OBEDIENCE

By the vow of obedience, the Religious woman gives her will into the hands of Christ, through the hands of her Religious superiors. Of course, determining the path of one's own life is a good thing. But being totally available for God's mission is better. The vow of obedience is lived in accordance with a rule of life approved by the Church. Since its purpose is to enable the Sister to unite her will to God's will, it can never contradict the laws of God and of the Church. A Sister can never be asked under her vow to do anything evil. In such a case, she would not be bound to obey.

The vow of obedience makes Religious Life an adventure. In our Community, we receive our assignments yearly. A Sister may teach in the same place year after year or may be sent somewhere new. When I am given my assignment, I may not know why it was given to me. What I do know is that I will be where Christ wants me to be that year. I will encounter those whom He wants my life to touch. My responsibility is to seek His face where He wants me to meet Him.

I occasionally come across people who think that the vow of obedience means that Religious give up thinking for themselves and become some sort of mindless robots who are no longer able to make decisions. This is not true. Yes, I have made a vow to choose to do the good that my superiors ask of me. But doing this requires all of my willpower, intelligence, and energy. For several years, my assignment has been to teach at Ave Maria University in Florida. To fulfill this assignment, I have to prepare lectures, teach classes, translate Latin, meet with students, and take on all sorts of other activities. The vow of obedience stretches and shapes each Sister. It does not make her stagnate.

Women who are members of Religious Institutes—we call them "Sisters"—contribute to the Church and her holiness by their persevering, public love and service of, and obedience to, the chaste Christ, the poor Christ, the obedient Christ. Add a communal life, a shared apostolate and a distinctive dress, and we have Sisters in name and in fact who spend themselves, like their model the Ever-Virgin Mary, in declaring for all of us to hear: Jesus Christ is Lord! How we need Sisters to point us to Heaven!
—Msgr. Charles M. Mangan, priest and Director of the Marian Apostolate in the Diocese of Sioux Falls

Religious Life as sign of the Kingdom

While only some make *vows* to live by the evangelical counsels, all Christians are called to live by the *spirit* of the evangelical counsels. Jesus told His followers that the greatest commandment was, "You shall love the Lord, your God, with all your heart, with all your being, with all your strength, and with all your mind, and your neighbor as yourself" (Lk. 10:27). All Christians must love God more than material things, must recognize that sexual love must be lived out in accordance with God's plan, and must seek the will of God in their lives. The laity (the baptized who are not priests or Religious) seek the Kingdom of God by using the things of the world. They are responsible for transforming the world through their involvement in it. They might participate in politics, business, law enforcement, and so on. Religious, who live the counsels in the radical form of the vows, step back from certain earthly goods in order to be a reminder to all Christians that the things of God come first.

Unlike the vocations to the priesthood and married life, Religious Life does not have an additional sacrament connected to it. Religious consecration is a deepening of the baptismal consecration. At Baptism, the grace of the Holy Spirit enters the soul and dynamically directs the newly baptized onto the path of holiness. Religious consecration involves a free choice to live the baptismal call to holiness in a radical way. St. Paul describes the Church as the "bride of Christ" as well as the "body of Christ." He tells the whole people of Corinth, "I betrothed you to one husband to present you as a chaste virgin to Christ" (2 Cor. 11:2). The whole Church is the bride of Christ; all Christians partake in Christ's love for His people. Yet, as a consecrated bride of Christ, the woman Religious lives within the reality of this love in a particularly intense way. She expresses the nature of the Church with her whole life. The Second Vatican Council underlined this by saying that Religious Life, "though it is not the hierarchical structure of the Church, nevertheless, undeniably belongs to its life and holiness."[2] If Religious Life died out in the Church, something essential would be missing. A necessary message about the attractive power of Christ's love would be lost.

After the resurrection of the dead, at the time of Christ's second coming, there will be no more marriage.

together, work together, and relax together. The common life supports and sustains the vows. It is in turn enriched by the love that the vows generate. Within our Dominican family, we live according to the Rule of St. Augustine and our Dominican Constitutions. This way of life, approved by the Church, gives a structure to my life where I can practice the vows and offer my life as a sacrifice to God. I am able to live out my vow of obedience by following our rule of life in accordance with the direction of my superiors. I am able to live out my vow of poverty by sharing both material goods and the daily rhythm of our simple life with my Sisters. The friendship of my Sisters supports my practice of the vow of chastity. Our Religious habit is a sign of our shared consecration to Christ and of our common Religious family. I love it when I meet people who immediately recognize my Community from my habit. It also reminds me who I am and how I have vowed to live. Enriched by divine charity, community life should reflect both the community of love within the Trinity and the nature of the Church.

Apostolate

The foremost duty of a Religious is "assiduous union with God in prayer."[4] We prayerfully offer the sacrifice of our lives in union with Christ's own sacrifice. A major component of the prayer life of a Religious is the Divine Office, a rotation of Psalms, petitions, and readings by which we sanctify the hours of our day. We pray for God's mercy upon the Church and the world. At every hour of every day, there are Religious and priests around the world raising their voices in prayer to God through the Divine Office. The laity are invited to join in this prayer but are not required to practice it.

The next way in which Religious serve the Church is through our common apostolate. Each Religious Community has a mission within the Church. The Second Vatican Council describes the different Religious families as fruit-bearing branches that grow on the tree of the Church: "Thus it has come about, that, as if on a tree which has grown in the field of the Lord, various forms of solidarity and community life, as well as various religious families have branched out in a marvelous and multiple way from this divinely given seed."[5] The apostolic mission of each Community flows from the "charism" or spiritual gift that God gave to the founder of the Community. This charism is confirmed through the approval of the hierarchy of the Church. The charism and apostolate of a Religious Community is the way in which that Community carries on the work of Christ in the Church. Christ's life had an indescribable richness: He preached the Gospel, cared for the poor, healed the sick, welcomed children, called sinners to conversion, spent time in prayer, and agonized in the Garden of Gethsemane. Each Religious Community expresses one aspect of Christ's life. As Dominicans, we share in the work of Christ the Teacher.

Mary

A final aspect of the life of a consecrated woman Religious is that it is lived in union with Mary. Mary lived in total availability to Christ in all of the feminine richness of her mind and body. She gave her *fiat* to the overshadowing of the Holy Spirit, which consecrated her life to God in a unique way. She lived at Nazareth in humble simplicity. She was faithful to the end, standing beneath the cross of

Christ, even when her heart was breaking. We look to Mary as the perfect example of a life of virginity and spiritual fruitfulness. She is our Mother and our model, the perfect disciple of Christ. Our prayer is that our lives will show her gentle love to the world.

Endnotes

[1] Sacred Congregation for Religious and for Secular Institutes, Essential Elements in the Church's Teaching on Religious Life as Applied to Institutes Dedicated to Works of the Apostolate, 5, Vatican May 31, 1983, http://www.vatican.va/roman_curia/congregations/ccscrlife/documents/rc_con_ccscrlife_doc_31051983_magisterium-on-religious-life_en.html.

[2] Second Vatican Council, *Lumen Gentium: Light of the Nations*, 44, Vatican, November 21, 1964, http://www.vatican.va/archive/hist_councils/ii_vatican_council/documents/vat-ii_const_19641121_lumen-gentium_en.html.

[3] Ibid.

[4] Code of Canon Law, c. 663.1, sec. II, III, http://www.vatican.va/archive/ENG1104/_INDEX.HTM.

[5] *Lumen Gentium*, 43.

Chapter 3

Happiness in Accord with Virtue...
Philosophy of Religious Life
—*Sr. Catherine Thomas Brennan, O.P.*

At first glance, Religious Life as a graced response to a divine call may seem to have little, if anything, to do with human philosophy. Religious Life is supernatural in both its origin and its goal and is lived on the level of faith. Philosophy is the human investigation of reality and life's meaning, the pursuit of wisdom according to human reason. Did not St. Paul indicate the futility of these exercises when he wrote to the Church at Corinth, "Has not God made the wisdom of the world foolish?...but we proclaim Christ crucified, a stumbling block to Jews and foolishness to Gentiles, but to those who are called, Jews and Greeks alike, Christ the power of God and the wisdom of God" (1 Cor. 1:20, 23–24). St. Jerome, the fourth–century Doctor of the Church who is best known for his translation of the Scriptures into Latin, was famously rebuked in a dream by the Lord Jesus Christ for being more of a follower of human learning than a Christian. When he awoke, he dedicated himself to the study of the Scriptures.

However, it is also the case that for many saints of every age of the Church's life—St. Justin Martyr, St. Augustine of Hippo, St. Thomas Aquinas, St. Edith Stein—the pursuit of philosophy not only prepared the way for a life radically consecrated to God, but also supported the living out of their "yes" to God lived on the level of faith. St. Thomas Aquinas, who seems to have been one of those saints who are holy from the cradle, went around as a child pestering those around him with the question, "What is God?"—a little philosopher from the start. Pope St. John Paul II extolled philosophy as "one of the noblest human tasks" and "the way to come to know fundamental truths about human life," an "indispensable help" for understanding and proclaiming the truth of the Gospel.[1] The very name *philosophy*, "love of wisdom", points to the love of Him who is the very Word of the Father, "Christ the power of God and the wisdom of God" (1 Cor. 1:24). For this reason philosophy is known as the "handmaid of theology." This chapter will investigate the ways in which insights culled from philosophy have informed the Church's teachings on consecrated life and continue to enrich the lived experience of consecration in today's world.

𝓕IRST INSIGHT: *AGERE SEQUITUR ESSE*

One well-known philosophical dictum is *agere sequitur esse*—"doing follows being." In other words, what something *does* follows or flows out of what the thing *is*; how one acts is a function of who (or what) one is. What a squirrel does is not what a tomato plant does, because they are two different kinds of beings. Different kinds of beings have different capacities and potentials for different kinds of actions: tomato plants can produce tomatoes, cheetahs can run, and human beings can build cathedrals. To be sure, what one *does* affects what one *is*; what we do can either develop our potential or thwart it. But that brings us right back to being. Our actions can either develop or diminish our being, but without some being that exists in the first place, there is nothing to develop or diminish. Take the following obvious examples of health:

One can eat well and exercise, and these actions help one to become healthy. One can fail to eat or move, and thus starve or atrophy. Thus, there are some actions that are necessary for a being to develop and flourish, and there are some actions that inhibit development and full flourishing. But unless some *being* exists in the first place, it would be nonsensical to speak about whether it is healthy or unhealthy.

The priority of being over doing is no idle philosophical speculation. This axiom has immediate and profound repercussions for daily life. We are meant to walk on our feet, not on our heads. If we reverse the priority to doing over being, attempting to walk with our feet in the air and our heads on the ground, the results will be painful. What would this look like in a culture that places high value upon success and possessions? What does this philosophical distinction look like in a culture that values hard work and the self-made man or woman—that is, a culture very much like twenty-first century America? It becomes all too easy to define yourself in terms of where you went to school, your GPA, your salary, what clothes you wear, the car you drive, and the items in the pocket of your size-whatever skinny jeans. Doing and having become the measure of being and identity: *the more I do/earn/have, the better and more valuable I am.*

It would be nice if a fervent Christian life or a vocation to Religious Life made one immune to this line of self-deception. It does not. Francis Xavier Nguyên Văn Thuân, the bishop of Saigon who was imprisoned for thirteen years in a Vietnamese Communist prison camp, testifies that it was only there that he began to learn to "choose God and not the works of God":

> I could not sleep because I was so tormented by the thought of being forced to abandon my diocese, and of the many works that I had begun for God now going to ruin... One night, from the depth of my heart, a voice said to me, "...You must distinguish between God and the works of God. Everything you have done and desire to continue doing...[t]hese are God's works, but *they* are not God! If God wants you to leave all of these works, do it right away and have faith in him! God can do things infinitely better than you can. He will entrust his works to others that are much more capable. You have chosen God alone, not his works!"[2]

The temptation to view one's identity in terms of work for the Kingdom of God and to view work for the Kingdom of God in terms of measurable success has a special edge for consecrated men and women. *I am a good Religious because I am on time for prayers and follow all the rubrics. I am reliable in my duties in Community, and I work hard in the apostolate...* All of these things are good; in fact, they are essential expressions of the total gift of self that Religious consecration is. But they are not the most essential. The essential of essentials for the consecrated woman is that she is a bride of Christ. From being a bride she becomes a spiritual mother, and spiritual motherhood entails a great deal of *doing*. But that *doing* is a natural overflow of her intimacy with Jesus.[3]

Pope St. John Paul II exhorts consecrated men and women to recall the "superiority of being over having."[4]

This remark, made in the context of the vow of poverty, fundamentally applies to the relationship between being and doing as well. The truths of creation and redemption are a beautiful reminder of the primacy of being over having and doing. God, who had no need of anything, created heaven and earth from nothing; the God who created us took on our own nature and saved us while we were dead in sin. We exist because we are loved; we are made God's beloved sons and daughters at our Baptism. We hear our fundamental identity proclaimed by Truth Himself: "This is my beloved Son, with whom I am well pleased" (Mt. 3:17); at the farthest extreme of this Love, God pours out His life for us on the cross and remains hidden in our tabernacles

> *I can think of no greater witness to God's goodness than a joyful Religious Sister. It is sometimes said that opposites attract, when more often the case is that likes attract likes. The virgin Christ is attracted to his virgin bride like no other, and their union fills the world with joy. As the Venerable Concepcion Cabrera de Armida tells us, "This is why virginity delights the Father, because He sees Himself in it. On earth, there is no fruitfulness greater than that of virgin souls who reflect the Father in themselves and replicate him. Looking upon the souls, He is pleased because He sees his image in them, a reflection of His very being."*
> —*Fr. James Mason, Rector of Kenrick-Glennon Seminary*

to give us this life in the Eucharist. While He pours out His life and love for all, He calls some to a special intimacy with Himself, in the spousal relationship of Religious consecration.

A Missionary of Charity Sister with whom I worked understood this truth well. We were selecting groceries, and a sticker reading "ninety-nine cents" somehow attached itself to her habit. I pulled it off, and her reaction was immediate and decisive: "Ninety-nine cents? No! I am worth all of the infinite blood of the Son of God!" The immediacy of her reaction struck me as profoundly as her words did. Here was a woman who understood where her value lay: not in what she had or did but in the fact that Love loved her to the end.

ꙅECOND INSIGHT: THE HAPPY LIFE IS CONTEMPLATIVE

"But we must not follow those who advise us, being men, to think of human things, and, being mortal, of mortal things, but must, so far as we can, make ourselves immortal, and strain every nerve to live in accordance with the best thing in us; for even if it be small in bulk, much more does it in power and worth surpass everything.... [T]hat which is proper to each thing is by nature best and most pleasant for each thing; for man, therefore, the life according to reason is best and pleasantest, since reason more than anything else is man. This life therefore is also the happiest."[5] —*Aristotle, 4th century B.C.*

In the last book of his *Nicomachean Ethics*, Aristotle makes an eloquent case for the joys of contemplation. For him, happiness is "activity in accord with virtue," where virtue is the excellence of our human capacities, our human powers honed for peak performance.[6] What kind of activity makes for authentic happiness? Aristotle distinguishes the different kinds of good things around which a person may center his life: pleasures of the body, active virtues such as contributing to civic life and providing for one's own needs and those of others, and the activity of contemplation, which he associates with "tak[ing] thought of things noble and divine."[7] For Aristotle, the power of reason "is man" and so the activity of reason is man living at the level of his truest self.

This may strike a twenty–first century ear as impossibly removed from reality. Who would spend spring break or a paid vacation just thinking? But Aristotle's claim is precisely that the activity of contemplation is not only the "noblest" but also the "pleasantest," and that this is true not merely for some intellectual elite but for human beings as human beings.[8] The joy of contemplation is even more intense and more continuous than the pleasures of the senses (with whose traditional categories of food, sex, and entertainment we could include shopping, coffee and cocktail bars, and movies). Contemplation as the activity of reason par excellence is not simply an intellectual exercise like a logic puzzle. Contemplation is the gaze of the mind in fascination and wonder at beauty, truth, and goodness. Anyone who has lost all track of time and felt stabs of joy and longing in the presence of some marvel of nature, or some masterpiece of human creativity, or in a fascinating conversation, or in a gaze of love on one's beloved, has had an experience of contemplation. Anyone who has had this contemplative experience wants more of it and can begin to see why he would "strain every nerve to live in accordance with the best thing in us; for even if it be small in bulk, much more does it in power and worth surpass everything."

The Christian life in general and Religious Life in particular draws upon the insight that contemplation is the most necessary and joyous activity in human life. According to the Second Vatican Council, the Church is "eager to act yet devoted to contemplation."[9] St. Thomas Aquinas echoes many noble strands of ancient and medieval tradition when he proclaims that human life can be divided into action and contemplation, where action refers to the external activities of life and contemplation to the activity of the soul.[10] This distinction hearkens back to the Gospel episode of Mary sitting at the Lord's feet while leaving her sister Martha busy with serving the guests (see Lk. 10:38–42). Christ draws the anxious gaze of Martha to Mary's choice of the "one thing necessary." St. Thérèse of Lisieux understands this to mean that "souls thus on fire cannot stand still. Like Mary, they may sit at the feet of Jesus, listening to His sweet and exciting words. Jesus does not, of course, blame Martha's work, but only her worrying about it. For His Mother humbly did the same jobs when she got the meals ready for the Holy Family."[11]

Martha's activity is not rejected as such; the dinner party with Jesus would have become awkward if no one prepared the food or thought about bringing Jesus water. Martha's works were needed if His voice flagged while speaking at length with Mary, who represents contemplation. But activity is not the most important thing. If everyone at the dinner party was so taken up with "what needs to be done" that no one sat with Jesus and listened to Him, it would have been a very sad party indeed. Action and contemplation are both important, but contemplation is the wellspring and the goal of action.

Christian contemplation is Trinitarian and Christological: a child of God the Father turns the eyes of mind and heart to Christ in the Spirit. The activity of the Church, of the Christian, and of the consecrated man or woman will be supernaturally effective only to the degree that they are saturated with the presence of God, and we become saturated by God only in prayer. Work without prayer is social work—valuable, good, praiseworthy, but limited to the horizons of this world. Sometimes we hear, rightly so, "My work is my prayer." This is good! Our work not only can be but must be a continuation of our self–offering to God. The Religious who leaves the chapel for the classroom or the kitchen or the hospital is going about her Father's business and is under His gaze. But she is fooling herself if work becomes a substitute for prayer, because this means that work has become a substitute for God, and she will only impoverish herself and others. Without contemplation, activity becomes a list of tasks to be checked off the to–do list, and persons become numbers on the list or interruptions to the list. Lists are well and good, but we were made for more than lists. The bride of Christ cannot give what she does not have. Work becomes work for the Kingdom (and hence prayer) when it is fed by an overflow of personal intimacy with Jesus.

Third insight: Friendship

> "Without friends no one would choose to live, though he had all other goods."[12] —Aristotle

The Second Vatican Council identified Religious Life with the "pursuit of perfect charity through the evangelical counsels."[13] As St. Thomas Aquinas begins his treatment of the theological virtue of charity in his great *Summa Theologiae*, he consciously adopts Aristotle's account of friendship in the latter's *Nicomachean Ethics*. Simply put, for St. Thomas, "charity is friendship," and he often draws upon Aristotle's insights into the nature of friendship to make the case that this is so.[14] Delving into these insights, then, will be of service to apprehending the nature of perfect charity to which the profession of the evangelical counsels of poverty, chastity, and obedience are directed. Aristotle's account of friendship can also illuminate our understanding of fraternal life in Community.

> *Human beings are created by God for more than this world. In contrast, our modern Western culture insists that this world is all there is, and that this world is the end of all things. This narrow perspective handicaps the human spirit, limits our horizons, and prevents our ability to flourish as God intended. Women Religious show us that this lie is false. By joyfully sacrificing some of the goods of this world on behalf of the Kingdom of God, they provide counter-evidence to the lie that nature is all there is and divine grace is a fiction. They bear witness to a reality that gives the lie to the world's claim to be all that exists. They are in the world but not of it. They open a window on Christ's Kingdom, and by so doing encourage all of us to resist being squeezed into this world's mold with its dehumanizing values and practices.*
> —Al Kresta, President and CEO of Ave Maria Radio

What is friendship? Aristotle contends that "[t]o be friends, then, they must be mutually recognized as bearing goodwill and wishing well to each other."[15] It is not enough for one person to wish well to another; the other must also wish well to him, or this would not be friendship. The well-wishing must be not only mutual but known to be mutual;

two people who admire each other from afar but have never met would not be called friends. Hence a certain sharing or communication is required for friendship.

Finally, the friends must desire what is good for the other for the other's sake rather than for his own. Aristotle delineates three main kinds of friendship based upon three different kinds of goods that the friends pursue: pleasure, utility, and virtue. In the case of friendships based upon pleasure and utility, the friend is not loved for himself but for whatever pleasure or usefulness one can get from him. In the case of friendship based upon virtue, what is loved is the virtue the two have in common; hence the friend is loved for his goodness. The friendship of the virtuous is also pleasant and useful to the friends, who delight in each other and seek each other's good as their own.

Interestingly, Aristotle actually denies that friendship is possible between man and God, since the two are too far removed to have sharing and communication.[16] Nevertheless it is precisely with *friendship* that St. Thomas elects to describe the love of God for human beings and of human beings for God. Admittedly, in using Aristotle's terms to describe friendship, St. Thomas radically elevates the definition. St. Thomas explains what makes it possible for human beings to have this kind of communication with God:

> [T]here is a communication between man and God, in-asmuch as He communicates His happiness to us, some kind of friendship must needs be based on this same communication, of which it is written (1 Cor. 1:9): "God is faithful: by Whom you are called unto the fellowship of His Son." The love which is based on this communica-tion, is charity: wherefore it is evident that charity is the friendship of man for God.[17]

Thus, man's friendship with God is the fruit of the Incarnation: fellowship with God in His Son, who took on our human nature and who says, "I have called you friends" (Jn. 15:15). God became man so that men might become sharers in the divine nature (2 Pet. 1:4).

According to St. Thomas, the soul loves God and others with the same love of friendship. This love is based upon fellowship in happiness, and so it extends to all who are capable of sharing in beatitude: one's self, the angels, and other human persons.[18] Thomas even includes one's own body[19] among the objects that we love with the love of charity, because he takes the resurrection of the body seriously. Our bodies are part of the "I" called to love God forever in heaven.

If fellowship in virtue is part and parcel of the human vocation, it is all the more so for the Religious vocation. By their consecration, Religious strive to pursue perfect charity, that is, the perfection of loving friendship with God in Christ and the extension to and inclusion of all others in that friendship. There is a great need for that friendship with God to be lived and experienced first by the individual Religious; she cannot give to others what she does not have. Here we begin to see why community life is so essential to the pursuit of perfect charity; this point was repeatedly emphasized by the Second Vatican Council and in the Church's post-conciliar teachings on Religious Life.[20]

Common life is the first witness that a Religious gives to the reality of God's transforming love. Common life makes this love evidently *real*, and the first to receive this transforming love is the Religious herself. This love turns total strangers into sisters and brothers. The new postulant or novice may be startled to hear herself addressed as "Sister," but so she is. Community life, like the life of a family, is the first place for the giving and receiving of love, forgiveness, acceptance, support, and good example. Christ first called His apostles together around Himself to be with Him, and when He did send them out, He sent them two by two. Hence, the first apostolate of all Religious is Community life.

Conclusion

The Virgin Mary could rightly be called the first Christian philosopher. She was the first to live the truths cherished by the philosophers in the light of Christ. She, the faithful and humble one, asks questions when her reason is stretched by a mystery she does not comprehend: "How can this be, since I have no relations with a man?" "Son, why have you done this to us?" (Lk. 1:34, 2:48). Ever ready to act in response to the needs of others, as at the Visitation or the wedding feast at Cana, she first puts the whole of her *being* in a posture of receptive readiness to her Lord's beck and call: "Behold, I am the handmaid of the Lord. May it be done to me according to your word" (Lk. 1:38). She is the first and perfect Christian contemplative, turning the gaze of her eyes, and of her mind and heart, to Jesus, treasuring His words and pondering Him in her heart (Lk. 2:19, 2:51). The Mother of the Church and Queen of Apostles waits in prayer with the disciples for the coming of the

Spirit of Truth, the Love of the Father and the Son, and this apostolic fellowship gathered in prayer with Mary and sent out afire is the icon of the Church and of Religious Life in every age.

Endnotes

[1] John Paul II, *Fides et Ratio, Encyclical Letter on Faith and Reason,* 3, 5, Vatican, September 14, 1998, http://w2.vatican.va/content/john-paul-ii/en/encyclicals/documents/hf_jp-ii_enc_14091998_fides-et-ratio.html.

[2] Francis Xavier Nguyên Văn Thuân, *Testimony of Hope,* trans. Julia Mary Darrenkam and Anne Eileen Heffernan, (Boston, MA.: Daughters of St. Paul, 2000), 42.

[3] "The purpose of the Religious Life is to help the members follow Christ and be united to God

through the profession of the evangelical counsels. It should be constantly kept in mind, therefore, that even the best adjustments made in accordance with the needs of our age will be ineffectual unless they are animated by a renewal of spirit. This must take precedence over even the active ministry." Second Vatican Council, Perfectae Caritatis, 2. Vatican. http://www. vatican.va/archive/hist_councils/ii_vatican_council/documents/vat-ii_decree_19651028_per fecae-caritatis_en.html.

[4] John Paul II, *Redemptionis Donum*, 4, Vatican, March 25, 1984, http://w2.vatican.va/content/ john-paul-ii/en/apost_exhortations/documents/hf_jp-ii_exh_25031984_redemptionis-donum. html.

[5] Aristotle, *Nicomachean Ethics*, sec. X.7, trans. W.D. Ross, MIT Classics Department, http://classics. mit.edu/Aristotle/nicomachaen.10.x.html.

[6] Ibid.

[7] Ibid.

[8] On the other hand, it is also the case that virtue or its absence shapes our desires. For the vicious or non-virtuous person, the true good can appear undesirable, and lesser goods can appear more satisfying than they really are, much as how a sick person may not be able to eat anything but pudding and saltines. The cure for this, of course, is not settling for lesser goods but striving for virtue, which makes us capable of living on the level of our greatest desires. Also, Aristotle does limit the number of persons who can, in practice, live the most happy con-templative life. Even for the virtuous person, contemplation requires leisure and the posses-sion of health, long life, and enough of this world's material goods to meet life's necessities (*Nicomachean Ethics* X.8).

[9] Second Vatican Council, *Sacrosanctum Concilium*, 1, Vatican, December 4, 1963, http://www. vatican.va/archive/hist_councils/ii_vatican_council/documents/vat-ii_const_19631204_sacro sanctum-concilium_en.html.

[10] Thomas Aquinas, *Summa Theologiae*, II-II q. 179.1.

[11] Thérèse of Lisieux, *The Story of a Soul*, trans. John Beevers, (New York, NY: Random House, 2001).

[12] Aristotle, *Nicomachean Ethics*, VIII.1.

[13] Second Vatican Council, Perfectae Caritatis Decree on the Adaptation and Renewal of Reli-gious Life: 1, Vatican, October 28, 1965, http://www.vatican.va/archive/hist_councils/ii_ vatican_council/documents/vat-ii_decree_19651028_perfectae-caritatis_en.html.

[14] "St. Thomas quotes Aristotle four separate times in a single brief article." Thomas Aquinas, *Summa Theologiae*, II-II q. 23 art. 1. http://dhspriory.org/thomas/summa/SS/SS023.htm l#SSQ23OUTP1.

[15] Aristotle, *Nicomachean Ethics*, VIII.2.

[16] "If there is a great interval in respect of virtue or vice or wealth or anything else between the parties; for then they are no longer friends, and do not even expect to be so. And this is most manifest in the case of the gods; for they surpass us most decisively in all good things. But it is clear also in the case of kings; for with them, too, men who are much their inferiors do not expect to be friends; nor do men of no account expect to be friends with the best or wisest men. In such cases it is not possible to define exactly up to what point friends can remain friends; for much can be taken away and friendship remain, but when one party is removed to a great distance, as God is, the possibility of friendship ceases" (Aristotle, *Nicomachean Ethics*, VIII.7).

[17] Aquinas, *Summa Theologiae*, II-II q. 23 art. 1.

[18] Aquinas, *Summa Theologiae,* II-II q. 23 art. 1; q. 24.

[19] Aquinas, *Summa Theologiae*, II-II q. 24 art. 5.

[20] See: *Perfectae Caritatis*, 15; *Evangelica Testificatio*, 47; *Essential Elements*, 19; *Christus Dominis*, 15; *Redemptionis Donum*, 15; *Vita Consecrata*, 41, 61; "Fraternal Life in Community," 2, 3, 8, 26, 68; "Directives on Formation in Religious Institutes," 26; *Ecclesiae Sanctae*, II 25-29.

Chapter 4

Vocations Beget Vocations...
The Story Behind the Statistics on Religious Life
—Sr. Teresa Christi Balek, O.P.

At the intersection of Rhode Island and Connecticut Avenues in Washington, D.C., stands a monument dedicated to the over 600 Religious Sisters from 12 Communities who served in field hospitals during the American Civil War. The monument's bronze relief depicts these "Angels of the Battlefield," and the etched granite stone above describes how "[t]hey comforted the dying, nursed the wounded, carried hope to the imprisoned, [and] gave in His name a drink of water to the thirsty." This monument hails the dedication of these valiant consecrated women who served the wounded of both sides during America's most bloody war. While many Americans were generally suspicious of the Catholic Church in the 19th century, the Sisters' brave service helped their fellow citizens see that a good Catholic could also be a good American.[1] In her recollections from the war, Mary Livermore—a prominent American journalist, abolitionist, and women's rights advocate—noted similar sentiments regarding the nursing Sisters she encountered:

> Never did I meet these Catholic Sisters in hospitals, on transports, or hospital steamers, without observing their devotion, faithfulness, and unobtrusiveness. They gave themselves no airs of superiority or holiness, shirked no duty, sought no easy place, bred no mischief. Sick and wounded men watched for their entrance into the wards at morning, and looked a regretful

farewell when they departed at night... Every patient gave hearty testimony to the skill and kindness of the Sisters. If I have ever felt prejudiced against these Sisters as nurses, my experience with them during the war would have dissipated it entirely.[2]

I had the opportunity to visit this monument on a hot day in May 2014, a few months before I renewed my temporary vows. I paused with deep reverence and gratitude for the Sisters who had gone before me. These Sisters had heroically built America's educational and healthcare systems with their bare hands and on their knees. In every way, I am aware of the spiritual giants on whose shoulders my vocation stands.

In the decades following the Civil War, Catholic immigrants came to America in astonishing numbers. The Catholic population in America increased from just over 6 million in 1880 to almost 16.5 million in 1910. Catholic immigrants contributed to half of the American population increase during these decades when the population rose from 75 million to 95 million.[3] As the American Catholic population grew, so did the number of Religious Sisters. There were 22,000 Religious Sisters in 1880 and 90,000 in 1920.[4] While prejudice against Catholics remained strong during these decades, the Sisters still played a vital role in teaching children and providing healthcare to poor and rich, Catholic and non-Catholic alike. Their practice of the spiritual and corporal works of mercy pointed many to the hope that is Jesus Christ and His Church. By the post-World War II era, Catholicism was socially acceptable in America and the Church was flourishing as a result of its well-built educational and health care institutions. Even popular culture lauded Catholicism and Religious Life through motion pictures such as *Going My Way* and *The Bells of St. Mary's* which earned a total of seventeen Academy Award nominations and won eight of these.[5]

By 1966, the Catholic Church in America boasted 181,421 Sisters; almost no Catholic hospital or school was without them.[6] Raised in that era, my mother fondly recalls the Sisters who taught her in the 1950s on the South Side of Chicago. She recalls how Sr. Inviolata taught the 60 children in her kindergarten class without blinking an eye. My mother was one of the over five million children taught in Catholic elementary and secondary schools in the 1950s and 1960s, where the large majority of the teachers were Sisters.[7] The Sisters' impact on millions of American Catholics, particularly children, was evident in the strength of the faith among Catholics in the pews and Catholic families.

God only knows the number of souls that Sisters touched by their apostolate, prayer, and mere presence as consecrated women Religious in the world. Undoubtedly, they influenced scores of priestly vocations at this time, particularly among the children they taught. An older Franciscan priest once told me of how enchanted he was by his

seventh-grade teacher, Sr. Mary Stephen, as she baton-twirled for the class after they earned so many good marks. He said that the Sisters who taught him encouraged his priestly vocation by their own example. Many priests of his generation speak of how a Sister in the schools they attended encouraged their vocation to the priesthood; vocations, faithfully and joyfully lived, beget vocations.

In addition to their encouragement of other Religious and priestly vocations in the Church, Sisters influenced those who served in the civil and secular realm as well. In his autobiography, *My Grandfather's Son: A Memoir*, Supreme Court Justice Clarence Thomas recalls his Catholic elementary and high school education and praises the Sisters who taught him "that God made all men equal."[8] The Sisters clearly taught him why he existed: "We learned that God made us to know, love, and serve Him in this world and to be happy with Him in the next."[9] The Sisters gave Justice Thomas not only a good education but a clear understanding of his human dignity, which undoubtedly laid the foundation for his future years of civil service to our country.

Today, many people, even Catholics, have never seen a Sister. Just recently I was stopped on the street by a mother and her young daughter. Despite her daughter's attendance at a Catholic school, the mother felt the need to make sure that her daughter knew who a Sister is. In 2015, there were 48,546 Sisters in the United States, less than half the number of Sisters just 15 years earlier in 1990.[10] Even more startling is that today only 1.8 percent of teachers in Catholic schools are Sisters, whereas they were the overwhelming majority just 50 years ago.[11]

The question of why there has been such a drastic decline is multifaceted, but not as complex as some make it out to be.[12] Some say that young women are simply not interested in Religious Life because they now have other career options. While it is true that women have more options now than they did in the 1950s, the truth of the matter is that the Religious Life is not one option among many, like choosing a university or career. A vocation to Religious Life is not the same as a career. It is a calling from God to which a young woman is invited to respond in love, no matter her other options. Indeed, God is still calling young women to the Religious Life and, thankfully, His invitation is not constrained by its apparent lack of popularity in our modern age.

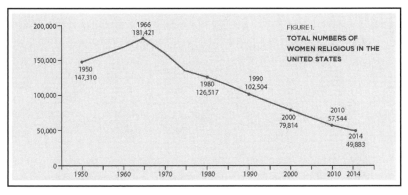

The number of women Religious in the United States peaked in the 1960 and has been declining ever since, according to a 2014 report by the Center for Applied Research in the Apostolate.

However, the modern age has brought with it some significant complexities for women discerning Religious Life, and these complexities have reached into some Religious Communities as well. The rapid changes of these times explain some of the shocking statistics. Some Communities were swept up in the social and political movements of "the Sixties" under the veil of the legitimate reforms of Religious Life called for by the Second Vatican Council.[13] As a result, many Sisters moved out of the traditional apostolates of teaching and health care, in addition to altering their practices of prayer, community life, and identifiable Religious dress.

After the great decline in the number of Religious Sisters in the 1960s and 1970s the first aftershock was that a generation of Catholics arose who were woefully catechized as never before. The second aftershock was that the cost of Catholic schools soared, so that we have been closing schools at an unprecedented rate without our Religious Sisters to teach and lead our schools. Catholic schools suffer from a twofold crisis: rising costs and a crisis of Catholic identity. Both of these are the direct result, in my mind, of the loss of Religious Sisters.

We desperately need holy and joyful Religious Sisters, in order to:

- *Give wholehearted and joy-filled witness to the love of God.*
- *Help the Church teach the beauty and splendor of the Faith.*
- *Save Catholic schools from runaway costs and a vacuum of Catholic identity.*
- *Heal the culture's "war on women" by giving witness to authentic and holy femininity.*

And finally, we need holy women Religious who have their flasks full of oil, good works, and love, to be ever-vigilant brides who are ready to welcome the return of the Lord, the Bridegroom of the Church!

—Dr. Tim Gray, author and President of the Augustine Institute

As Sisters disappeared from the classrooms and hospitals, many young women were left without a concrete witness to the beauty of Religious Life. They began to move through their formative years not knowing what to do with the aching in their heart for the eternal "more" that characterizes an authentic Religious vocation. To a world that prizes material and professional success, the vows of poverty, chastity, and obedience seem ridiculous, even cruel. It is easy for a young woman to become distracted by both the good and not-so-good options presented to her by the modern world, leaving her unable to cultivate a quiet heart that listens to God. Thus, she fails to understand that her vocation is the most important thing in her life, something she needs to discover and whole-heartedly embrace. She may have an inkling of the call, but without the presence of Sisters (or a priest) in her life, she may not find any support or anyone who can adequately direct her. For these reasons, and many others, the number of young women consecrating their lives to God for the good of the Church and the salvation of souls has declined drastically in the past fifty years.

It certainly is a new age when it comes to Religious vocations. Since very few young women come into contact with Sisters in their school years, the way they discern a call and meet a Religious Community is different than it was fifty years ago. What attracts a young woman to a particular Community and its way of life is indicative of both the desires that God puts in her heart and the essential aspects of a Religious Community.

In 2015, the average woman entering Religious Life was eighteen years old when she first started considering a vocation. Of young women who entered Communities in 2015, 42 percent were under the age of twenty-five, and thirty-seven percent were between twenty-six and thirty-six years old. Studies have also considered where these young women were born: 77 percent were born in the United States, 9 percent were born in Latin America, and 4 percent were born in Asia and Africa each. They have a variety of experiences before entering the convent; 4 percent were converts to Catholicism and 55 percent received a Catholic education in at least elementary school, and 49 percent have undergraduate degrees. Of those who attended college, an overwhelming majority were involved in their campus ministry programs: 81 percent participated

in retreats, and 41 percent participated in the March for Life, an annual pro-life event in Washington, D.C. Another 23 percent have attended a World Youth Day, an international gathering of Catholic youths started by Pope St. John Paul II in 1985. About half of them also participated in parish youth groups in high school.

The number of Religious Sisters is, in my view, among the best indicators of the spiritual health of the Church. Sisters reflect the spousal image of the Church in a profound way. Their self-gift, in prayer and ministry, offers a vital witness to the world in our time.
—Fr. Steve Mattson, Pastor of Resurrection Catholic Church in Lansing, Michigan

Young women who enter Religious Life say they received encouragement from members within their chosen Community during their discernment. The vast majority, 84 percent, said that a vocations director aided them greatly in their discernment and 72 percent attended a "come and see" retreat offered by the Community, which is an opportunity for interested women to experience firsthand the Community and their way of life. Also, 80 percent said they were encouraged by priests and 72 percent by a campus minister. Of their family members, 61 percent felt encouraged by their parents.

The way a young woman first met the Community she entered varies: 35 percent encountered their future Community through a friend or advisor; 21 percent through an institution in which the Sisters serve. In this age of technology, it is not surprising that 33 percent first encountered their future Community through the Community's website, and 41 percent said that their Community's social media posts were influential in their discernment.[14]

Overall, a clear institutional identity and mission, dedication to communal prayer, and life in community are what over 90 percent of young women find attractive in a Religious Community. For example, 86 percent state that the Community's fidelity to the Church's teachings are important to them. Of the 92 percent who desire communal prayer, 96 percent desire daily Mass and the Liturgy of the Hours, and 92 percent say that Eucharistic adoration is an important practice of prayer. Other devotional prayers, such as the Rosary, are favored by 84 percent of young women discerning Religious Life. The wearing of identifiable Religious dress is a positive factor in the discernment of 87 percent of young women. The sharing of a communal life with other members, which includes living, praying, recreating, working, and sharing meals together, is desired by over 90 percent of young women. Commitment to an apostolate and a sense of identity as Religious are desired by 79 and 75 percent, respectively.[15]

The future of Religious Life in the United States is a bright one, because the young women entering are walking on firm ground. While they are significantly fewer in number than in the past, these young women understand and seek the authentic forms of prayer, community, and apostolic life that the Church holds up as essential to the consecrated life. Many of them have discerned their call in a much different way than in the past. Vocations directors, "come and see" retreats, college campus ministry, websites, and social media are now prominent aids in discernment, and even in posing the initial question: "Have you ever thought about Religious Life?"

These statistics show us that the Church needs more Sisters, not only to support its institutions, but also to be a light in this very dark world. The presence of a Religious Sister—whether it be in the classroom, soup kitchen, or in the hidden sacrifices that she offers for a starving world—transforms people's hearts. Passing a Sister on the street or having an encounter with her may be the whisper from God that a person needs for conversion. God is still calling young women to this way of life; it is a matter of being able to listen for that call and respond to it with courage. A vocation lived in love necessarily encourages more young people to follow this way to holiness, for a consecrated woman's heart simply must give—to Jesus Christ and to the world—in a total way.

Endnotes

[1] For a general history of the Catholic Church in America, see: Jay P. Dolan, *The American Catholic Experience: A History from Colonial Times to the Present* (Garden City, New York: Doubleday, 1985).

[2] Mary Livermore, *What Shall We Tell Our Daughters: Superfluous Women and Other Lectures* (Boston: Lee and Shepard, 1883), p. 177-178.

[3] James Hennesey, S.J., *American Catholics: A History of the Roman Catholic Community in the United States*, (Oxford: Oxford University Press, 1981), p. 173.

[4] George C. Stewart, *Marvels of Charity: History of American Sisters and Nuns* (Huntington, IN: Our Sunday Visitor, 1994) p. 565.

[5] The Academy of Motion Picture Arts and Sciences, "The 17th Academy Awards: 1945," *Oscars Ceremonies*, 2015. http://www.oscars.org/oscars/ceremonies/1945; "The 18th Academy Awards: 1946," *Oscars Ceremonies*, 2015. http://www.oscars.org/oscars/ceremonies/1946. For more on Catholic culture at this time, see Mark S. Massa, S.J., Catholics and American Culture: *Fulton Sheen, Dorothy Day, and the Notre Dame Football Team* (New York: Crossroad, 1999).

[6] National Catholic Educational Association, "United States Catholic Elementary and Secondary Schools 2015-2016: The Annual Statistical Report on Schools, Enrollment, and Staffing," *Public Policy and Data*, 2013. https://www.ncea.org/data-information/catholic-school-data.

[7] *Ibid.*

[8] Clarence Thomas, *My Grandfather's Son: A Memoir* (New York: HarperCollins, 2007), p. 14-15, 29.

[9] Ibid., p. 15.

[10] Center for Applied Research in the Apostolate, "Clergy, Religious, and Lay Leaders; Leaders in Formation," *Frequently Requested Church Statistics*, 2015. http://cara.georgetown.edu/frequently-requested-church-statistics/.

[11] National Catholic Educational Association, "United States Catholic Elementary and Secondary Schools 2015-2016: The Annual Statistical Report on Schools, Enrollment, and Staffing," *Public Policy and Data*, 2013. https://www.ncea.org/data-information/catholic-school-data.

[12] Erick Berrelleza, S.J., Mary L. Gautier, Ph.D., and Mark M. Gray, Ph.D. "Special Report: Population Trends Among Religious Institutes of Women." *Center for Applied Research in the Apostolate* (2014), p. 2. http://cara.georgetown.edu/WomenReligious.pdf.

[13] For more discussion on the history of religious life in the post-Vatican II era, see Ann Carey, *Sisters in Crisis Revisited: From Unraveling to Reform and Renewal* (San Francisco: Ignatius Press, 2013). Also, see *Perfectae Caritatis*, the Decree on the Adaptation and Renewal of Religious Life (1965), issued by the Second Vatican Council.

[14] Mary L. Gautier, Ph.D. and Thu T. Do, LHC, M.A., "Women and Men Entering Religious Life: The Entrance Class of 2015," *Center for Applied Research in the Apostolate* (2016), p. 8-11, 14- 20, 29. http://cara.georgetown.edu/2015EntranceClass.pdf. This report represents 68 percent of the 174 reported entrants into women's religious communities in 2015.

[15] *Ibid.* p. 23, 31- 35, 40.

array can be rather daunting to consider, as each Religious order or congregation has a unique charism at the service of the Church.

Perhaps the best way to think about the great variety of Religious is to consider it in the same way St. Thomas Aquinas does in speaking of the multiplicity of creation:

> Because [God's] goodness could not be adequately represented by one creature alone, He produced many and diverse creatures, that what was wanting to one in the representation of the divine goodness might be supplied by another. For goodness, which in God is simple and uniform, in creatures is manifold and divided and hence the whole universe together participates the divine goodness more perfectly, and represents it better, than any single creature whatever.[2]

If we simply substitute "Religious charism" for "creature" in this passage we see the reason for the great variety among Religious orders: they represent God's infinite goodness. Once we recognize the purpose of having diverse charisms and Communities, we then have to ask: "Where do I fit?" While the Church's history has been blessed by countless orders and congregations, we will briefly discuss a few main orders and their charisms.

$\mathcal{B}$ENEDICTINES

While not specifically an order, the Benedictine tradition traces its history to the founder of Western monasticism, St. Benedict of Nursia. The Benedictine tradition of *ora et labora* (prayer and work) has attracted people for one thousand years. Others who follow the Rule of St. Benedict include the Cistercians and the Trappists, both of which began as a reform of the monastic life intended by St. Benedict. Saints such as St. Gregory the Great, St. Bernard of Clairvaux, St. Scholastica, and St. Gertrude all found their way to holiness through this spirituality.

CARMELITES

Tracing their spiritual heritage to Elijah and the hermits of Mt. Carmel, the Carmelite Order is perhaps best understood through the lives and work of some of its many saints: St. Teresa of Avila, St. John of the Cross, St. Thérèse of Lisieux, St. Elizabeth of the Trinity, and St. Teresa Benedicta of the Cross (Edith Stein). The Carmelite spirituality centers on a direct experience of God in prayer. In works such as *The Way of Perfection* and *The Dark Night of the Soul*, Carmelite saints highlight that each individual comes to know God more deeply through progressive purification.

FRANCISCANS

The Franciscans, who were founded by St. Francis of Assisi in the early thirteenth century, are one of the great mendicant orders, along with the Dominicans and the Carmelites. This means that they supported themselves by begging. The hallmark of the Franciscan life is poverty—St. Francis would often speak fondly of "Lady Poverty." While Franciscans may be found teaching and nursing, they are best known for their work with the poor. The Franciscan order is home to many great saints, including St. Anthony of Padua, St. Bonaventure, St. Clare, and St. Agnes of Prague.

$\mathscr{D}$OMINICANS

The Order of Preachers (Dominicans) was founded by St. Dominic in 1216. For eight hundred years Dominicans have been living the charism of the order—to preach and teach the truth—in many different ways. As study is an essential part of the charism, they are often involved in education at some level. The saints of the Dominican order give witness to a great variety of gifts: scholars, such as St. Thomas Aquinas and St. Albert the Great; artists, such as Bl. Fra Angelico; and preachers, such as St. Vincent Ferrer and St. Hyacinth. The women saints of the Order of Preachers are no less illustrious: St. Catherine of Siena, St. Rose of Lima, Bl. Imelda, and St. Catherine de Ricci.

$\mathscr{F}$INDING THE RIGHT FAMILY: RELIGIOUS CONGREGATIONS

When I was discerning Religious Life, I had a good friend at the university who was also discerning. We both decided to attend the retreat held by the Dominican Sisters of Mary, Mother of the Eucharist, in Ann Arbor, Michigan. We arrived with two different frames of mind: she was pretty sure this was the Community she was going to enter, while I did not really know where God wanted me and was not overly interested in teaching. God had other plans for both of us. I left the retreat with application papers, and she left knowing that she was called to Religious Life, but not in this specific Community. She is now a Sister of Life.

While my friend and I each discerned Religious Life in Communities who have very different charisms, the same scenario can occur when we discern congregations that share a basic charism or spirituality. Each Dominican,

Franciscan, or other congregation is unique. While they share the basic charism of their order, it is manifested in each congregation in varied ways; rather like families, no two congregations are exactly alike.

> *The presence of Religious Sisters gives a diocese additional witnesses of feminine holiness and virtue, as the different vocations all speak of the richness of Christ's Church. These consecrated women express a total commitment to the Lord as his chosen brides. Such witnesses cannot but help encourage other vocations in their respective commitments of love.*
> —Fr. Shane Deman, Director of Vocations, Diocese of Sioux City

I had the opportunity to study this past summer with Dominican Sisters from two other congregations. While there is great joy when we meet to study or pray together, at the same time these gatherings highlight the differences that make our different congregations unique. Some of our Sisters, as well as those from other Dominican Communities, have said that when they first visited a Dominican congregation, they knew they were called to be a Dominican, but knew that it was not in that specific Community.

What does this all mean for a young woman discerning Religious Life? First, remember that no two Communities are exactly alike. If you are attracted to the basic charism and spirituality of an order, don't be worried if the first Community you visit doesn't seem to be the perfect fit. If it seems close, perhaps you should continue looking at other Communities which are tied to the same order, whether Dominican, Franciscan, Carmelite, Benedictine, or something else. If you find that it is not so much a question of the right "family spirit," but more a question of the larger way that order lives Religious Life, perhaps you should take some time to look at other Communities outside of that specific order.

Second, remember that you are not in charge. God has a way of surprising us and inviting us to a life that we might not have thought about or preferred on a natural level. The amazing thing is that as we say "yes" to the call to Religious Life in the congregation to which God has called us, we grow ever more deeply in love with Him through living and assimilating the charism of our specific congregation.

*P*ART II: LIVING THE CHARISM—THE ROAD TO HEAVEN

In this second part of the chapter, we discuss what happens once a young woman crosses the threshold of the convent to begin her Religious Life. By entering Religious Life, she is saying, in effect, that she believes this is the way God is calling her to get to Heaven. When she makes her final profession of vows, she knows this definitively. Her whole Religious Life is shaped and lived according to the specific charism of her Religious Community. A Sister's whole life, whether she is in initial formation or under final vows, is spent learning and deepening her understanding of the specific charism of her Community. The basic building blocks of Religious Life, which we mentioned in the first part of this chapter, now resolve into greater clarity as they are refined in the practice of a specific charism.

One of the most poignant ways this occurs is through the observance of the vows. The three vows of poverty, chastity, and obedience are joined in some congregations by a fourth vow, usually related to the Community's charism. For example, the Religious Sisters of Mercy of Alma, Michigan, vow "to serve the poor, sick and ignorant,"[3] while the Sisters of Life make a fourth vow "to protect and enhance the sacredness of human life,"[4] and the Missionaries of Charity profess "wholehearted and free service to the poorest of the poor."[5] Conversely, the Dominican nuns, following the tradition of the Dominican order, profess only obedience, because poverty and chastity are both considered to be contained within the vow of obedience.

Getting to heaven the Dominican way: The Dominican life and charism in detail

To demonstrate how the charism of a Religious Community shapes the foundational elements of Religious Life in more depth, I will use the example of the Dominican charism as it is lived by the Dominican Sisters of Mary, Mother of the Eucharist, since this is the charism with which I am most familiar. Although our practice may differ slightly from other Dominican congregations, the main aspects of the Dominican charism will be the same.

Consecration

While the Dominican nuns and friars profess only the vow of obedience, active Religious Sisters profess the three vows of poverty, chastity, and obedience. As Dominicans, we are called to preach and teach the truth of Christ to all, and so the way we live out our vows is consonant with that end. Here is a brief look at a Dominican understanding of the three vows.

$\mathcal{P}$OVERTY

Dominican poverty is modeled on the poverty of Christ and the apostles who were itinerant preachers. Our lack of material goods makes it easier for us to "get up and go" wherever we may be sent. It is a reminder to others and to ourselves that Christ is our greatest treasure. Dominican poverty is poverty for mission. Material things are not bad, but our renouncing them frees us to be available to bring God's message of truth *to* the world without being caught up *in* the world.

CHASTITY

Dominican chastity is founded in the essential good-ness of the human being as body and soul. St. Dominic founded the Order of Preachers while combating the Albi-gensian heresy, which was rampant in the Languedoc region of France at the beginning of the thirteenth century. One of the major tenets of the Albigensians was the belief that all matter was evil. Thus, they held that even the human body and marriage were evil. St. Dominic challenged the beliefs of the Albigensians by proclaiming that the body is good. St. Dominic is still known for his nine ways of prayer, which are ways of praying using both body and soul.

The vow of chastity is an essential aid to Dominican study and contemplation. Chastity frees us to love God with our whole heart and to love others with His love. Chastity helps us to guard our purity of heart, which, according to St. Thomas, assists us in our contemplation of God as the practice of the virtues render us more like Him.[6]

OBEDIENCE

Obedience is the hallmark of Dominican life. As previously mentioned, the Dominican nuns and friars only profess the vow of obedience, since the vows of poverty and chastity and all they entail fall under obedience.

Obedience gives us the assurance of using our talents for the salvation of souls. In living a life of obedience, we are configured ever more closely to Christ, who became "obedient to death, even death on a cross" (Phil. 2:8). At no moment of His life was Christ the Preacher more eloquent than in the few words He spoke from the cross. It is through our conformity to Christ on the cross by our vow of obedience that our preaching and teaching are made effective. Through this conformity to Christ we are truly able to recognize that our lives are not about us or what we are able to do on our own. Rather, the Order's work for the salvation of souls is really about allowing the Lord to use us as He knows best, through the mediation of our superiors.

Dominicans, in love with truth, place great emphasis on the fact that obedience must be intelligent. We are not automatons, and we recognize that our intellect and will are gifts which render us capable of knowing God through grace. The early desert fathers' tests of obedience—which often featured ridiculous or futile tasks like planting things upside down, just to see if the subject would obey—do not find a home in a modern Dominican Community. I have never yet met any Dominican who was asked to plant cabbages upside down!

*P*RAYER: PREACHING TO THE PREACHERS

Prayer, both communal and private, is essential to the Dominican life. Before founding the Order of Preachers, St. Dominic was a canon—a priest dedicated to the celebration of the liturgy—in the cathedral church of Osma, Spain. Because of his deep formation in and devotion to the liturgy, he bequeathed to the whole Order a great love for the Mass and the Liturgy of the Hours. As a Community, we gather daily in the chapel to pray the hours of Lauds, Daytime Prayer, Vespers, and Compline together.

Perhaps the best summation of the role of the Divine Office in the life of a Dominican Community comes from Fr. Bruno Cadoré, Master of the Order of Preachers:

> The liturgical celebration of the Hours, repeated several times a day in community, must be a time when the Word of God, and not ourselves, comes to be our center. It is when we allow the Word to seize us, to take hold of our desire to give our life and enable this desire to do far more that we could ever do ourselves. This celebration repeated each day and in each liturgical Hour gives us the courage to expose ourselves to the Word; to listen to the words of Scripture and the prayers of the tradition; to become accustomed to the familiarity that the Word wants to have with us; to discern through the words of Scripture the face of the Son that is revealed and who is the very source of obedience. We need constantly to regain our strength,

to take heart. It is in this mystery of the liturgy that we learn how to do this, or better, in the liturgy we can implore the Lord to do it in us.[7]

The rhythm of prayer for a Dominican is an essential part of the interplay between our life of contemplation and our active life in the apostolate. As Fr. Cadoré continues, "The liturgical celebration of the Hours is the place *par excellence* where our communities bring into the presence of God our aspirations for the world to which we are sent as Preachers."[8] The work of the apostolate fuels our prayer, yet at the same time our life of prayer and contemplation of God fuel our apostolic desire to go out and make God's love known to others.

The Dominican method of praying the Office is itself designed to lead us to contemplation and to foster zeal for souls. The Community chants the psalms in two choirs facing each other. During the psalms, the two sides of the choir alternate sitting and standing, which symbolizes the proclamation of the Word to each other. During the Glory Be to the Father at the end of each psalm, we bow profoundly, as did St. Dominic, humbling ourselves before the majesty of God. In the very gestures of our prayers we preach to ourselves, and to those who may join us for prayer, the great goodness of God and the respect that we owe Him.

Within the setting of the hours of the Divine Office, the jewel of the Eucharist shines out. As a Community, we have an hour of Eucharistic adoration daily, allowing us time face-to-face with our Spouse. The Community Mass is the high point of our day. It is from here that we derive the strength for our apostolate. It is only fitting that immediately after receiving the Lord in Holy Communion, we go out to our work for the day. It reminds us that we are to bring, not ourselves, but Christ to souls.

Another aspect of our Community prayer that is deeply rooted in the Dominican tradition is devotion to Mary. This occurs *par excellence* in the daily communal renewal of each Sister's Marian consecration. The recitation of the Rosary is also given an important place, prayed as a Community, immediately after Vespers. Tradition holds that the Rosary was given to St. Dominic by the Blessed Mother as a weapon in the fight against heresy. Throughout history, Dominicans have been at the forefront of preaching about the Rosary. This devotion provides an avenue for contemplating the mysteries of Christ's life with His mother, helping us to grow deeper in our love and knowledge of God.

Apostolate: Preaching the Word

The year 2016 marked the 800th jubilee of the Order of Preachers. Dominicans today are still following the charism and apostolate that St. Dominic first laid out in 1216. Over time, some Religious orders either cease to exist or, like the military orders of the Middle Ages, have had to change their apostolate, since their original apostolate is no longer necessary. Preaching the truth, however, is always in season, and so there is always work for Dominicans to do!

The Dominican apostolate can be summed up in the various mottos of the Order: *Veritas* (Truth), *Contemplare et contemplata aliis tradere* (to contemplate and to give to others the fruit of one's contemplation), and *Laudare, Benedicere, Praedicare* (Praise, Bless, Preach). At first glance, these may seem rather broad ideas from which to distill a concrete apostolate, but they all point to the same reality of preaching and teaching truth.

The apostolate of holy preaching takes on a different hue in each Dominican congregation. As women Religious,

we do not preach in the strict sense of preaching during Mass, but in the broader sense of proclaiming truth. The main manifestation of the preaching charism in our Community is through Christian education. As teachers, we bring our love of truth to our students, helping them to encounter Christ in their studies. Dominicans recognize that all truth is a participation in the first Truth, who is God. Thus the study of any discipline, when approached with humility and openness, can lead us to a deeper knowledge of God. Seeing the order of creation through the sciences leads us to contemplate God's wisdom; the beauty of art and music help us to know God's beauty. In math, graphing limits, which approach infinity but never reach it, can lead us to ponder what it means to say God is infinite. Building on this implicit preaching within mainstream academic disciplines, Dominicans explicitly preach the faith. We aim to teach our students both the doctrines of the faith and also how to live them by cultivating a life of virtue.

Outside of the classroom, we preach the truth by giving retreats and talks, writing, singing, and many other activities. Preaching occurs within everyday encounters; sometimes it is explicit, and sometimes we preach through the example of our lives. Whether it is answering someone's questions on a plane or interacting with fellow students while studying at a university, we are always seeking to bring people to an encounter with Jesus Christ, who is Truth.

In order to preach the truth, Dominicans must first come to know it. Thus, study is an essential part of the Dominican charism. This first means the study of theology, but it extends to other subjects as well, particularly those needed for our work of teaching. Dominican study is not simply an intellectual exercise but rather an avenue to contemplation. It is not as though a chasm separates the choir and the classroom; they are multiple expressions of one reality.

As was mentioned in the discussion of prayer, contemplation of divine truth and the active work of preaching are intimately linked. We sometimes speak of balancing these two aspects as though they were two sides of a coin, where only one side is visible at a time. While making the point that contemplation and action are equally part of the Dominican life, this analogy falls flat in that it introduces a false dichotomy, as though one can be contemplative *or* active but not both at once.

I would like to propose as an alternative the image of the ocean tides. The ebb and flow of the tide is very much like the Dominican life. We are always to be centered on God and in the contemplation of truth, but we are often pulled out into the world to meet the needs of our fellow man. Similarly, when the tide comes in it does not lose its connection to the rest of the ocean, but brings the ocean to the dry land. The tidal ebb can be seen as our return from the world to the cloister at the end of the day. What I find attractive in this analogy is the fact that if we see our contemplation of truth as the essential aspect of our life, then we see can see the ocean as our Dominican life. What changes with the tides is not the ocean itself, but the location of the water—being pulled out of itself toward the land and then returning to the depths. What changes in Dominican life is, in like measure, the location and expression of our contemplation of truth.

COMMUNITY LIFE

Community life is an essential part of the Dominican life. St. Dominic sent his first friars out two by two, in the tradition of Jesus sending out the 72 disciples two by two, to preach the Gospel. Living in community strengthens us in our vocation and intensifies the witness of our lives.

No one can live in isolation, and this is an essential truth in Religious Life as well. We need the other members of our Community—just as those in the world need the members of their family—to call us out of ourselves to a life of self-giving love. Community life strengthens each Sister in her own vocation through the faithful witness of her fellow Sisters. We find support when times are challenging, and we give that support to others as well. Community calls us on to holiness.

Spending time with our Sisters also strengthens us by giving us time for leisure. Each evening we spend an hour of recreation together. This can involve anything from playing board games or working on crafts to simply sitting and talking. How we spend the time is less important than the fact that we are able to be together and rest from the work of the day.

While community life is essential to the living of our vocation within the convent, it is also an important part of our apostolate as well. We have a corporate apostolate—

not in the sense of a corporation, but in the sense of a body: we share an apostolate as a Community. Normally we have at least two, and in some cases as many as five or six Sisters in a school in which we teach. When we work together at a school, we give witness not only to the fact that God exists, but also to the reality that the following of Christ is a deeply fulfilling and joyful way of life.

Monastic life within an active Community

In addition to the elements shared by all Religious congregations, Dominicans also have an additional wellspring of tradition that provides an important dimension of living our charism as preachers of truth. From the beginning, St. Dominic included certain monastic observances in the life of the order. These all contribute to building and sustaining within the convent an atmosphere conducive to contemplation and sacred study, so that in the classroom and elsewhere, we can be effective preachers and teachers. St. Dominic gave to these monastic practices, already well established in Religious orders in his time, a specific orientation toward the salvation of souls.

Silence is golden

The Order's saying, *Silentium pater praedicatorum,* means that silence is the father of preachers. In observing times and places of silence, we are given the physical and mental space necessary to pray, study, and live in God's presence without external distractions. It is this climate that fosters the contemplation necessary to the life of a Dominican; our prayer fuels our apostolic work, and we share with others what we have first spent time contemplating in silence. As Dominican Sisters of Mary, Mother of the Eucharist, we observe silence daily in the morning before leaving the convent for the apostolate, as well as after Compline in the evenings. Our meals are normally taken in silence while a Sister reads aloud from a spiritual book. This spiritual reading allows us to feed our minds upon truth even as we feed our bodies. On special feast days and holidays, dispensation from the usual silence allows us to live the liturgical year with greater intensity. Even on feast days, however, we maintain silence in certain places in the convent, including the chapel, sacristy, and cells. This designates these locations as very special places set aside for encounter with and contemplation of God, regardless of the time or day.

CLOISTER

The word *cloister* usually conjures up images of nuns who never leave their monastery. Certainly, the most well-known kind of cloister is that lived by contemplatives who neither leave the convent nor invite others to come into the enclosure. As an active Religious Community, we are not cloistered in this sense, because we must leave the convent during the day in order to teach and study. However, there are still parts of our convent designated as "cloister," meaning that they are reserved for the exclusive use of the Sisters. While we go out to the world to preach and teach, we do not allow the world full access to our life. This separation provides a protected space, away from the bustle of the world, for us to be alone with God and with our Sisters. Without this space for our prayer and Religious Life, we simply could not serve the souls entrusted to us.

𝒫ENANCE

No life, whether Religious or lay, is complete without some form of sacrifice. We see this vividly in family life: for example, parents waking up in the middle of the night to care for a sick child, or spouses making compromises for each other's good. In the Dominican charism, penance, like every other aspect of our life, is at the service of the salvation of souls. St. Dominic prayed and sacrificed nightly in reparation for his own sins and those of others. Unfortunately, today penance is often viewed with distaste or mistrust. But recall for a moment the aforementioned sacrifices of parents. Would they say that they would rather dispose of their child and be comfortable? No. Usually the answer is, "It's worth it. It may be hard, but it's worth it."

Penance in Religious Life ought to follow a similar pattern. It is not about great acts of mortification but about living each aspect of our life faithfully and embracing the small and big sacrifices that flow naturally each day from that fidelity. These sacrifices open our hearts to love God and souls with a purer love. We also should be able to say, "It's worth it."

𝒥T IS WORTH IT!

Yes, it is worth it! Religious Life, lived with fidelity to the founding charism, brings all sorts of challenges, adventures, and surprises. But when we are living the life to which we are called and for which we are made, we will experience the joy Christ wishes to share with us. The Lord reminded the apostles that in His Father's house there are many mansions (Jn. 14:2), just as in our mother the Church, there are many Religious orders and charisms. The Lord's promise to prepare a place for the apostles applies equally to each young woman called to Religious Life. If He calls you to Religious Life, He will prepare a place for you—not a one–size–fits–all answer, but a place in a specific congregation, following a specific charism and path to holiness.

Endnotes

[1] Catholic Church, Code of Canon Law Latin-English Edition (Washington, DC: Canon Law Society of America, 1995), 663§1.

[2] Thomas Aquinas, Summa Theologica, trans. Fathers of the English Dominican Province, (Benzinger Brothers, 1947), I Q.47 a. 1. http://dhspriory.org/thomas/summa/FP/FP047.html#FPQ47OUTP1.

[3] "Vows," Religious Sisters of Mercy, Alma, Michigan, http://rsmofalma.org/vows/vows.html.

[4] "About Us," Sisters of Life, http://www.sistersoflife.org/about-the-sisters-of-life.

[5] "Missionaries of Charity—Region of the Immaculate Conception—East Coast/USA & Canada," Council of Major Superiors of Women Religious, http://cmswr.org/member-communities/member-communities/74-missionaries-of-charity-region-of-the-immaculate-conception east-coast-usa-canada.

[6] Thomas Aquinas, Super Evangelium S. Matthaei lectura, trans. R.F. Larcher, O.P., 5-2, http://dhspriory.org/thomas/SSMatthew.htm#5.

[7] Bruno Cadoré, O.P., "Laudare, Praedicare, Benedicere: Letter on the Liturgical Celebrations of the Hours," 4, (Rome, 2012), http://www.op.org/sites/www.op.org/files/public/documents/fichier/cadore_letter_hours-en.pdf. Emphasis in the original.

[8] Ibid, 2.

Chapter 6

No "How-to" Manual...
Formation of Young Women in the Novitiate
—Sr. John Mary Corbett, O. P.

> Peter said to him in reply, "Lord, if it is you, command
> me to come to you on the water." He said, "Come." Pe-
> ter got out of the boat and began to walk on the water
> toward Jesus. But when he saw how [strong] the wind
> was he became frightened; and, beginning to sink, he
> cried out, "Lord, save me!" Immediately, Jesus stretched
> out his hand and caught him, and said to him, "O you of
> little faith, why did you doubt?" (Mt. 14:28–31).

What did Peter see in the eyes of Jesus as he met His
approaching gaze while walking toward Him on the sea?
The Scriptures do not reveal an answer to this question.
What we do know is that Peter trusted Jesus enough to
come at His bidding and follow Him out onto the water. As
Peter fixed his gaze on the Lord, he stepped out into the unknown, and walked on the water toward Jesus, something
impossible by his own power. When Peter diverted his attention from Jesus and noticed the wind, his faith wavered,
and he began to slip. But not a moment passed before his
cry was heard, and the strong hand of Jesus raised him up
and drew him to Himself, back into the safety of the boat.

Many fruitful insights can and have been gleaned from
this poignant account in St. Matthew's Gospel. Who cannot
recall a time in her following of Christ when her faith was

shaken by the experience of her own weakness or perhaps painful suffering or circumstances in the family, and when she was subsequently buoyed up by the saving hand of Christ, either through prayer, the grace of the sacraments, or the advice and support of a friend? This Gospel passage may also serve as a valuable point of departure for observations about another area at the heart of the Church's life, which necessitates no less courage or faith: the formation of young women entering Religious Communities today as postulants and novices.

STEPPING INTO AND OUT OF THE BOAT

The young woman accepted into a Religious Community makes an initial, radical choice for Christ in response to a supernatural call of grace. Likewise, when we meet Peter in this narrative, he has already been called by Christ; he is already in the boat. It is as if he is a few months into his "postulancy." He is evidently one of Christ's followers, but we know that he is not yet ready to lay down his life for Christ. His faith has to be tested, and he has much more to learn from living closely with Christ as His disciple. The time of formation as a postulant and novice in Religious Life may be likened to the time of preparation and instruction that Peter and the apostles spent with Christ during the three years of His public ministry. This time affords the Sister the precious opportunity to test her vocation and to discern, under the guidance of her superiors, if indeed He is calling her to a particular Community. After responding to the initial call by entering a Community, or "getting into the boat," so to speak, she must then step out in faith onto the water and live out her vocation in the Community by fully engaging in the formation process. She will not be alone and will have others to assist her in keeping her eyes fixed on Christ as she moves forward in the adventure that is Religious Life.

A GIFT FROM ABOVE

There is something observable about one who is deeply in love: She has a one-track mind, or rather, a one-*person* mind. She is preoccupied with her beloved. He is the center of her thoughts and desires. She wishes only to please him and is happiest when she is with him. The same may be said of the bride of Christ who has found happiness in her vocation. The vocation to belong to Christ as His bride in Religious Life is a response to a divine call for a more radical union with Christ patterned after His own way of loving. This vocation is a gift from God and invites an ongoing response in freedom.

One of my favorite musicals as a child was *Annie*, and the song "It's a Hard-Knock Life," was also much-loved. This song has come back to me frequently, and I have often thought that one song a Religious could appropriately sing in her heart would be: "It's a supernatural life for us!" As long as the Religious is humbly aware of her calling's unique origin, she will seek Him above all else and be able to live her vocation with great joy and freedom, relating all things in this life to Him as He desires. The Religious Life makes no sense if we lose sight of its supernatural dimension. During my years serving as a postulant mistress and novice mistress, I sought to draw the Sisters' attention as frequently as possible to this fundamental reality.

The papal apostolic exhortation *Vita Consecrata* states beautifully, "Formation should therefore have a profound effect on individuals, so that their every attitude and action, at important moments as well as in the ordinary events of life, will show that they belong completely and joyfully to God."[1] The postulant and novice became daughters of God at their Baptism. As Religious, they are called to a deepening of their baptismal promises through the profession of Religious vows, by which they will belong to Christ even more intimately.

St. John Paul II teaches: "Christian tradition has always spoken of the objective superiority of the consecrated life" (Vita Consecrata 18). If you are someone thinking about the possibility of pursuing a religious consecration, know that you have much encouragement. In fact, the encouragement comes from Jesus himself, poor, chaste, and obedient, who offers counsels, not commandments, to be close to him in poverty, chastity, and obedience. The world needs more consecrated persons to remind us of the life of Jesus Christ. How beautiful it is to see a Sister, a Bride of Christ, sharing our Lord's own life! What could be greater?
—Fr. Andrew Hofer, O.P., Assistant Professor of Patristics and Ancient Languages at the Pontifical Faculty of the Immaculate Conception

The young woman accepted into the Religious Community is responding to this divine call from God, Whom she believes is inviting her to love Him more perfectly in this life unto the next. She enters into Religious Life knowing that He is inviting her to sacrifice the great goods of an earthly marriage and children, free use of material possessions, and self–determination for the sake of higher, supernatural goods. These sacrifices are only possible by God's grace and in response to His call, with humble awareness that He will sustain her.

*T*HE GIFT OF TIME

Jesus does not mince words when He tells His disciples, "And everyone who has given up houses or brothers or sisters or father or mother or children or lands for the sake of my name will receive a hundred times more, and will inherit eternal life" (Mt. 19:29). The young women do, indeed, leave behind what is familiar to begin on their entrance day a new life out of love for Christ, and they learn quickly that this radical surrender is not a "once and for all" experience. The Lord will call them to a lifetime of "fiats," and each day will bring new opportunities to renew their "yes" as they come to understand more intimately Who it is that has called them and the life He has called them to embrace. Emboldened by his budding faith, St. Peter left his father and his fishing nets to follow Jesus, but he still had much to learn about discipleship and what it meant to take up the cross. Jesus bade him to come toward Him, but Peter

was distracted and saw the "wind" and began to sink. He was not yet ready for his ultimate vocation that would culminate in leading the Church as the first Pope and to his martyrdom. He needed to be formed.

All this points to the treasured time and gift of the novitiate in the Religious Life. While some Religious Communities require both a postulancy and two years as novices for their Sisters, the Church at minimum requires a canonical novitiate of one year of all Religious. This is precious time safeguarded by the Church. Each stage of formation has its specific end or purpose, and the Sister is called to throw herself 100 percent into the life, cooperating generously with the means of formation offered to her. The great Dominican Biblical scholar Père Marie-Joseph Lagrange, O.P. reflected back on the time of his novitiate as follows:

> The novitiate is a time of hidden life. And I did indeed spend this year seeking God. Why then speak of it to others? Because I am convinced that the graces I then received provided me with such light that the faith was more firmly rooted in my spirit.[2]

It is notable that Jesus did not hand the disciples a "how-to" manual on discipleship. He did not sit them down for an all–nighter on day one and spell out for them what the next several years would hold. There were few explicit details that would dispel their fears or the concerns of family members. Just as Jesus expected His first followers to come and remain with Him, without knowing entirely what the future held, so too is the Religious in formation called to trust the Community and cooperate in the formation process. This involves a gradual unfolding of the Religious Life to the candidate who over time more completely participates in the life of the institute. Formation is gradual for a reason. As eager as the young Sister may be to learn everything all at once, and regardless of how seemingly ready or ill-equipped she may feel (or truly be) at the time of entrance, in time she will be given the guidance and grace to meet the demands that Religious Life inevitably brings. The

Directives on Formation states, "It certainly is not required that a candidate for the religious life be able to assume all of the obligations of the religious life immediately, but he or she should be found capable of doing so progressively." [3] The Church is a wise Mother and knows best from experience that a firm foundation laid over time will bear fruit in a strong Religious Life that can weather any storm.

A GOD OF SURPRISES AND VARIETY

Members of the Dominican family often remark that they cannot be pigeonholed into a "mold" in terms of personality or talents. Meet one Dominican and you have met only one Dominican! At the same time, it is our hope that after spending some time among our Sisters, one will perceive a shared spirit that flows from our charism as well as common ideals and fidelity to common observances. As a Formator, it was a joy to witness a young Sister growing in her Religious identity and to see her unique personality start shining through as she lives her Dominican vocation! This was a gift to be welcomed, not stifled!

Each group that has entered our Community has been characterized by a variety of ages, educational backgrounds, and experiences. Within one postulant group, there might be a few eighteen-year-olds, a handful of young women who have come in the middle of their college studies, and some who have entered after working for a few years after college. Some grew up in intact families; others have divorced parents. A few Sisters may be converts to the faith. The personal experiences of each new Sister will be as vastly different as their family and education backgrounds. Once the postulants don their "blues" on entrance day, they all become part of the same group and start on equal footing. What binds them together from henceforth will be the pursuit of God's will in this Religious Community.

The Church has increasingly emphasized the personal dimension of Religious formation, recognizing the uniqueness of each person God calls, in the context of the formation that so necessarily takes places in community. The role of the postulant or novice mistress is a vital one, and she above all seeks God's will for the young women under her care, ever mindful that the Holy Spirit is the primary agent of formation.[4] One of my favorite intercessors, St. Thérèse of Lisieux, related the following from her time in the Lisieux Carmel working with the novices:

> From the beginning I realized that all souls have more or less the same battles to fight, but on the other hand I saw that since no two souls were exactly alike, each one must be dealt with differently.[5]

My experiences working with the young women who enter our Community resonated with this insight from St. Thérèse. The postulant and novice mistress should have a great reverence for the unique working of God in the individual souls of her Sisters. Recognizing the precious gift of a Religious vocation, she will pray and sacrifice for her Sisters and get to know each individually. The Formator is one who seeks to channel the Sister along the path the Lord is calling her. The Sister in formation is "invited unceasingly to give an attentive, new, and responsible reply."[6] In other words, the Sister has a vital role in her own formation, and only she can say "yes" to God and live out her vocation each day. The Formator cannot say "yes" for her!

Returning to the above narrative of Peter's attempt to walk on the water, the role of the Formator could be likened to that of one who is constantly pointing out the way to keep one's eyes fixed on Jesus, the goal of all our striving. She points out the pitfalls, gives advice about how to withstand the wind, and provides timely encouragement on how to keep moving forward despite, at times, feeling one's unworthiness, or perhaps not even seeing Jesus ahead or hearing His voice.

THE BLUES ARE BACK!

"It's so good to have the blues back!" This phrase is often heard around our Motherhouse during the first few weeks after our postulants' entrance each year at the end of August. The "blues" refer to the postulants, or more explicitly to the navy blue polyester outfits that distinguish them from the rest of the Community. Each Sister in the Community who no longer wears blue, and now wears white, can recall her own days of wearing the "blues" and especially all that she learned in the joyful "blur" of her first few weeks a postulant. While there is only a four-week window in our Community when we are "without" postulants each year (the period after the previous years' postulants receive the habit and became novices at the end of July and the entrance of a new postulant group in late August), there is something about the presence of postulants in the Community that seems to make life at the Motherhouse joyfully complete. Everything is new for the postulants. When we witness their delight and awe at our family customs as they experience them for the first time, we are reminded of our own first Christmas as postulants, for example, or when we first fumbled at table-waiting, and the encouraging smiles that the other Sisters gave us, which heartened us to keep trying. We have all been in their shoes, and as we get to know them and pray with them and for them, they truly become our Sisters in Christ.

GETTING TO KNOW THE COMMUNITY: POSTULANCY

Pope Benedict XVI is attributed as saying to the youth of the Church, "The world offers you comfort. But you were not made for comfort. You were made for greatness."[7] Pope Benedict recognized in young people—as did his predecessor, Pope St. John Paul II—a capacity for greatness, and frequently called upon them to move beyond the lies of relativism that dominate our culture. He challenged them to seek the fullness of Truth in the Person of Jesus Christ.

As postulant mistress and novice mistress, I have encountered young women who have heeded the calls of these great pontiffs. They are not strangers to the culture, and have come to encounter the Person of Jesus Christ in a variety of ways. They have not come to the convent seeking a life of comfort, but with a profound desire to give themselves unreservedly to Christ in the service of the Church. I have been humbled over and over again by the generosity of these young women when they first enter the convent. They have so much joy and willingly hand over all the material things that were once of value to them in the world. They leave cell phones behind, turn in their credit cards, and are eager to make every preliminary sacrifice in order to begin learning the ins and outs of convent life.

The main purpose of postulancy, the stage of formation preceding the novice years, is to assist the postulant in transitioning from lay life in the world to the Religious Life, which officially begins when she becomes a novice.

As postulant mistress, it was my primary role to introduce the postulants to the essentials of the Religious Life. This combined practical matters like learning the rubrics of the Divine Office (how we chant our prayers, when we bow, etc.) with a variety of classes in theological and catechetical subjects. Initially, the postulant's focus is upon learning what she needs to do and where she needs to be day in and day out. As she gradually becomes more at ease with the schedule and the rhythm of the life, she becomes more free to see and understand the purpose behind the various practices of our daily life, all of which are potential means to glorify the Lord and deepen her relationship with Him. For example: the invitation to unite her own prayers to those of the whole Church five times a day in community prayer will likely become more meaningful when the postulant is more confident finding her place in the breviary, the book she uses to pray the Liturgy of the Hours.

The postulancy is also a very important time for human formation. All aspects of formation are ongoing, and human formation should continue for each Religious well beyond her initial years of formation. However, her postulancy is a time when she begins to take on her identity as a Religious Sister and so is a particularly crucial time for human formation. The Church teaches that Formators, in union with the Father and the Holy Spirit, are called to shape "the attitude of the Son in the hearts of young men and women."[8] Hence, the whole of formation and the principal task of Formators is to create a firm grounding in a Sister's identity as a Religious.

The Church recognizes that sound human formation within Religious Life is of great urgency today, perhaps more so than in years past. The breakdown of many families and a pervasive secular culture often leave young people with deep wounds, of which they may or may not be aware. It is not unusual that young women with Religious vocations enter the convent, only to discover over time that they lack the necessary freedoms in certain areas of their lives to give themselves fully and peacefully to God and their neighbor, or to make the lifetime commitment that the vocation requires. These wounds need to be healed before they are able to surrender themselves fully to their vocation.

There is also a crisis of maturity among some young people entering Religious Life today. These young women are emerging from a secular culture that perpetuates indecision and a kind of arrested development among an age demographic who, a generation earlier, were settling down, having children, and making other important and permanent commitments. I often reminded the postulants and novices that they were adult Catholic Christian women. This may sound obvious, but it is a mindset that is often lacking, even among young women in their late twenties.

We would do well to consider what it means to be an adult Catholic Christian woman today. What is their prior experience of being a Catholic woman in the world? I encouraged them to reflect upon the reality that they should think of themselves this way, and that they would be treated as adult women in our Community and expected to relate to one another in the same regard. We could discuss personally any difficulties or challenges. Even if perhaps their family members or friends did not view them or treat them as adults, the Sisters could still respond in an adult manner. Religious Life must be embraced as adult Catholic Christian women.

We would then go further into the essence of Catholic womanhood and the gift of femininity. Formation in this area is ongoing in the life of every Religious woman. This is essential for living with other women in the Community and laying the foundation for how we relate to one another. We seek to communicate with each other and those outside the Community as mature women. A healthy identity as Religious depends upon this fundamental truth. Also, when the Sisters study the vows as novices, they come to understand how each vow specifically must be lived with an adult maturity. We seek to be childlike as Jesus called us—not to be childish.

$\mathcal{B}$RIDES-TO-BE: NOVICE YEARS

About a year ago, I had the unique experience of being mistaken for a bride at a photo shoot while at a state park with the postulants for a picnic. A woman caught sight of me in my white habit from a distance (perhaps she did not notice the black veil?) and inquired of the postulants as they approached if they were the bridesmaids for my wedding. The postulants kindly explained that they were Sisters, and pointed out my religious habit. They further clarified that they did not have the habit yet (but God-willing, soon!), and that we were there for a picnic.

Afterwards, the Sisters and I had a laugh about that, and we suspected that the woman in the park likely never had encountered Religious Sisters in habit before. We also wondered what she thought about the postulants' "blues" as potential bridesmaids' dresses! Finally, we acknowledged the bit of truth in the woman's observations. While not the type of bride she thought me to be, I was, indeed, wearing my wedding garment, the Religious habit I received on my reception day as a novice. The start of the novitiate in most

Communities is marked by a ceremony in which the Sister receives the habit of the Community and a new Religious name. Postulants long for this day to come, and in many Communities, great speculation (and suggestions) abound regarding the potential names the new novices will receive.

The new Religious habit, the white veil of the novice, and the new Religious name distinguish the Sister as a member of the specific Religious Community. In consequence, the new novice represents no longer herself, but the Church and her specific Community in a whole new way. The dramatic change of the habit and the new name reflects the beginning of a new level of responsibility as she begins to prepare for Religious profession. She is a public witness to the primacy of Christ by the habit she wears and a reminder of God and life eternal to all those who see her.

The canonical year of the novitiate that the Church requires is of particular importance and is dedicated to deepening the novices' prayer life and to studying the vows. While Community living begins as postulants, the novices grow in self-knowledge and have concrete opportunities to practice the virtues as they live and work closely with their fellow novices, day in and day out. Along these lines, *Fraternal Life in Community* states the following:

Religious community is the place where the daily and patient passage from "me" to "us" takes place, from my commitment to a commitment entrusted to the community, from seeking "my things" to seeking "the things of Christ."[9]

The novice years may be likened to a courtship in a relationship, in which the Sister is given precious time to get to know her Spouse-to-be very intimately. As the novice takes on more duties and comes to a deeper understanding of the vows and the Community's particular charism, she should be seeking above all the Lord's will. Is the Lord calling me to love Him in this way as a Religious? Am I willing to make the sacrifices this life requires? Do I have the necessary freedom to make a complete gift of myself to God and to others for the love of God? Learning to be comfortable in silence is also essential for the novices, and they need to be taught in this area. This becomes even a more urgent necessity in our age inundated by social media and noise.

On the level of Community, she is being guided and formed. The Church emphasizes the importance of ongoing dialogue with Formators who assist the young Sisters in discerning God's will. In addition to prayer, study of the vows, and silence, most Communities limit the novices' contacts with relatives and friends to a greater extent during the years as a novice. During my years working in formation, the Sisters struggled at times with missing family and the human element of this separation. That was certainly normal and understandable. However, these same Sisters most often also welcomed and saw the importance of having a time that freed them to focus more on their relationship with Christ and understood why the Church safeguarded the novitiate in this way.

On the other hand, while many families do support their daughters and sisters and respect the regulations of the Religious Life, I have seen just as many offer vocal resistance to the way of life that these young women have chosen. Some express ongoing displeasure and accuse their daughter or sister of hurting her family by her choice to enter Religious Life. While I do not wish to underestimate the sacrifice that a family makes in supporting the Religious vocation of a loved one, I can attest that these young women are keenly aware of how their families feel and the pain they may be causing them by their choice.

I hope everyone realizes that entering a convent or seminary is a discernment process and will help the individual grow in their relationship with Jesus Christ. I always tell young people that I will celebrate when they go to discern. I will also celebrate if they leave because they took the time to discern. Please do not be afraid to see if Religious Life might be right for you. Our family feels greatly blessed to have a Religious vocation and we pray that many young people will take the time to discern their calling in life.
—Judy Cozzens, mother of Bishop Andrew Cozzens, and President-Elect of the USA Council of Serra International

I encourage family members who may struggle with their relative's decision to enter Religious Life to prayerfully consider that her choice is an adult choice made freely. As families often struggle with this, I also encourage openness to understanding that choice over time. My own family, as well as the families of many other Sisters, can verify that they slowly found out that they did not lose a daughter when she entered the convent. Rather, they gained more daughters than they ever could have imagined! A hundred plus and more! Each Sister's family becomes part of a larger family when she enters Religious Life, and the Lord will bless parents and siblings for the sacrifice they make in supporting their loved one's Religious vocation. It takes time, trust, and sacrifice. And they will receive many, many prayers!

A final note about the novice years is that many Communities have a second year in addition to the canonical year. In my own Community, we call this year the "apostolic" year. This year, when provided, calls for the novice to experience the apostolate of the Community. She is to be given a taste of what she eventually will experience on a larger scale as a professed Religious. At the same time, the time of the novice's prayer is to be safeguarded, and she is not to be given the full responsibility of a professed Sister. Our Community is a teaching order, so our apostolic novices spend one day a week at our schools: observing in the classrooms, assisting the teachers, working with the children, and at times teaching lessons. Additionally, the novices have opportunities to go on apostolic trips with professed Sisters throughout the year for vocations and bear witness to Christ in a variety of settings. All the while, they are being guided by the novice mistress at the Motherhouse and are seeking to interiorize all that they are learning both inside and outside the classroom. After two years as a novice, if she believes herself ready and is accepted by the Community, the novice professes her first vows of poverty, chastity, and obedience, and becomes officially a bride of Christ!

$\mathcal{M}$ARY, STAR OF THE SEA

Returning to the scene of the Gospels in which Peter moved forward toward Jesus on the water, it is true to note that Peter did walk on water, however briefly. While I am not seeking to give an exact equivalence of formation or Religious Life to walking on the water, the words of Pope Benedict bear repeating: God calls us to greatness! The Lord chooses whom He wills. We respond only with the help of His grace and move forward not by our own power, but by keeping our eyes firmly fixed on Him. If He calls you or someone you love to the Religious Life, please encourage them to seek His will, which will undoubtedly bring the greatest happiness and everlasting joy. As we all move forward toward Christ on our paths to holiness, may we be strengthened by Mary, Star of the Sea, who illuminates our path to her Son and never ceases to pray for us!

Endnotes

[1] John Paul II, *Vita Consecrata*, 65. (Boston, MA: Pauline Books and Media, 1996).

[2] Marie-Joseph Lagrange, Père Lagrange: Personal Reflections and Memoirs (New York, NY: Paulist Press, 1985), p. 217

[3] Congregation for Institutes of Consecrated Life and Societies of Apostolic Life. Directives on Formation in Religious Institutes 42, (Boston, MA: Pauline Books and Media, 1990).

[4] *Directives on Formation*, 19.

[5] Thérèse of Lisieux, *Story of a Soul: Autobiography of St. Thérèse of Lisieux*, 3rd ed., trans. John Clarke (Washington, D.C.: ICS Publications, 1997), pp. 239–240.

[6] *Directives on Formation*, 29.

[7] Scott Kallal, "The Legacy of Benedict XVI." *Focus on Campus,* last modified March 12, 2013, https://focusoncampus.org/content/the-legacy-of-benedict-xvi.

[8] *Vita Consecrata*, 66.

[9] Congregation for Institutes of Consecrated Life and Societies of Apostolic Life, *Fraternal Life in Community*, 39 (Boston, MA: Pauline Books and Media, 1990).

Chapter 7

Merciful Love...
Personal Formation for the Apostolate
—Sr. Thomas Aquinas Betlewski, O.P.

> "Those who are well do not need a physician, but the sick do. Go and learn the meaning of the words, 'I desire mercy, not sacrifice.' I did not come to call the righteous but sinners." (Mt. 9:12–13)

At the heart of every Religious vocation is a definitive acceptance of God's infinite mercy. A Sister cannot "call herself" to Religious Life; such a self-willed project would be a chimera. A vocation is a demonstration of Divine Mercy in that it is a free gift, given in spite of the lowliness, sinfulness, and poverty that is at the core of all human existence. A Religious woman is *called* to accept the mercy that is her vocation, a vocation to an exclusive intimacy with Christ and a participation in His mission for the salvation of souls. She is called *by name*, that is, uniquely and irrevocably, in the context of her own subjectivity, despite any resistance she experiences within herself, or any external pressure from the society from which she comes.

Through my Religious Life, I see myself in this dynamic of Divine Mercy. As I don my Religious habit each morning and make my way to the chapel for morning Holy Hour, I am reminded of the mercy that is at the heart of my vocation. I do not deserve to number myself among those chosen by Christ for His purpose. As I kneel before the Eucharist in those first moments of the day, I *know* a deep joy, despite the fatigue or distractions, a joy that springs from the mercy that pours into me. Other Religious—within both my own and other Communities—also speak of this joy, which is a gift from the Bridegroom and a fulfillment even now of the spousal intimacy with Jesus to which we are called.

I believe the Church needs more Sisters because it is a unique way of life through which Jesus wishes to manifest His love and compassion for all people. First and foremost, a woman who enters consecrated life reminds everyone of important spiritual truths that are countercultural. For example: Happiness is not to be found in wealth, fame, or materialism, but can be found in a life of sacrifice, prayer, and service. Placing one's life in the hands of an order and its leadership is a profound statement of trust in God's love and providence. Sisters do this by their presence and the many ministries in which they serve.
—*Fr. Michael Caruso, S.J., President of St. Ignatius College Prep in Chicago, Illinois*

This experience of Divine Mercy is at the heart of my vocation, and it is also a call to share with others the message, meaning, and power of God's mercy. All Religious women are called to proclaim to others the beautiful line from Our Lady's Magnificat: "The Mighty One has done great things for me, and holy is his name. His mercy is from age to age, to those who fear him" (Lk. 1:50). Among Dominicans, this proclamation takes on the unique form of teaching and, for me specifically, teaching at the high school level.

Giving a living witness to mercy is at the heart of a Sister's teaching. The message of mercy is more necessary than ever for the young people entrusted to our care. In a world of fierce competition, high expectations for an almost unattainable perfection, and frequent incidence of family breakdown and teenage depression, anxiety, and suicide, the reality of God's loving mercy is desperately needed. The living witness of one whose entire existence and work attests to the loving mercy of God—the Religious woman—provides an ideal answer and image for our young people today. In sum, this is the essential meaning of the Religious woman at the high school level: to proclaim the infinite mercy of God in a world that is hurting.

This is not to say that a Sister is the same as a campus minister, or that she ought to assume the role of a therapist for her students. She is first and foremost a teacher, and her daily task is to educate the minds and hearts of future generations. Nevertheless, the dynamic of her Religious vocation enables her to give a profound witness to mercy; in the midst of her daily teaching, whether in geometry, world literature, physics, Spanish, or United States history, her being speaks to her students of God's mercy. She teaches not merely a subject but a way of life, showing how the acceptance of God's mercy sets the human personality on the path toward holiness. When she lives in joyful surrender to grace, she becomes a model of the pursuit of virtue. The sole motivator for a Sister's effort in the apostolate is to fulfill the will of God lovingly and thus strive to be of one mind and heart with Jesus Christ.

𝒯HE FEMININE GENIUS AND SPIRITUAL MOTHERHOOD

A woman's innate vocation is to motherhood, whether physical or spiritual; the very design of her body and her manner of love show her the truth of her vocation to motherhood. This feminine vocation brings a particular *genius* to the classroom that is both different from and complementary to her male counterparts. Pope St. John Paul II, in his *Letter to Women,* describes the beautiful link between motherhood and education:

> I would like to call to mind woman as teacher. It is a well-founded hope, if one considers the deep meaning of education, which cannot be reduced to the dry imparting of concepts but must aim at the full growth of man in all his dimensions. In this respect, how can we fail to understand the importance of the feminine genius? She has a unique capacity to see the person as an individual, to understand his aspirations and needs with special insight, and she is able to face up to problems with deep involvement. The universal values themselves, which any sound education must always present, are offered by feminine sensitivity. Wherever the work of education is called for, we can note that women are ever ready and willing to give themselves generously to others, especially in serving the weakest and most defenseless. In this work they exhibit a kind of affective, cultural, and spiritual motherhood which has inestimable value for the development of individuals and the future of society.[1]

This remarkable passage is a charter for all women, but especially for Religious women who have devoted their lives to the classroom. By living out her call to spiritual motherhood, in service of her witness to mercy, a Religious woman becomes more than just a teacher. Of course, like any teacher, a Sister relies on professional and human development, years of experience in the classroom, and advanced degrees in her subject area. Yet a Sister also combines *feminine genius* and *spiritual motherhood* with her experience of God's mercy and her intimacy with Jesus. This unique and powerful synthesis is the extraordinary gift that a Sister gives her students and the school community she serves.

I think of the countless times in my own life of *giving a mother's heart* to students through my prayer. I remember in particular a young man who was talented on the soccer field and very popular among his peers. He did not ask directly for prayers, probably because he did not want to appear weak or vulnerable. Yet he knew that no matter how he made the request, I would come through with my support. He came into my classroom, took a piece of paper and wrote down the name of his father, and slid this piece of paper across my desk to my hand. Although I didn't know exactly why he was giving me the paper, I just knew this young man needed my *spiritual motherhood* through loving prayer. A few weeks later I received word that his father had died of an aggressive stomach cancer. When I saw him at the funeral Mass, he gave me a hug and said simply, "Thank you."

A Religious woman gives witness to mercy wherever she goes, but for our Community, one of the principal ways this is done is in her classroom and broader school community. By means of her spiritual motherhood, a Sister becomes a channel of grace for her students and fellow teachers.

Communion

Perhaps the most noticeable gift a Religious woman brings to her teaching is the witness she gives of mercy received and lived *in community*. I was recently at a store with the three Sisters on my mission, and we passed a young dad holding his little daughter by the hand. When she saw the four of us in our habits, she exclaimed, "Look! They are all one!" We laughed at this delightful moment, but later reflection revealed the profundity of this little girl's exclamation. She meant, "They are all wearing the same thing!" She touched on the deeper unity signified externally by the wearing of the habit.

So often our students comment on the amount of time we must spend together, and they ask why we do not ever seem to argue or fight. How do we get along? Due to the frequency with which this question is asked, I believe that our witness of healthy Community life does more than support our own Religious Life; it also helps our students to see that unity of life and friendship is both possible and rewarding. Our Community life is a blessing and requires effort and sacrifice to nurture its growth. We are not always able to come to every basketball game or to chaperone the homecoming dance. Our time in Community is a priority which often leads us to sacrifice involvement in the active extracurricular and athletic world of our students for the sake of Community activities and prayer. We make time for community because we desire to be "all one" in the words of the little girl at the store. We have the conviction that Community life is the "habitat" in which authentic communion lives and grows, and it is authentic communion among the Sisters that in turn supports and nourishes our consecration to God.

The witness we give of knowing and loving one another is tangible to the students and communicates to them the possibility of finding and maintaining human friendship and love throughout one's life. Throughout their high school years, young people are forging new bonds of friendship with one another and exploring the dimensions and complexities of relationships with the opposite sex. They find that relating to one another authentically requires effort and involves making mistakes. Oftentimes students approach the Sisters for advice in the area of human relations, because they instinctively see the Sisters as "experts" at communion. The questions they ask involve how to interact with others and to secure their own identity in the process, and a Sister provides ideal accompaniment in this delicate development.

*J*NTELLECTUAL VIRTUES

Integrated into the Sister's fundamental desire to do God's will is her love for truth, which I have found powerfully expressed in my own Community's Dominican charism. I have lived and taught with Sisters who served in mathematics and science departments, in the humanities, and in my own department of theology. These Sisters continuously inspire me by their efforts to advance human knowledge and to introduce their students to the nobility of the intellectual life. They take their academic subjects seriously and teach with thoroughness and passion. Their students learn the disciplines while being trained in the intellectual virtues. A life of the mind requires diligence, perseverance, and industry, and these virtues are modeled by the Sisters on a daily basis. Like our Holy Father, St. Dominic, we strive to be preachers and teachers of truth and grace, and it is our joy to see high school students discover their interests and passions.

Furthermore, in a world where *objective and subjective truth* are often confused and absolute moral norms are clouded by relativistic ideas, the necessity of teaching philosophical principles has become essential.

THE VOWS

Perhaps the preeminent witness of mercy that a Religious woman gives is her living of the evangelical counsels of poverty, chastity, and obedience. As markers of her consecrated existence, these vows are the distinguishing signs of her total belonging to God and her surrender to His infinite and loving mercy. They also serve as powerful signs of contradiction for her students.

In our world today, the message is clear: the more you have, the happier you will be. We are constantly bombarded by empty promises of happiness arising from material possessions. This lifestyle is "costly," not only in a material sense, but also on the human and spiritual levels. I have observed in the lives of my students and their families the deep spiritual and emotional poverty that often accompanies the amassing of possessions and money. In this culture, the vow of poverty starts profound conversations. My students are shocked that I do not own a smartphone, and that I only use a tablet or laptop insofar as teaching requires them. My vow of poverty exudes the simplicity that has become my "home," so to speak. The students recognize—often in spite of themselves—that possessions only increase feelings of isolation and, when used out without purpose and moderation, may dehumanize. The fact that Religious women live without these distractions causes our students to stop and consider embracing moderation in the use of material goods. They recognize this desire to "give up" possessions as a way to "have more" spiritually; thus is fostered a dynamic maturity and independence which even the youth find refreshing. Further, I have found that students from lower-income families have a special identification with the Sisters, as we see beyond possessions, style, and popularity to our students as persons.

The vow of chastity is likewise a powerful witness of God's mercy to young people today. Even if her subject area does not include Catholic sexual morality, a Religious woman teaches the value of chastity by her very presence. Chastity is not simply about abstinence; the joy and calm that radiate from an integrated chastity demonstrate that chastity embraces interpersonal relations and our respect for self and others. I have often explained to my students that I see my vow of chastity not as a "no" to sex and marriage but as a "yes" to a full life of love consecrated to Jesus Christ. Chastity is personal, not impersonal. It is dynamic, not static. Sexual behavior among teenagers today remains on the rise, and what better way to introduce high school students to the beauty and fulfillment of a chaste life than through the witness of a Religious woman? In my own classes, students have asked me frankly if real love is possible. Because of the witness of my consecrated life, I believe the answers I give are especially credible.

Self-assertion and actualization are the prized end-result of democratic education—more than ever before, students are encouraged to "define themselves." Even community service is meant to assist students to "feel good" about themselves as participants in "making the world a better place." Planning one's future is the principal task of today's high school graduate, and self-determination is seen as the ultimate goal of adulthood. What a challenge the vow of obedience provides to these standards of self-importance! My students are amazed that the Sisters can be happy while surrendering their wills, their futures, and their plans to the will of another human being! The peaceful manner in which a Sister embraces her assignment each year shows students the inestimable value of emptying oneself for God and for His work. When moving from one school to another, with His grace, and with our daily "yes" to the Divine plan, we trust that we will meet these young people once again, and pray that we will be with them for all eternity. The vow of obedience frees me to love the students I teach each year as chosen gifts from Christ for me.

$\mathcal{P}$RAYER

The life of a Religious is above all a life dedicated to prayer. Whether a Religious lives a cloistered life or teaches in a classroom, her primary work is to lift her heart and mind daily to God in prayer. The Divine Office, mental prayer, spiritual reading, and *lectio divina*—all of these punctuate her day to remind her of her duty to praise and adore her God. These periods of prayer are the expressions of her spousal bond with Christ and cannot be set aside as extra or secondary to her work as a teacher. Perhaps one of the most rewarding aspects of teaching remains the dedicated task of praying for my students. As we take this seriously, students know that in a unique way we belong to them, and one way we honor this bond is through prayer. I love when a student entrusts me with a special intention, whether for a family member, an upcoming final exam, or some kind of personal difficulty. As a Religious, I am entirely free to dedicate my time of prayer to students who I think are struggling or who suffer from some unarticulated burden. Our prayer reaches where we cannot go, and one of the chief means of expressing our spiritual motherhood is prayer and sacrifice.

By living my Religious Life, as embraced and articulated by my particular Community, I give witness to the infinite mercy and goodness of God. I show forth the value of a life given to God, and by wearing the Religious habit, I witness to my students how important my Religious Life is to me and to the world today. Despite my imperfections, God has called me to Religious life. He had mercy on me. Through His merciful love, I witness to this Divine Mercy in the very weaknesses of my humanity, and tell forth, like Our Lady, the great things God has done for me.

CONCLUSION

As Sisters in a high school classroom, we enter the youthful fray each morning, reinforced by the prayers we have already offered to the Lord on behalf of each of our students. Although we bring our own human hopes, desires, and frailties, we do not come alone; we come with Christ. The Sister's role is to represent her Spouse, Jesus Christ; through the work of the apostolate and spiritual motherhood, she seeks to bring as many of His young people to Him as possible in her lifetime. Sisters in the classroom educate for heaven, because we believe that our students are offered and can accept the same gift we have received, the inestimable gift of the gracious Mercy of God.

Endnotes

[1] John Paul II, *Mulieris Dignitatem*, 9, Vatican, August 15, 1988, https://w2.vatican.va/content/john-paul-ii/en/apost_letters/1988/documents/hf_jp-ii_apl_19880815_mulieris-dignitatem.html.

Part 2: Lived Experiences

Chapter 8

Bridging over Troubled to Untroubled Waters...
Finding Fulfillment in God's Plan
—Sr. Maximilian Marie Garretson, O.P.

FAITH AND FASHION

It was a Friday morning in Lent 2016, and I was reminded that my life as a consecrated Religious vowed to Christ is not at all bland, but replete with vivid contrasts and paradoxes.

A spectacular blue sky and a nip in the air found me walking across Sant'Angelo Bridge in Rome, Italy. I was clad in my black mantle, its hem whipping at my ankles in response to my clipped pace. Traditionally traveled by Christian pilgrims, the bridge was the only passageway to get to the Basilica of St. Peter. It was a routine walk to the Pontifical North American College where I serve as the librarian. I turned the corner onto the bridge. It was strangely empty. I walked between the ten angelic statues holding the instruments of Christ's passion—a perfect complement to the Sorrowful Mysteries I was praying that day. My attention was drawn to the Lord within, still glowing and warm, hidden in the taste of bread.

I continued walking along the bridge and came upon the backside of an ultra-lean figure, feminine and lightly clad. Her single-layer, skin-toned dress was the length of my t-shirt (the first of four layers I was wearing). It was more sparkles and sequins than fabric, glistening in the rising sun. She was standing midway on the bridge facing Castel Sant'Angelo. I took in this odd scene as I approached her, concerned about the chill on her bare legs and arms. Then, at the far end of the bridge, I noticed a mob of darkly dressed videographers and photographers. Looking at them, I realized my adolescent-girl dream to be a model in Italy was finally coming true!

Reining in every dormant—but suddenly waking—trace of vanity in me, I attempted to focus on the rosary beads I was working through my gloved fingers. I kept my eyes on the dome of the Basilica. My gaze was intercepted by the angelic statue towering over us both, holding its passion instruments, while my thoughts were whisked away to both the present scene and my childhood aspirations. I was struck by the contrast between the face and figure of the woman and mine on the Ponte Sant'Angelo catwalk this morning. Her defined eyebrows, "perfectly tousled" blonde hair, and flawless complexion were stunning. Her lips, all shine and pout; mine, colorless and lined only with a slight smile. Her eyes were dark and defined: empty and starved. My eyes were clear of all "mocha-mist" eye shadow, but shining from the afterglow of a heavenly banquet. My meditation came back to the Stations of the Cross, especially Christ stripped of His garments, and I wondered what my layers of black-and-white habit looked like against her imperceptible dress (both in tone and expanse), not to mention its incongruity with her near-nakedness in the chilled air. Nearly stripped bare, the woman was clothed in the glamour of this world. Stripped of the world but clothed with Christ, I wore three layers of a Dominican habit! My caped mystery strode past her posed curves, and I was struck by the irony of what the stone angel towering over us held: the "garments and dice" of our Lord's passion.

As a consecrated Religious, my "garments and dice" are now in the loving hands of Christ. At one time, however, my greatest aspiration was to be that Italian beauty—glamorous and dressed to kill. It was the means, I thought, to personal happiness and perfect fulfillment.

*F*ASHION AND DESIRE

I was raised in the state of Oregon by faithful Catholic parents in the 1980s and 1990s. One of six children and the youngest of the three girls, my life was always a funky blend of faith and fads. On my nightstand, the fashion magazines lay beside my Bible, spiritual books, and rosary. Next to my Hard Rock Café shot glass collection, on the wall opposite the crucifix hung a life-sized door poster of Patrick Swayze. A tangle of hoop earrings and bangle-bracelets shared the shelf with images of the Immaculate Heart of Mary and the Sacred Heart of Jesus.

Glamour demanded no small amount of sacrifice and perseverance. Thanks to the living witness of my parents, I had an understanding of and practiced both. Under the influence of my older sisters, I applied these admirable virtues to clothes and fashion. Just as athletes learn sacrifice and perseverance through their sport, I learned and applied them through elaborate beauty regimens rather than in my spiritual life. Uncomfortable, even painful, shoes were a small price to pay for a perfect outfit. If two hours of aerobics per day was what it would take to look great in that prom dress, then sign me up. Working a second job to offset the expense of a sheepskin jacket was worth it. Some outfits required the inevitable freezing fits or sweating sessions—to wear a coat over your Easter dress was just not an option. Even though back–to–school pictures were scheduled during an Indian summer, I still wore my new autumn sweater.

Underneath this fashion frenzy, for as long as I can remember, was a deep desire to be a wife and mother. The perfect outfit, hair, and makeup seemed to be sure–fire tools to find the perfect man who would fulfill my longing for intimacy and motherhood. In my plastic–perfect world of Barbie and Ken, it all seemed to go together: the perfect outfit, perfect looks, perfect man, and perfect life. Somewhat shy around boys, "crushes" were safe and kept me motivated toward this end. Moreover, my imaginary world of serial crushes fueled my wardrobe, and my wardrobe fueled my imaginary world. The latest crush would influence the wardrobe: the soccer player, the band member, the outdoors man, the actor. There was a direct correlation between what I wore and whom I loved at the time. By age sixteen, my closet was bursting.

If someone had told me then that the love of my life and my fulfillment as a mother would find me wearing a Religious habit, I would NOT have believed them! The navy blue polyester skirt and vest, white button–down blouse, and plain black shoes of a postulant would never have made it into my closet.

DESIRE AND SERVICE

My adolescent obsession for fashion came to a climax shortly after high school graduation. All year I had saved my money to go on a two-week graduation trip to Hawaii with five of my friends. We had a few organizational meetings and preparation sessions. But what I remember most is the time, energy, and delight I invested in coordinating the wardrobe I would need to accommodate all the dreamy happenings of a tropical escapade. I imagined the moment I would descend the small plane and be welcomed with a lei placed over my head. Suddenly I realized I needed a new sundress to go with it. Where did I put that Talbot's catalogue? I would picture enchanted evenings spent beside pools lined with tiki torches, but I had nothing suitable to wear at a pool lined with tiki torches! Off I would go to the fabric store to purchase a bolt of sarong material. I would look forward to snorkeling in aquamarine waters and sunbathing on white, sandy beaches and decide I needed a few extra swimsuits for that much water activity. Off to the mall I went. And, while shopping at the mall, I realized I needed the perfect outfit to wear while shopping in Hawaii.

Externally, Hawaii was everything I had imagined and hoped for, but somehow it was still not enough. My perfect vacation and my perfect wardrobe left me feeling empty. I did not realize this until I had a contrasting experience of an altogether different kind of trip which left me filled with inner joy.

Upon returning home from Hawaii, not nearly as tanned as I had hoped and having worn only one-third of the clothing I packed, a phone message was waiting for me. Through our parish I was invited to be a part of a service trip called "Los Embajadores," named after St. Paul's "ambassadors for Christ" (2 Cor. 5:20). It was a mission trip in which young people were given the opportunity to serve in the poorest parts of Tijuana, Mexico. This trip would be two weeks, not of beaches and shopping, but of service and simplicity. While I had saved and spent so much money on the Hawaii trip, this trip was a gratuitous gift paid for by generous benefactors. I went to Hawaii with friends, but this would be a group of twenty-five people I had never met before. We were limited in our luggage allowances and encouraged to pack lightly and simply. After a few days of training and bonding, we all piled into two fifteen-passenger vans. Somewhere on the I-5 Freeway in California, our leaders—a devout married couple—encouraged and even challenged the girls to go without makeup for the trip as a daily sacrifice, adding that it would free us from being concerned about looks while serving the poor. It was no blue polyester postulant outfit, but what I had actually signed up for began to sink in.

In Tijuana, when we were not laying foundations for schools, making repairs to fences, running electrical wiring, or painting, we were praying in common, attending daily Mass, playing soccer with the children, having meals with the families in their homes, and being treated to popsicles by grateful boys and girls who were themselves abjectly poor. At the end of each day, as we went to bed on mattresses in a cement compound, my new friends in Christ and I were absolutely exhausted and absolutely full of life. When I returned home two weeks later, I realized I had never been as happy as when I was serving others and living simply. Whether I realized it or not, the living Person, Jesus Christ, was real and bursting into my illusory world. I had come back empty from my dream vacation to Hawaii but returned from Tijuana with a heart brimming with joy and hope. It was the taste of hopeful joy that made me long for the "more" of life. I began to understand "that God is the true wealth of the human heart."[1]

SERVICE AND REALITY

Old habits die hard. Gradually I returned to my old ways, means, and methods to find personal fulfillment. My innate and sincere search for happiness continued to contend and blend with the cultural inclination to "live in my head," exclude reality, and avoid sacrifice. Until this point in my life, I read mostly magazines, the backs of cereal boxes, and banal fiction. I searched for the reasons behind things, to be sure. However, the questions I asked did not probe the meaning of life. Instead my mind was occupied with questions like "Why exactly was I grounded (yet again)?" or "What do I need to do to pass this class?" and "Why can't I go out dressed like this?"

After a few years of career changes, serial boyfriends, and severe heartbreaks, I decided to enroll at Magdalen College, a small Catholic college in New Hampshire. Arriving on campus in 1994 as a freshman at age twenty-one, I began to sober up from my surface-level living and learn how to love and to live a more honest, authentic life.

By immersing myself in both the academic program and a sacramental life, I began to put into words my experiences of past emptiness and to recognize partial "truths" I had accepted and lived as absolutes. I began to distinguish true happiness from fictionalized fantasies. I began to see through the "all-glamour-and-fun" lifestyles plastered on billboards and magazine racks. From the movie and television screen, I could see the seductive autonomy and false sexuality that promoted "happiness" and hear the superficial sensuality blaring over the radio. Most importantly, I recognized the evidence of its impact in the very way I spoke, thought, and lived.

Within a year's time, I was exposed to (and exposed by) a variety of works of universally acclaimed authors. This experience opened me to examining the fundamental questions of life: "Who am I?" "Where have I come from?" "Where am I going?"

The apathy of Albert Camus' title character in *The Stranger* seemed somewhat normal to me. But, when read alongside Victor Frankl's *Man's Search for Meaning*, I was struck by the Stranger's incapacity for intimate relationships and the meaninglessness of life without them. My world view was altered by the striking contrast between his apathy juxtaposed with the transcendent effect of Dr. Frankl's love for his wife and the transforming power of beauty in his experience as a death camp prisoner.

I was floored that Alexis de Tocqueville, a French aristocrat, could visit America in 1830 and describe me and my friends: "alike and equal, constantly circling around in pursuit of petty and banal pleasures."[2] I lived and breathed the extreme individualism depicted by his exposé in *Democracy in America* and saw the sad evidence that "each man is forever thrown back onto himself alone, and there is danger that he may be shut up in the solitude of his own heart."[3] It led me to examine my life and wonder if I wanted to live a life governed by a "calm and considered feeling which disposes each citizen to isolate himself from the mass of his fellows and withdraw into the circle of family and friends."[4]

I found answers in Aristotle's polis. The realization that we are social by nature and cannot live well outside of community resonated within me. Moreover, his explanation of the nature of virtue, the importance of character, and the role of friendship was like wind in my sails. Yet, for my part I more often lived out the Great Gatsby's formula for personality: an "unbroken series of successful gestures."[5] I had adopted this formula and let it define me.

I remember the moment I saw the immaterial beauty and order of Euclid's Proposition 47. I, who had spent most of my tenth–grade lunch period in remedial geometry, rediscovered the reality of an immaterial world and of my immortal soul through the Pythagorean Theorem.

The devastation wrought by the unbridled passions of the boys in the *Lord of the Flies* opened my eyes to the darkness and sin lurking in the human heart and the need for a savior. I knew what it meant to be "voted off the island" and, in good time, return the favor. When I read George McDonald's *Wise Woman*, I was tricked into looking into the mirror of fallen human nature and my own depravity through the characters of Rosamond and Agnes and encouraged to embark on the painful yet beautiful transformation that comes through true self-knowledge.

Most of all, I identified with the disillusionment of Socrates' cave dweller in Plato's *Republic*, his fear of truth and the painful process of emerging from the darkness. The many shafts of light radiating from these books and cutting through my darkness were challenging and painful. "Why," I asked with St. Augustine, "does the truth call forth hatred?" I liked my self-made fetters and wore them like jewelry. I was comfortable with my shadow-play "reality" on the wall. All this annoying light from outside was hurting my eyes, and I was developing a crick in my neck from an uncontrollable urge to jerk my head back to discover its source.

I understood the Grand Inquisitor's philosophy of blissful ignorance and *The Brothers Karamazov*'s painful yet liberating life lesson: the Truth will set you free. I rode alongside Don Quixote as he chased illusory giants, and I saw the nature of the human person through the lens of Shakespeare. I was finally given answers and also hope in St. Augustine's *Confessions*: "My heart is restless until it rests in thee."

As I wrestled with these great works and others over the next four years in the context of personal friendships and community life, I think I learned to be truly human for the first time. A childlike wonder reawakened in me as grace began to perfect my newly discovered human nature.

REALITY AND FAITH

One day at Mass in the chapel on campus, after receiving Holy Eucharist, I gazed up at the crucifix and realized how much Christ loved me. The reality of the crucifix and of the Holy Eucharist took hold of me—sacrificial love and selflessness. I had seen, known, and consumed Him my whole life, but never with such deep meaning. He loves me as I am—with or without the beauty regime or the perfect outfit. His total outpouring of love demanded a radical response from me: sanctity. Not just as a wife and mother, but as a holy wife and mother.

From this point on and by God's grace, I became a woman of faith and a daily communicant who was in love with the living Person, Jesus Christ. No longer did I find my security in the externals and the castles I had built up in my head. My identity was rooted in Christ, my Lord, and in His Catholic Church. Now, I had a firm foundation to stand on. But my plan to be a saintly wife and mother was being thwarted by God Himself! It seemed that almost every virtuous man (i.e., potential husband!) He put in my life ended up discerning a call to the priesthood. It was nine months after a near-engagement that I found myself on my knees before the Eucharist in total surrender to His plan. In this desperate moment of prayer, He took the inch I gave Him and stretched it six thousand miles—all the way to Rome in the year 2000 for the Jubilee Year World Youth Day.

The world hungers for authentic motherhood, especially spiritual motherhood. Yet our Lord's loving call to women to be consecrated to Him as His bride—and therefore a spiritual mother—can be difficult to hear and difficult to answer. We are in great need of more women who will give their the courageous "Yes" to be the bride of Christ, so that with His grace new spiritual life may spring up and flourish in the Church. Wherever the bride of Christ is, salvation quickens.
— Msgr. John Cihak, Papal Master of Ceremonies and Professor of Theology at the Pontifical Gregorian University in Rome

FAITH AND VOCATION

At twenty-six, I was a single laywoman working as a parish youth coordinator. The youth group and I were among the twenty thousand graced pilgrims who passed through the Holy Doors of Saint Peter's every hour during that World Youth Day. The chaplain for our group of twenty young pilgrims was Fr. John, a newly ordained priest from Oregon. During Mass, I heard for the first time a homily about the nature of the priesthood and Religious Life. His words matched up with my every longing. But wasn't Religious Life a thing of the past? I quickly attempted to stifle the stirring in my heart. It didn't conform to my lifelong dream to be a wife and mother. I prayed: "Please, God—no." I knew I was called to marriage and motherhood, but surely someone in this group was being called to Religious Life. His homily was for them. As we waited in the fields of Tor Vergata for the arrival of Pope St. John Paul II, I thought it was the perfect time to ask him, "Father, how do you know if you have a Religious vocation?" I watched the eyes of the young listeners as he explained using phrases like "intimacy with Christ," "bride of Christ," and "spiritual motherhood," which resonated in my searching heart. He explained that "it is a call to a universal spiritual motherhood and intimacy with Christ. He calls those with a particular capacity for love and motherhood." Again, I prayed: "Please, God—no! *No!*"

Still shaken, we waited with the other two million pilgrims for the Vigil with the Holy Father. Pope St. John Paul II spoke these words to the young people, pointing to Him who is our happiness and satisfaction:

> It is Jesus in fact that you seek when you dream of happiness, He is waiting for you when nothing else you find satisfies you; He is the beauty to which you are so attracted. It is He who provokes you with that thirst for fullness that will not let you settle for compromise; it is He who urges you to shed the masks of a false life;

it is He who reads in your hearts your most genuine choices, the choices others try to stifle. It is Jesus who stirs in you the desire to do something great with your lives, the will to follow an ideal, the refusal to allow yourselves to be grounded down by mediocrity, the courage to commit yourselves humbly and patiently to improving yourselves and society, making the world more human and fraternal.

I silently prayed: "Please, please, God—really?"

After receiving the Eucharist at the World Youth Day Mass, kneeling in prayer, in the depths of my heart, the Eucharistic Christ came. He beckoned me. He invited me. He called me to be His alone—intimately and exclusively. My response? Shock, awe, and wonder. Also, fear of giving my unreserved yes to something I did not yet understand or know how to navigate.

Two days later, over a cheeseburger in the airport, I explained to Father John the details of my life's journey. When I got to the part of the stirring in my heart in response to his preaching and the unmistakable invitation to give myself exclusively to Christ, he went deadpan. The all–American burger and fries lost all interest for him. I knew it was serious when he seemed as surprised as me. Not many people witness a young woman's call to Religious Life in the prime of her life. I took in his expression, and my heart harbored an interesting mix of horror and hope. He looked me straight in the eye and said, "I think the Lord might be inviting you to Religious Life." I did not know whether to laugh or cry.

Days after having experienced the Lord's invitation in Rome, I attended a college friend's wedding in southern California. There Christ Jesus laid out before me the contending desires of my heart. In the wedding party was another college friend, who was leaving the very next day to join the Dominican Community in Ann Arbor, Michigan. There, in that little mission church, the Lord presented to me the beauty of two vocations: marriage and consecrated Religious Life. As I witnessed the wedding vows, my childhood dream played out before my eyes. There seemed to be so much to surrender: wardrobe, makeup, hair, wedding dress, the "perfect" husband, angelic children. On the other hand, my friend entering a Religious Community was not at all homely and boring, which shattered my false perception of consecrated Religious. I was drawn to the fire blazing in her heart to give all to Christ with zeal for souls. I had a long drive home and much to think about. I thumbed through the newsletter my soon-to-be-Religious friend gave me as she departed for Ann Arbor. I saw the joy of the Sisters, their habits, and the school children. In these faces gazing back at me, I saw a simple truth: "In Christ it is possible to love God with all one's heart, putting Him above every other love, and, thus, to love every creature with the freedom of God!"[7] As I prayed a Rosary for clarity and courage, Christ took my greatest fears and turned them into hopes, my romantic daydreams and turned them into realities that only He could fulfill perfectly.

In those moments and in so many words, I understood "the chastity of celibates and virgins, as a manifestation of dedication to God with an undivided heart."[8] It is a reflection of the infinite love to which the Jesus bears witness, even to the point of giving His life. "The love of God has been poured out into our hearts through the Holy Spirit that has been given to us" (Rom. 5:5). This elicits a response of total "love for God and the brethren."[9] Right there, in my shiny

Volkswagen Jetta, I gave my response freely: "Yes, Lord—let it be done unto me according to your will!"

$\mathcal{V}$OCATION AND LOVE

On a recent October morning, I found myself walking once again across the Sant'Angelo Bridge. As I stepped onto the bridge, I laughed to myself at the irony of the scene before me, especially in light of my earlier "photo shoot" with the Italian model. I was approaching a young bride posed and exuding radiant joy. Though no man was present, the glorious white dress symbolized to everyone walking by that she was in love and about to dedicate her life to another. With the medieval Castel Sant'Angelo as the backdrop, one had the feeling that Prince Charming would ride up at any moment, claim his bride, and it would thus begin: the first day of the rest of her life living happily ever after. The bridal gown and sheer veil floating on the breeze communicated the timeless and transcendent desire of every woman: to be known and loved intimately for all eternity; the desire and possibility of bearing and nurturing new life and the purpose and fulfillment of life to be loved and to love.

Seeing smiles escape from the lips of every woman that strode alongside the stony expressions of a workaday rush hour crowd, I winked at her as I passed, as one bride to another. Remembering the "garments and dice" of my previous photo shoot, I inspected the stone angel hovering over this young woman. Indeed, there he stood. Her angel held a crown of thorns as if ready to exchange it in the future for her bridal veil. The crown of thorns—suffering—is always part of the fabric of love in this world, whether in the physical suffering of childbirth, the emotional suffering in relationships, or the suffering of personal loss. Christ embraces His beloved and, in that loving embrace, the thorns of His crown pierce the beloved's brow.

Fueled by this meditation, I continued on the pilgrim path to St. Peter's Basilica. I stood before the Pieta and its five-foot eight-inches of vulnerability etched in stone.

Mary's right hand with graceful strength firmly supports her Son, the open palm of her left hand seeming to echo the words she first spoke a few decades earlier, "Behold, I am the handmaid of the Lord. May it be done to me according to your word" (Lk. 1:38). There, as I pondered, I was struck by the paradoxical nature of her lap serving, no longer as the throne for her baby king, but now as a bier for His dead body. An imperceptible layer of linen interrupted the flesh-to-flesh contact as she stabilizes His body on her lap.

I dwelt upon the stone-cut portrayal of the Sorrowful Mother, remembering that she was in actual size much larger than the marble Christ figure. Indeed, if Mary with all those draped folds and flowing fabric was to stand erect, she would tower over her Son and the rest of us. Surely, Michelangelo's reason for this was practical: a massive lap to cradle gracefully a full-grown man. Even so, it is as if her expansive lap was an altar of sacrifice and she, clothed with a corporal, cradled Him in the sacred linen on which the priest today confects the Eucharist.

Mary, in the Pieta, ensconced in a corporal, cradling the Lamb of God, communicates who she is and her perfect fulfillment as mother and bride. What she "wears" perfectly correlates to her expansive heart, and lap as well as to the vulnerability of her vocation to love.

I am happy to discover that in Religious Life, perhaps inspired by Mary, mother and bride, there is still a direct correlation between what I wear and whom I love. And though what I wear is not the cause of perfect fulfillment, it is most certainly a means and a sign of that fulfillment. What I wear is a living witness to Jesus, my Lord—the One I truly love and the One who loves me truly.

Mary, Mother of the Eucharist, pray for us!

Endnotes

[1] John Paul II. *Vita Consecrata*, 90. Vatican. March 25, 1996, http://w2.vatican.va/content/john-paul-ii/en/apost_exhortations/documents/hf_jp-ii_exh_25031996_vita-consecrata.html.

[2] Alexis de Tocqueville, *Democracy in America*, trans. George Lawrence, (New York, NY: Anchor, 1969), 692.

[3] Ibid, 508.

[4] Ibid, 506.

[5] F. Scott Fitzgerald, *The Great Gatsby*, (New York, NY: Scribner, 1953), 2.

[6] John Paul II, "Address of the Holy Father John Paul II, Vigil of Prayer, 15th World Youth Day." Vatican. August 19, 2000, http://w2.vatican.va/content/john-paul-ii/en/speeches/2000/jul-sep/documents/hf_jp-ii_spe_20000819_gmg-veglia.html.

[7] Vita Consecrata, 88.

[8] Ibid., 21; cf. 1 Cor 7:32-34.

[9] Ibid., 21.

Chapter 9

So Many Plans of My Own...
From Homeschooling to Convent
—*Sr. Rene Noel Blanchard, O.P.*

Why me? I sometimes find myself asking this question, and the answer is always bafflingly and profoundly simple: because God loves me. There are as many different ways for God to call someone as there are people in the world, and His love for each of us is as unique as we are! When we are honest with ourselves, we realize that there is an aching longing planted deep in our hearts for that fulfillment of love. God has allowed this "heavenly homesickness" to draw us back to Himself. St. Augustine said it best: "You have made us for Yourself, O Lord, and our heart is restless until it rests in You."

My heart is full of gratitude as I look back on the ways God has used everything in my life to lead me right back into His arms: the relationships, the trials, the joys, the surprises. May my life echo Mary's cry of joy in some small way: "The Almighty has done great things for me, and holy is His name!"

IN THE HEART OF THE FAMILY

I am the second oldest of six children raised in a non-traditional traditional family. My family has always been one of those that crushes stereotypes right and left: we were all homeschooled, yet every one of us alone is loud enough to be a party of eight. We were always late to everything except Sunday Mass (daily Mass was hit or miss), and yet we never missed anything either. A party wasn't really a party until the Blanchards showed up! We prayed the Rosary, fought over who had to unload the dishwasher, and agonized over math homework.

Our interests were vast and varied. We were involved in 4-H, Toastmasters, historical balls and reenacting, church groups, basketball, and soccer. From the time I was young, we balanced (and sometimes did not) a busy schedule of six kids' interests.

In the tussle of sibling squabbles, chores, and workbooks, we became a close-knit family. My siblings and I were best friends growing up, and we still are. A mere ten years separates the oldest from the youngest.

Dominic is the oldest. He is a deep thinker, a passionate philosopher at heart. I learned much from him about what it means to listen, especially to God. He is a leader, with a strong and courageous manner of "taking up his Cross daily."

Right after me is Rachel. Her childlike trust in God continues to convict me to this day. Rachel and I would spend hours making each other laugh and coming up with clever games. We played such fascinating games with our Barbie dolls that the younger siblings begged to be allowed to watch us play. One favorite game was pretending that our Ken dolls were Franciscan friars who had to go into the witness protection program and pretend to be college students at a secular university!

The next youngest is Nathan. I was always very protective of Nathan. He sometimes got on my nerves, but with his round freckled face and shining blue eyes, I could never stay mad for long. Nathan has always been sensitive to the beautiful, with a heart easily moved to compassion.

Our gentle and compassionate Anna comes next. When she was six months old, I asked Mom and Dad to "send her back" because I couldn't stand the crying anymore. She grew out of that stage and into a beautiful young woman who is probably the smartest of all of us. In days gone by, we would wake up early and eat breakfast together on the back deck, watching as the woods behind our house flushed rose and then gold. I sometimes think that my leaving for the convent hit her hardest.

Benny is the baby of the family and the only other sibling who has brown eyes and brown hair like me. Benny is easygoing, with a great sense of humor; excellent traits for the youngest of six kids.

I share this about my siblings because they have shaped who I am. My relationships with my immediate family were the first ways God opened my heart to form me and my vocation. When we know ourselves to be so completely loved by other human beings, it starts to seem possible that God might actually love us, too. Later on we realize that we are only able to love anyone because God has first loved us. Believing in God's individual and very personal love is the first step everyone must take in his or her vocational journey, because every vocation is a response to love.

Against the backdrop of the care and love of my upbringing, God placed the first hints of a Religious vocation. My mom claims Rachel and I played "Sisters" when we were little and danced around with pillow cases on our heads. One time we locked ourselves in the closet to play "monks," and I remember at least once packing saltines and wanting to run away and be a hermit like St. Catherine of Siena. The idea of Religious Life was definitely in my head.

Yet, for all of this, I don't remember my parents ever directly asking me or bringing up the topic of vocation when I was growing up. I am convinced that they nourished my vocation in the simplest, most effective way possible: through their prayer and example. Being of deep faith and with deliberate expression of this, I understood they were fellow travelers on the way: disciples just like us. They never preached but encouraged us in our spiritual growth as those who understood where we were because they had been there, too. My parents, too, are always seeking to grow and mature in their relationship with Christ.

Sadly, I didn't fully appreciate or even notice my mom's daily example of sacrifice and perseverance while I was growing up. Now, I see the million ways she daily put aside her own wants, and sometimes needs, to tend to ours. Mom was not the kind of "supermom" who home-schooled the kids, kept a spotless house, and always had dinner ready at six o'clock on the dot. But she was a "supermom" in the sense that she was always ready to listen and to make prayer a priority. She was more concerned about her kids' souls than anything else, and helped to form us, not just teach us. Mom has, to this day, a peaceful and practical wisdom: a true gift from God for raising a large family.

So that we could homeschool, Dad worked a job that could support all eight of us on his single salary. When he got home he would help us with math or science while Mom got dinner on the table. One of the highlights during the day was always when Dad would call Mom to say "hi," usually around lunchtime, simply because he loved her. Dad also made prayer a priority and took his role as head of the household seriously. With humility, to this day he is always ready to learn something new, even from someone younger or less experienced. He always enjoys the little splendors in life, and his wonder at the natural beauty of creation is a cherished gift he worked to pass on to his children.

My parents did not want us simply to know about the faith, but to love it and live it as well. They wanted it to touch our hearts. So, along with saying a family Rosary when we could, they often packed everyone in the car (with schoolbooks) and made the trip to daily Mass. Our parents would take turns going to a nocturnal holy hour on Tuesdays, and any of the kids who wanted to was welcome to come. This quiet time with Jesus, before I even fully understood what it meant, was pivotal in my being able to discern my vocation at a young age. I am sure it was in these quiet hours, or the moments during Lent when we prayed the Stations of the Cross, that Jesus first planted the seeds of a Religious vocation in my heart.

I began thinking about being a Sister explicitly and clearly in middle school, when we relocated to Flagstaff. It was a dramatic shift for our family, even though it was only two hours away from where we had been living in Phoenix. Little did I know how much God had in store for me in that beloved city of pines and mountains!

OPEN AND SHUT

As high school approached, I started to push any idea of becoming a Sister to the back burner. I was already fighting homeschooler stereotypes in my Life Teen group and my theatre group. I did not want to add the "future nun" label to the ones I already had. No one was particularly mean or unkind, but I did occasionally resent my lack of knowledge of "the real world." I suppose I felt all the normal pressures of wanting to fit in, to know and do what everyone else knows and does. Discerning a call to Religious Life did not exactly fit that bill.

When I was an incoming freshman, I went on my first Steubenville West Conference. It was a powerful experience and made me realize that though I lived my Catholic identity faithfully, Jesus was calling me to a personal relationship with Him. I was completely blown away by grace that weekend and stood up for the altar call for those who thought they might have a Religious or Priestly vocation. I told myself I was open to whatever God's plans were. After all, my parents had read me many a saint story, and I knew what Religious Life was all about...didn't I?

I realized later that I thought I was "open" because I was sure I was called to marriage. I told my friends at the time "God wants us to be happy, and He's not going to call us to something we simply do not want to do. I do not want to be a Sister; therefore, God must be calling me to marriage." The problems with my logic were easy to spot; I had been profoundly influenced by the comfortable lies our culture tells us.

While God does indeed seek our true happiness, this often looks very different from what we have in mind. He wants us to be joyful, but with the joy that comes from Him, a joy that can very easily coexist with sadness and suffering. It sounds contradictory, but that is because we have such shallow notions of happiness and joy. True joy is knowing and doing God's will; He gives a deep peace that no tempest on the surface can shake.

He also knows us infinitely better than we know ourselves. We think we know what will make us happy, but only God really knows that. Sometimes it is necessary to trust and do something that we initially do not want to do. Only later do we realize that what God asked of us did make us happy, but not in the way we expected.

In addition, our desires are not always 100 percent on the mark. Though God does speak to us through them, they are often skewed and twisted by disordered attachments. Only God can purify our desires so that we want what is truly best for us, which is always His will.

The next summer I went to Steubenville West again. It was another powerful experience, but not quite as uplifting as my first one: I came face-to-face with the realization that I was, in fact, not open to God's plan if it included Religious Life. I had so many plans of my own and left no room for God's. Or at least, not without limits.

There were also many lurking fears that kept me from being open to Religious Life. Chief among them was the lie that becoming a Sister would mean giving up love. I would have to give up my family, my friends, and a future husband. I saw Religious Life as one enormous, tedious sacrifice. Part of the reason was that I had almost no contact with actual Sisters. I think if I had seen their joyous witness, I would have realized that there was nothing strictly negative about it. It is a life of total giving, but also of infinite receiving: Sisters give themselves to Christ and receive Christ Himself in return!

In spite of these fears, Jesus continued to draw me deeper. I continued to pray at holy hours with my parents on occasion. I loved attending Mass, especially during the week. After a few months of hesitation and prayer, I asked God for help to be open to His will for me, even if it meant being a Sister.

*W*HAT DO YOU DESIRE?

The summer before my last year of high school, I went on the Steubenville retreat with high expectations. I had been thinking about Religious Life here and there over the past couple of months, but rather unwillingly and somewhat bitterly. It was on this retreat that I first realized clearly that God was calling me to Religious Life. I had reached a point where I was not so much terrified as upset. I did not want it. I did not understand what God was asking. I did not understand what He was giving. In a moment of grace, I prayed with all my heart: "Lord, if you want this, make me want it too, because I do not right now, and I am scared."

It may seem like a dumb prayer, but usually our honest prayers are the ones that end up being the most efficacious. An honest acknowledgment of precisely how you feel about a certain situation is sometimes exactly what Jesus is waiting to hear from your lips. He will never fail us, especially when we put childlike faith in Him.

With that prayer still echoing in my heart, I plunged into my last year of high school. I began to be drawn to Our Lady and Eucharistic adoration more than ever. I started to say the St. Louis de Montfort prayer of consecration to Mary every day. I did not know what the prayer was, nor did I realize it was the prayer you are supposed to use to renew your consecration after having made it, but I prayed it faithfully, and I am sure Mary used it to guide me.

Suddenly, in January 2010, during a Life Teen adoration night, it was as if a cloud lifted. I could see that my vocation was Religious Life, and, more importantly, I wanted it more than I had ever wanted anything in my life...which was saying something! I was longing for it. It felt like Jesus had torn open my heart and poured in a double-strength dose of His love. I began to desire to give everything I had to Jesus. I started to live for Mass and the Eucharist and would go as often as I could, practically daily. He became the center and soul of every day, and I could not live without Him. The desire burned so strongly that I sought desperately for the one thing that could begin to quench it: following my vocation.

That spring I went on a diocesan retreat and met our Community. I had always had a strong inclination towards the Dominicans, since my dad had encountered Dominicans at his Newman Center in college and loved their spirituality. A Dominican concelebrated my parents' wedding, and they named my older brother and me, their first two children, after Dominican saints. I was thrilled finally to meet Dominicans in person and immediately felt drawn to their charism. Once I found out that only this Community of Dominicans had a daily Eucharistic holy hour and made the St. Louis de Montfort Marian consecration, there was practically no doubt in my mind that this specific family of Dominicans was where God was calling me.

The Sisters invited me to come on the May discernment retreat in Ann Arbor, Michigan. However, as much as I wanted to go, it is not cheap to get a round-trip ticket from Arizona to Michigan. My parents said they would not be able to afford it. I told my pastor of the predicament, and he assured me he would take care of it. The very next day at daily Mass, he told me he had found an anonymous sponsor to pay for the ticket. The miracle confirmed for me the necessity of visiting this Community.

I went on the retreat with an attitude of peaceful joy. I loved the Community immediately and knew this was where God was calling me to enter. Of course, the Lord's plans are often more exciting than we might imagine, and my peaceful weekend was thrown into turmoil when I was asked by the Vocation Directress about my plans for next year.

That weekend was my opportunity to trust God's plans fully, not only in what He wanted but when He wanted, as well. I realized I had been excited about being a Sister, but on my own time and in my own way. God wanted me to abandon myself completely that weekend and trust solely in Him. He was not calling me to be a Sister "sometime down the road" but now—in fact, this year. The power, reality, and love of that "now" took my breath away. Up until that moment it had been a nice theory. Now it became an unshakable, beautiful, staring-me-in-the-face reality, and I had to choose. Praised be Jesus Christ forever that I responded to the grace that weekend to say my own "yes." I came home from the retreat with application papers for August and three months to prepare.

Every big yes in life is usually the build up of a series of little yeses and is followed by many more to make the big yes a reality. Though my family supported my decision to enter in August, they did not understand it immediately, and others tried to discourage me. They told me that I had not "seen the world." I had not even visited any other Communities of Sisters. How could I possibly know myself and what I wanted when I was so young? Shouldn't I go to college first? In a way, they were all valid concerns.

A Sister once wrote me, "It is a singular grace to give your youth to God; it is also a singular cross." I have found this to be true a million times over. Though there are surely experiences I will never have in the world simply because I entered right out of high school, I have never once regretted the decision. God has given me infinitely more than the world ever could. As the Psalmist says, "Better one day within Your courts/than a thousand elsewhere" (Ps. 84:11). I am blessed to have encountered only slight pushback against my vocation in some quarters. What opposition I did face I was able to consider a means of purifying my decision.

There is a terrible trend these days among spiritual people of "trusting" in the Lord to the point of total passivity, even paralysis. I have met people who, when faced with an obstacle to doing something good, simply throw in the towel, saying, "Well, it must not be God's will." They think that anything God wants them to do will be easily and speedily accomplished because He will pave the way and add neon lights! Sometimes God does work that way, but often He speaks to us in much more subtle ways. We have to pray and listen quietly to know His will; then we must persevere in honesty and through substantial significant obstacles to carry it out.

As many spiritual masters have pointed out, Jesus never promised it would be easy to be His disciple. What He did promise was that He would be with us the entire way.

When we encounter obstacles in following God's will, they can actually be signs that we are on the right track. We are experiencing His Cross, and that is where Jesus is truly found.

It would be a lie to say that the few months leading up to my entrance day were easy. There were moments of ecstatic joy as I thought about the life that lay ahead of me. There were also moments of wrenching pain, the pain of the Cross, as the reality of leaving home sunk in. Entering out of high school brings a special cross, particularly in the sector of family attachments. I was used to seeing my parents and my siblings daily, practically all day, every day, since I was homeschooled. It was a very real, and very tough, transition for my family when we realized that those days were coming to a close.

My older brother left for his first year of college a few weeks before I entered the convent. There were tears, from me and from my family, but there was also immense grace. God sustained my family in all that He was asking of us. Through it all, I knew this was what God wanted of me, and the yes that I had steadfastly given anchored a deep peace in my soul. I never questioned whether this was actually what God wanted. By His grace I was filled with a tremendous peace, joy, and confidence that carried me swiftly to my entrance day.

THE JOURNEY BEGINS

I entered the Dominican Sisters of Mary, Mother of the Eucharist, on August 28, 2010. It was a day I will treasure as one of the happiest of my life, and also one of the most profound. My mom was the only family member with me; it would have been too expensive for the whole family to fly out to Michigan.

Lying in bed later that night, I asked myself, "What in the world did you just do?" I cried a little, prayed a little, laughed at myself, then rolled over and fell asleep quickly. Though I really had no idea what lay ahead, I knew God was with me. Together with Him, this was going to be a grand adventure!

Adjusting to Religious Life has its difficulties and joys for everyone. They are different based on each Sister's individual personality and background. One advantage of entering right out of high school is that you are already used to living with the same other people and sharing a daily schedule and routine. I was used to having to eat at a certain time, study at another time, and turn out my light at a predetermined time. While some Sisters find it hard to get into the swing of a common routine (called the "horarium") after living on their own for years, this was easy for me.

On the other hand, I had never lived away from home. I had to learn how to be a Religious while being separated from my family for the first time in my life. This was difficult, but I found great consolation in the joy of Community life with my Sisters and the letters I exchanged with my family.

A purifying moment came about two months after I entered. My cousin Renée passed away. She was the joy and delight of our extended family, beloved by us all. Renée had Down syndrome and cystic fibrosis, a combination which many doctors sought, in our culture of death, to give up on right away. But my aunt and uncle, even in the midst of suffering and occasional opposition, heroically fought for her life. No one expected her to survive to her birth or first year. Renée lived to be ten, surrounded by constant care and affection.

I have a great picture of Renée that I keep in my photo album. She is in her swimsuit by the pool and looks like she is almost dancing for the camera. Her hands are flung in the air and she has a grin on her face, the same purely joyful and delightfully mischievous one she often wore. It captures her personality well. Renée had a pure soul, lots of love, and a great sense of humor. I ask for her prayers a lot. May I dance through life as she did, with the same joy, zest, and childlike innocence!

The news of Renée's death hit me hard, coupled with the homesickness I'd already been dealing with as a result of entering the convent. I wasn't able to go to the funeral. However, God took all my sacrifices for her and made it a grace for me and my grieving loved ones.

As I was mourning, my Sisters in the convent surrounded me with their prayers. I was upset that I couldn't be physically present to my aunt, uncle, and cousin (Renée's brother). Yet after praying about it, I realized that God is the greatest comforter. What better place to rally a prayer army than in a convent? My Sisters helped me put together a beautiful card full of prayers and messages for Renée's immediate family. Because of the time difference, Renée's funeral began right as my Sisters and I were praying our afternoon Rosary.

Through all of this I began to realize what it truly meant to love my family. It did not hinge on physical closeness, but rather in lifting them up in prayer for their spiritual good. Through the communion of saints, Renée could be with me more than she ever had before. The night after I learned she had died, I sat staring out my darkened window at the stars. Tears streaked down my face, but a strange calm began to creep into my heart. *Be with me, Renée, I prayed. You're the family member I can have most present to me now.*

When the separation with my family feels particularly acute, I commend them even more to God and His loving care. After all, He can take care of them no matter where I am; He is God. It is important to remember Jesus' warning in Scripture that whoever loves father or mother more than Him is not worthy to follow Him. I am more than willing to give up the human, earthly pleasure of having my family always near, so that I may one day have the joy of receiving them back forever in heaven.

I have been in my religious Community for just over six years. Every day is filled with new blessings and graces. I do not always recognize them in the moment, but Jesus is my Spouse and Master, and He leads me to see His hand in every circumstance. This vocation is truly incredible. It is not natural—it is supernatural.

The joys and struggles of living Religious Life day in and day out are probably similar to those of a marriage. We get tired and frustrated. We also have great times with our Sisters and enjoy living life together. In whatever vocation we are called to, holiness lies in the daily yes. The moments that seem small are what Jesus was talking about when He

I like to call the Motherhouse in Ann Arbor "The Happiest Place on Earth." Why is this description accurate? I think it lies in the reality that our world today is very good at emphasizing and increasing pleasure, but impoverished when it comes to cultivating true and lasting joy. Sisters are living witnesses to the fact that our fulfillment does not lie in the attainment and multiplication of pleasure, but rather in loving and serving our Lord, and letting that love and service flow out into our encounters with our fellow man. The Church needs Sisters because people need witnesses, and these women, rooted in the love of Jesus Christ are some of the best witnesses I have ever met at proclaiming by what they say and do that we can have so much more than mere pleasure. They show us that we can have happiness in this life and live a foretaste of the joy of the world to come.
— Fr. John Eckert, priest of the Diocese of Charlotte

told us to take up our cross and follow Him. It is easy to feel that we are not making a difference in the world, that our daily humdrum life is too insignificant to affect anyone else. We have such difficulty seeing the spiritual power of one who lives her life in quiet, self-effacing fidelity. But if we are open to these realities, our eyes will see the immense treasures we can store up in heaven through our seemingly "tiny lot." God takes everything we give Him and multiplies it, even if it is as small as five loaves and two fish.

"COME FOLLOW ME"

If you are reading this because you yourself are considering a Religious vocation, be courageous in your trust. God sometimes asks us to step far outside our comfort zone and our plans, whether it be in the when or the how of following Him. Your friends and family may tell you that you are crazy, wasting your life or talents, or simply "in a phase," especially if you are young. They might say you are going too fast or too far. Yet, for all their well-meaning advice, only you know what God is asking in the depths of your heart.

Is His "Come follow me" resounding on the shores of your soul? What nets do you cling to that He is asking you to leave behind? Being afraid of what God asks of us boils down to being afraid of Him. If we really trusted that He loves us and wants what is best for us, we would do anything for Him in a heartbeat. We would follow Him recklessly, as the saints do. We fear not the task but the One asking, afraid that He is somehow in competition with us for our own happiness. But the One asking is also the Giver of all good gifts, the Lover of all souls, and the One who died so that we might live in Him. Be not afraid.

Chapter 10

The Unromantic Romance...
Living Religious Life at Eighteen Years Old
—Sr. Maria Frassati Jakupcak, O.P.

It was a refreshingly cool evening on Rome's Via della Conciliazione, and the sunset behind St. Peter's was a glorious riot of color. I sat on the curb watching the street cleaners, marveling that my heart could hold so much happiness. On my left was a handsome young man with fine green eyes who, after we had been talking for hours, finally worked up the courage to ask if he could buy me a drink. In no time the two of us were ensconced at a tiny Italian café table which is, incidentally, one of the best places for talking about life's big questions. Caught up in the excitement of the day, I leaned eagerly over the table and spoke of my fondest hope. I told my friend, with all the fervor of a seventeen-year-old hopelessly in love, how ardently I wished to enter the convent.

All right, that was slightly unfair—both as a beginning to this chapter and to the friend I was with at World Youth Day in the Jubilee Year 2000. I will excuse myself on the first point by saying that there are not a lot of especially colorful moments involved in my story of entering the convent at eighteen, so I have to make the most of the ones I have. As to my handsome friend, well, all I can say is that a woman in love is sometimes rather naive, and I was certainly very in love with the Lord on that particular evening after getting up close and personal with Pope St. John Paul II. The story of how I entered the convent does not begin on that evening in Rome, but rather on the day of my baptism. However, due to space constraints, I will just share some highlights of how God has worked in my life. I do this in the hopes that it might help others to see and accept God's work in their own lives or in the lives of those close to them.

$\mathscr{D}$IVINE ROMANCE IS NOT WHAT YOU THINK

My childhood, quite frankly, was mundane and blasé. That is worth saying because I often meet people who think that my upbringing must have been extraordinary in some way, maybe something of a mix between the *Diary of Saint Faustina* and *The Sound of Music*. But it was nothing of the sort. I have been Catholic all my life and, like many cradle Catholics, the faith was something I took for granted. Apart from the nonnegotiable Sunday Mass and my weekly attendance at CCD, I never really gave the faith a lot of thought. True, my Grandma Mary taught me to love the Blessed Mother and occasionally took me along with her to daily Mass, but I did not think of these things as "Catholic." It was simply what one did, part of growing up.

So, while I admit that I used to collect handfuls of violets for my Grandma Mary's May altar, outside of this there was not a lot of picturesque Catholic paraphernalia in my childhood. Sometimes people find this disappointing. Apparently, the Lord's pursuit of a soul should be obvious. Exciting. Romantic.

Personally, I do think it was romantic, but I have to clarify what I mean by that. No, I never heard a voice or saw a vision as a young child. But my childhood was filled with simple love, flooded by people who cared for me and wanted me to be happy. I never performed heroic works of penance, but I learned to make myself useful. I liked school and always made the honor roll. I loved to ride my bike and hike. I attempted to play softball and volleyball and discovered I am not much of an asset to a sports team. I discovered a knack for theater and spent a lot of time at it. I made friends and lost them. I fought with my older sister. I laughed and cried and got angry. I was something of a Goody Two-Shoes. I never practiced piano as I should have, but I practiced singing anywhere and everywhere, and especially in the car on beautiful days. All pretty prosaic stuff.

However, all of this prose was driven by a deeper poetry. Think of it this way: Any nice man can give you flowers, but only God can plan in what family you'll live. A knight in shining armor might plan a perfect moment, or day, or date. But God loved me enough to map out each and every detail of my entire life—*my entire life*! Even as I type this, I find it staggering. That He should arrange things so that I grew up in a particular way in a particular place with particular people...it is just marvelous. And romantic, though admittedly in a boy-next-door way rather than a Byronic-hero-who-sweeps-you-off-your-feet way.

*H*IS SURPRISING WAYS

It was all of this loving, if unnoticed, arrangement on God's part that led to my choosing to attend our local Catholic high school, Marquette. As a freshman, I was slightly terrified about sitting down in my first-period religion class with kids who had gone to Catholic school their entire lives. How was my once–a–week CCD going to compete with their eight years of daily instruction?

As it turned out, I held my own. Not because I knew everything about Catholicism, but because, as I began to realize, I believed it. All of it.

For instance, when we were learning about the Real Presence of Christ in the Eucharist, a hand shot up. James was rather forward. And forceful. He decidedly declared that the Eucharist was a nice symbol, but could not possibly really be Jesus. It was too absurd. There was nothing different about the host after consecration than before. If you scientifically examined it, it would be just the same.

And this, I thought self–righteously to myself, *is what eight years of Catholic schooling does. This punk kid went to religion class every day, and he doesn't even know that Christ is truly present in the Eucharist.*

I don't know if you have thought about this lately, but that is a pretty astonishing truth. As in flip–your–world–upside–down astonishing. That day, in the face of that lame argument, I realized that I believed that Christ was really present in the Eucharist. And I was astonished. Not just because it was true, but because I believed it was true.

That realization was a game–changer for me. If Christ is truly present in the Eucharist, He was present in my school chapel. If He was present in the chapel, He was present at Mass, and present when I received Him at Mass. Consequently, I had better think hard about the state in which I received Him.

That day God worked through the unlikely instrument of a skeptical kid in my first–hour religion class. He used that student's doubt to inspire my faith.

Another big moment happened for me that year after I had begun to pray every day. This was another case of

God working through unlikely instruments—in this case, my own pride.

The priest who taught freshman religion challenged his classes by saying that there were three things every Catholic had to do if they wanted to be a "real" Catholic. His list was as follows:

1. Carry a rosary at all times
2. Have statues and incense in your room
3. Pray every day

Here I was, a nice little freshman who had always gone to Mass and hardly ever missed Wednesday night CCD and this priest, this black-leather-wearing, let-me-take-a-smoke-break, motorcycle-riding priest who certainly did not fit my stereotype of what a priest should be, was telling me I was not a "real" Catholic because I could not check off the boxes on his arbitrary list. I was furious. I decided I would show *him* who the real Catholic was. Like many a furious female before me, I took action:

- I found a rosary from my first Holy Communion. Check.
- I moved a charming statue of the Holy Family from our living room to my bedroom and dug up some (non-ecclesiastical) incense. Check.
- I began to pray every day. Check.

I had no idea, really, how to pray. I figured I would just tell God what happened in my day. This seemed awfully silly since, of course, He already knew. But I was determined. Every requirement had to be checked.

What I did not realize is how transformative that time before that little statue each evening would become.

Slowly, I began to have more to say to the Lord. I began to think about Him more and to ask some big questions. One of the first questions I vividly remember asking was about eternity.

Eternity, I realized, is going to be *long*. As in very long. As in forever. Eternal. If the Church is right, there are only two places you can spend it: Heaven or Hell. Getting this right suddenly seemed important. Very, *very* important. I took a quick look around the world and wondered if there were any sure-fire ways to get into Heaven. Martyrdom? That did not seem likely. Amazing virtue? Even less likely. Becoming a Sister? This, I thought, had possibilities. I mean, St. Peter was probably waving all the ladies in veils through the Pearly Gates, right?

Except that becoming a Sister would mean, well, becoming a Sister. Renouncing my own will and all that. Giving up all my plans for myself. A future. A family.

"No, no, no. Forget I ever thought that, please, Lord," I prayed. "Let's take another look at that virtue thing. Maybe I could do that instead. Because nobody does that whole Sister thing nowadays anyway. So, once again, let's just forget that thought and move on. OK? Amen."

Fast–forward from that prayer to my sophomore year. As I was considering what I ought to do for Lent, I remembered going to daily Mass with Grandma Mary occasionally. I did some research and discovered that there was a 7:00 a.m. Mass at a local church. I could go before classes began for the day. I decided that I would try it.

I got to my first Mass late. Normally getting to Mass five minutes late is not a big deal, but I quickly learned that Father was known for his seventeen-minute Mass, and so five minutes cost me the entire Liturgy of the Word. In any event, I slowly figured it out: when to leave, where to park, and so on. By the end of that first week, I noticed a classmate of mine in the back of the church with her mom. Genevieve noticed me, too, and at school she told me she was going to go to spend a weekend on retreat. Did I want to come?

I certainly did. After all, this whole going to daily Mass business was mostly about me feeling good about how far I was advancing in virtue, so I figured I would get extra goodness points if I went on a retreat, too. I did not know it then, but it would be another one of those life-changing decisions.

When we walked into the retreat, I was immediately struck by the sight of a few hundred teenagers kneeling on carpet squares in adoration of the Blessed Sacrament. It was moving. There were talks, songs, prayers, and, in the evening, Confession. I decided that one must go to Confession on retreat, so off I went to get in line. I did not have anything particularly soul-searching to say; in fact, I had been to Confession relatively recently at school. However, here I was, in a dark little confessional on the left side of a stage in a gym.

My Confession was routine, with nothing particularly earth-shattering. That is, except when my confessor suddenly asked, "Have you ever thought about Religious Life?"

This was a particularly sticky question because, of course, I had. However, I knew that wanting a free pass into Heaven could not be the right reason to think about it. I did not want to say yes, but "no" was not strictly true. And I could not lie because that would defeat the whole purpose of being in confession. So, I was stuck. I settled on the shortest possible answer: "Yes, Father." "Well, I want you to pray about it," he said, "and I will pray for you."

This is where he pulled out Sneaky Priest Trick #473. "For your penance, go back out into Eucharistic adoration and pray about whether or not you have a Religious vocation."

See what I mean? Sneaky! Because now I *had* to pray about it. The nerve! I could not just brush it off as something Father said to every penitent at a youth retreat. It had to be done. But I decidedly did not want to do it.

I walked, rather stunned, back out to my carpet square and looked up at the Blessed Sacrament. This was just too much. I could not jump right into such a big question, so I decided to lead up to it by telling God all about my plan for my life. Not that He did not know, but I figured it could not hurt to remind Him. So I did. I told Him all about how I was going to go to the University of Illinois like everyone else in my family, study science, meet the perfect Catholic man at the Newman Center, have lots of kids, teach, and generally be contented and useful. It was a good plan, and I liked it a lot. In fact, I had rarely considered anything else.

I knelt there for a while, holding that plan up to God. As I did, I realized that I still had not done my penance; this was all telling and no asking. But I did not want to ask in case I did not like the answer. So I kept holding up my plan, turning it over and over and admiring it.

Then, slowly, I began to see a big problem with the plan: It was all mine. It suddenly hit me that I could not make this plan because I was not there when I was made. I could not write the instruction manual for my life because I did not know what I was made *for*. Only God knew that. And God, I reasoned, made me to be happy. Whatever He made me for was what would make me the happiest, because I would be doing what I was made to do. Who does not want to have superlative happiness? I wanted it desperately, at any rate, and I was willing to risk asking God this question about Religious Life. Because if Religious Life was His plan for my happiness, well then, I was going to do it. Religious Life was what God made me for. The conversation shifted: It was His plan for my happiness. I would do it.

That level of certainty in that short a time was a gift. I see that now. At the time, it felt perfectly natural. I simply looked around my life and thought, "Oh! So that's it!" It was as though all these jagged edges of things I did not understand suddenly came together and made a complete picture. Or as though I had been standing on my head and now suddenly saw things right side up for the first time. Everything just fit.

I find people often are not satisfied with that explanation, and I understand. A parallel situation might help. When my dad describes meeting my mom for the first time he says, "I knew in the first five minutes that she was the woman I was going to spend the rest of my life with."

Sure, Dad, I used to think. But lightning–quick life decisions must run in the family, because after my prayer that night, I knew just what Dad had meant.

Much of the rest of that weekend is a blur of tears, happiness, and profound peace. I was peaceful because it was all so clear. All I had to do was find a convent to enter. *Voila!* God's will is done; I get to be happy, and everyone rides merrily into the sunset.

I knew so little about vocational discernment that I was totally devoid of the fear I might have felt at sharing this news with my parents. My mom's version of the story is that I came home from that retreat saying, "I want to be a Sister. I want to teach. I want to wear the habit."

"Be a Sister and teach, OK," my dad said, "but the habit? I don't think anyone does that anymore."

"Oh yes, they do. I'll find them."

I am not sure that is a literal account of what happened, but that certainly was the sense of the announcement. I knew God's will, and I did not want to do anything by halves. My parents' reaction was beautiful. They wanted me to be happy, and this certainly seemed to make me happy, at least for now.

"*I*T IS JUST A PHASE"

Notwithstanding my parents' generous response, they thought this was a phase. Dad was pretty sure that once someone asked me to Homecoming, I would realize that decisions like this had consequences I might not like. My friends, for their part, were used to hearing me declare that I wanted this one week and that the next. How were they to know that this time I really meant it?

I was terribly resentful of this at the time, angry that nobody seemed to realize how serious I was, but at this distance I think the "just a phase" attitude was excusable. After all, I had wanted to be an astronaut one week and an architect the next, so it made perfect sense to think that this "becoming a Sister" aspiration was transitory too. Teenagers are flighty, and there was no real reason, from the outside, to think this would be a lasting passion. I knew what I knew, but the only way to prove it was to stick it out until everyone could see that I was serious.

An attentive reader will have noticed by now that there was a whole lot of "me" in my conviction about my Religious vocation; I was attracted to it because I knew it would make *me* happy. It suited *my* talents, *my* desires. This is not a terrible place to begin, but it is only a beginning. We cannot go about loving God for what we get out of it. Which meant, for me, that it was time for a trial. You see, all true vocations are put to trial in some way. Sometimes people have great opposition from their family. Sometimes there are health issues to overcome. And sometimes you have a story like mine.

THE INEVITABLE TRIAL

Something I found rather strange immediately followed this moment of newfound confidence in God's will for me. Despite judging his glaring ignorance about the Eucharist, I'd had a crush on James since practically the first day of high school. Shortly after the retreat, James was suddenly playing opposite me in the spring musical, *Cinderella*. Then, of all crazy things, he started to talk to me. And be nice to me. And generally make himself agreeable. In retrospect, I think that knowing God's will gave me a new confidence and a new self-assurance that was attractive and made me easy to talk to. In any case, whatever the reason it some-how came up that I was going to daily Mass at his parish. Then one morning, he appeared at 7:00 a.m. Mass.

He told me later that he knew I was driving in from the next town, and he reasoned that if he could not get himself up and make a five-minute drive over, then he was probably going to Hell. Which, as previously mentioned, is not a nice thought. So there he was at early Mass.

Genevieve, predictably, concluded that James had a crush on me. I was not amused by the Lord's timing. Because if I had a religious vocation—and I knew I did—I had no business dating anyone, no matter how much I wanted the relationship.

Really? I thought, and not without a tinge of bitterness, *"he couldn't have noticed me, say, a month ago before I knew this about myself? Argh!"*

As it turned out, Genevieve was wrong. James was friendly, but he was clearly in pursuit of other girls. And that was (somewhat) okay with me.

The following fall, during a quiet moment on a school retreat, I told James how glad I was that he came to daily Mass. He was a popular student, and some kids had started to join him at church. He told me he was glad as well, and we chatted about this and that. I cannot remember quite how I ended up telling him about the retreat I was going on in Ann Arbor with the Dominican Sisters of Mary, Mother of the Eucharist, but somehow I told him. I was totally floored when he said, "Well, that is interesting, because I've been thinking about the priesthood."

What? Seriously? This could not be happening. James was, after all, the same kid whose doubts about the Real Presence revealed to me my own belief. He could not be serious. But he was.

That evening's discussion was the beginning of what eventually became a beautiful friendship. My memory here is awash in images. James and I eating breakfast at the rectory after Friday morning Mass. Seeing James at church in the evening after my thirty minutes of mental prayer; his coming was timed to signal when I was done, because he knew it distracted me to wear a watch. An unfortunate dance picture of junior prom where we both look terrible. An evening when both of us realized that we wanted to pursue a romantic relationship but that, under the circumstances, it would not be right. His applying to seminary; my applying to the convent.

That friendship did, and does, mean a great deal to me, though now I only touch base with James every couple of years. However, his friendship taught me, as almost nothing else could have taught me, that I was lovable. I was worthy of love, not in a generic, impersonal way, but just as I was, with all my faults.

My parents, of course, love me just as personally, but there was something important in feeling this connection with someone outside of my family. I saw that I was loved by someone who was not obliged to love me by virtue of our shared DNA. It taught me about God's love for me, and I could not be more grateful to have had that experience.

It is a little bit anticlimactic to say that James left seminary in his third year, but he did. I stayed put, still totally sure of God's plan for me, but James remains in my grateful prayers, and he knows it. And now I have the added bonus of praying for his wife, his children, and his safety in the line of duty as a police officer.

Unlike the beginning of this chapter, I am not just sharing this to heighten the drama of my prosaic life. I share it because, after entering the convent, I discovered that this experience is extraordinarily typical for young women thinking about Religious Life. If you are seriously thinking about entering a convent, do not be surprised when, the minute you realize you are being called by God to a life of poverty, chastity, and obedience, Mr. Man-of-Your-Dreams walks in from stage left. It is almost inevitable, particularly if you are not being tried in some other way via your family or your health.

My point is that vocations must be tried in some way and, though it is difficult, it is all to the good. If following God's will were all sunshine and roses, everyone would do it, but not because we love God. I can see now that God was using James (and later, in a similar way, my handsome friend from World Youth Day) to purify my love for Him. The Lord was allowing me to experience the joy and beauty of human love so I would fully understand the sacrifice I was making. Some people will be tempted by career, opportunity, success, or even, as I was in the week before I entered, by something as simple as looking really amazing in a new dress. If you are discerning, you can expect a proliferation of whatever temptations will appeal most to you. The Lord wants to know that you are serious about pursuing His will and not just your own contentment.

There were other trials, of course. If you are going to enter out of high school, it can be difficult not to be applying to colleges like everyone else. Or planning your perfect dorm room. Or winning scholarships and awards. People might treat you more like a breakable doll than like yourself, and that can be isolating. At the end of high school, it feels like all the roads are open before you, and you may be beset by "what ifs." But if you truly have a vocation, you also have the grace to overcome all of this. Just bring it all to the Lord, and He will help you through it.

"*T*HROWING YOUR LIFE AWAY"

As my high school career progressed, it became clearer to everyone in my life that this was not a phase that was going away. At this point, I began to experience some real resistance.

For instance, if you ever want people to exaggerate your good qualities, just tell them you are going to enter a convent. Though you may previously have been the most ordinary girl, suddenly you are too smart, too young, too talented, too funny, and possibly even—as the grandmother of a good friend commented after seeing me in the spring musical—too beautiful. It seems to be a universal opinion that God could not really want you to "throw your life away."

"Please!" a wise priest friend of mine said at the time. "As if God only called old, ugly, unintelligent people." That was really helpful to hear.

There were other lines of attack, though. Here are some of the most common I experienced, and what I can say about them now after over fifteen years in Religious Life.

"*W*HAT ABOUT YOUR EDUCATION?"

I cannot speak for every Community, but this is a baseless fear for someone entering the Dominicans. We are educators and, as such, are well educated. For myself, when I am not working on this book chapter, I am working on my doctoral dissertation for a PhD in English. This will not be the path of every Sister or of every Community, but if an active Community allows someone without a college degree to enter, it is possible they may provide for further studies.

Religious Sisters are such a witness to a world in need of faith, hope, and love. While our world says that possessions, romantic relationships, or license masked as "freedom" bring us true happiness, Religious Sisters' vows of poverty, chastity, and obedience prove that God alone is enough, and He alone is the one who can bring true peace and joy. I don't know if anyone who meets a radiant Sister who is fully alive in Christ could deny that there is a God who loves us!
— *Jackie Francois-Angel, singer, songwriter, and speaker*

However, speaking more generally for all Communities, I will also add that there are more kinds of education than the ones that add initials after your name. In the Middle Ages, well-to-do families used to send their daughters to a convent for a year as part of their education, and I can understand why. Not only do we study Scripture, the *Catechism*, the vows, and various Church documents, but all of us also end up learning a lot about sewing, cooking, yard work, laundry, carpentry, event planning, and especially house cleaning. We always laugh about how a year or two in the convent would be the best preparation for marriage!

Even more importantly, however, living in community is an education in and of itself. Any Sister will tell you that the best part and worst part of our life is community. At the Motherhouse, we live in close quarters with as many as a hundred Sisters at a time, all of whom have good days and bad days. Inevitably, there will be Sisters who differ from you in temperament, age, background, experience, likes and dislikes; it teaches you a lot about yourself, believe me. For instance, when I was a twenty-year-old novice, I was assigned as head sacristan, and my assistant was a woman in her forties who had been a high-powered lawyer in New York City. It took the two of us a long time to learn how to communicate; for a while, whenever she asked me a polite question, I thought she was furiously angry. Eventually she and I both learned that people from New York communicate differently than twenty-year-olds from small-town Illinois. My point is that, in terms of education in human interactions, there is no better school than the convent. Even if a young woman does not stay in the Community, her time there will have provided experience and skills that will be a boon to her in any walk of life.

"*YOU* ARE JOINING A CULT! THEY WILL BRAINWASH YOU!"

Religious Life is so removed from most people's everyday experience that this is an understandable worry. Cults are real things, and they really do brainwash people. However, Religious Life is not a cult. I think our best defense against this accusation is probably those women who discern that God is not calling them to remain in Religious Life. Many women who enter in good faith find, though prayer and their time in the Community, that this is not, in fact, the life to which God is calling them. And so they move on. There is a regular crowd of one-time Sisters who attend events at the Motherhouse with their beautiful and happy families. They retain their love for the Community, and we retain our love for them. No one is ever forced to stay in the Community.

Of course, not everyone who leaves is happy about it. In fact, it is sometimes the difficult job of the Community to *un–brainwash* someone and help them see that this life is not a good fit for them. Women are especially prone, I think, to bearing up under difficulties even when we are miserable. So it is sometimes the uncomfortable job of a Formator to help a young woman notice that she is making herself miserable by hanging on to a life to which she is not called. When a woman has her heart set on a Religious vocation, this news can be crushing to her. However, the Community has her best interest at heart, and most young women come to see that in time.

"*You* DO NOT HAVE ENOUGH EXPERIENCE TO MAKE THIS DECISION"

Frankly, yes, this one is true. It was especially brought home to me once I began to work with college students at The Catholic University of America. It happened over and over that I would think, *They are just so young!* and then I would remember that at their age I was already in the convent. So, yes, someone entering young is inexperienced. But honestly, it does not matter. First, because no great thing in life comes to those who wait until they are experienced enough to receive it. Second, you cannot experience entering Religious Life unless you do it. And once you do, the Community is there with loads of personal experience and centuries of tradition to help you navigate the decision.

The Community is committed to your making the right decision, even when you perhaps are not. We all understand that while it is certainly true that most eighteen–year–olds are not, properly speaking, grown up, it is also true that the convent is a pretty great place to finish growing up. Certainly, in some ways, it is easier to navigate than the college campuses that greet most eighteen-year-olds when they leave home for the first time! For some women, the best decision is entering right out of high school. Others might be asked to wait until after a year or two of college. If the Community thinks you are ready, trust it. If they think you need to wait, trust that. The bottom line is that you can trust the experience of the Community in these matters more than you can your own.

THOUGHTS ON DISCERNMENT

Entering the convent right out of high school is wonderful in many ways. It is easier for a young woman to settle into Religious Life than it is for someone who was living on her own for years before entering. And while there is always beauty in giving God the good fruit our lives bear, there is something especially beautiful about giving Him the blossoms which precede the fruit as well. It gives Him more freedom to shape us to our maximum potential.

There are, of course, particular difficulties that come with entering young but, as I have said, there are particular difficulties for anyone who enters Religious Life. My advice to those discerning is to worry less about difficulties and more about desire. Dominicans are particularly averse to the idea of "discernment" as it is often lived these days...a kind of sitting at a bus stop and watching things pass you by until you are really, really sure of what God wants. Discernment should not be like this. Rather, it should be an examination of your desires. Not your transitory desires for this friendship or that job, but those deeper desires that animate your whole being. This sounds selfish, but it is not.

God manifests His work in us by giving us strong desires, because what we want the most is exactly what God wants the most: our happiness. The trick is that we have to learn, most of us gradually, that happiness does not come from filling ourselves up with good things, even if that good thing is God. Rather, happiness comes from giving ourselves away, without reserve. If you follow your desire for self-gift where it leads you, you can trust our Lord to work out the rest.

For myself, I went to the priests at my high school and told them I was called to Religious Life. I wanted to know what to do next. They told me to contact Communities, visit them, and go on retreats. I already went to daily Mass, but I also added regular time for mental prayer and Eucharistic adoration. It was early in my junior year when I first went on retreat in Ann Arbor, Michigan. Although it was not as instantaneous as my discovery of my vocation, it did not take me long to figure out that this is where I felt the most at home. It was clear that I belonged; this was my family. That, finally, is what anyone looking to enter Religious Life should seek: that at-home feeling. If you find it and discover that you want to enter a particular Community, trust that God is at work in that desire.

ℬE NOT AFRAID

Earlier on that evening in Rome during the great Jubilee, I was blessed to be a few feet from Pope St. John Paul II as he drove up the Via Della Conciliazione on his way to St. Peter's. In his address to the World Youth Day attendees that evening, he asked us a question: "What have you come here to find?" I think that is the right question for anyone sincerely coming to God and seeking His will. "What have you come in search of?" He continued, "Or rather, whom have you come here to find? There can only be one answer to that: You have come in search of Jesus Christ! But Jesus Christ has first gone in search of you."[1] That is the key thing to remember, whatever your walk of life: Jesus sought you first. His greatest desire is your happiness, and He helps guide your desires in the same path. Just trust His work in you, and you will not regret it. I know I do not.

Endnotes

[1] John Paul II. "Address at the Welcoming Ceremony, 15th World Youth Day." Vatican. August 15, 2000, http://w2.vatican.va/content/en/speeches/2000/jul-sep/documents/hf_jp-ii_spe_20000815_gmg-accoglienza2.html.

Chapter 11

Ivy along My Way...
Life after Harvard
—Sr. Maria Veritas Marks, O.P.

Dear college student,

Well, that is an awkward way to address a letter, but there was not much choice, was there? If I knew your name, I would use it, with all the affection of my heart.

God knows your name. Not only the name your parents gave you but also the name you will receive as a Sister if He is calling you to a Community where it is custom to receive a new Religious name when you receive your habit. He also knows the name you will have in Heaven: St. Elizabeth of the Trinity mused that her name would be "praise of His glory" (Eph. 1:12). Not many of us have as strong an intuition about that heavenly name we will receive (Rev. 2:17), but He knows what it is.

His knowing you is a most important truth. You have nothing to hide, because He knows it all already. You do not have to pretend to be holier or smarter or more put together than you are, because He knows better. And you do not have to fear, because God's knowledge is love. Among us fallen humans, knowledge filtered through wills still warped by sin can turn to derision or fear. God's knowledge of you, on the other hand, is why you exist at this moment. His knowledge is love: a love not of your defects, of course, but of you, now, as you are, with deficiencies, and of the perfect and healed and whole you He wishes you to become.

Knowledge is at the root of vocation, as well. It is because God knows a soul and how she will best come to know Him that He places in her the desire for Religious Life and the ability to live it—and in other souls the desire for marriage and in their lives the prerequisites for pursuing marriage. Each soul's vocation is the manifestation of God's knowledge of and love for her, and it is also her path to knowing Him. All of human life is coming to know and love Him more deeply, in preparation for the heavenly ecstasy of being "like Him, for we shall see Him as He is" (1 Jn. 3:2).

You will forgive my didacticism; I am, after all, a Dominican, so study is one privileged encounter with my Spouse, and teaching, the overflow of study, is another. If you have a Dominican vocation, you understand, or will eventually. But there are many other beautiful Religious orders gracing the Church like gems, each making its own unique contribution to the world's salvation.

I am writing to you because we have some things in common. You are in college and considering Religious Life. At this point in your life, a wide range of rewarding career choices await your enthusiasm, your intelligence, your generosity—just as they did me on May 27, 2010, the day after my twenty-second birthday, when I looked out upon a crowd of thousands, gathered in great pomp and circumstance for Harvard's 359th commencement, and delivered the salutatory address.

God may be calling you, as He did me, to only one of those choices, to one that demands not only all you can give, but all you are. If you are like me, you have considered this one option surreptitiously for a long time, even yielded to some extent to the conviction that it is the only way to happiness for you, but the thousand legitimate distractions of your life allow you to evade serious pursuit of it. Or, if you are like another one of my Sisters, you never considered it at all—only to have it suddenly arrive at your doorstep, unexpected, unannounced, and demanding immediate attention. You may be like another Sister who always knew and always said yes. She entered our Community as soon as circumstances allowed and has found happiness, along with all of us who took more circuitous routes and possessed less perceptive and docile temperaments.

Most of what is worth saying about a Religious vocation has already been said—two thousand years ago—by the One whose life it imitates. The only original element I can add is the story of grace in my own life, as precious and unique a story as yours is. I will interweave that story with His teaching.

Demystifying Discernment

First off, let's talk about this "discernment" thing. If you have already waded into the vocation waters, you will have heard the term, used to describe the process by which a young woman tries to determine if God is calling her to Religious Life. All I would say is: Do not try too hard.

By that I mean: Do not make things too complicated. If there burns within you a desire to spend more time with God, even to spend your whole life with Him, or if you know Sisters and are drawn to their way of life, embrace this desire. If you recognize the beauty of married love and still feel somehow a longing for more, accept this longing. It is good. Thank God for it and pursue it; talk to your parish priest or college chaplain, visit a convent, make a retreat. Most of all, frequent the Sacraments and make time for prayer. Go to Confession once a month, attend Mass as often as you can, and always on Sundays. Take five or ten minutes out of your day to talk to Love Himself and to His Mother.

Do not get tied up in knots about your unworthiness. We all have faults and failings; we all carry wounds from those who have hurt us. None of us is perfect, either exteriorly or interiorly. If God only called the perfect to Religious Life, there would be no Religious in Religious Life.

Obviously, you need a certain level of physical and mental health, as well as the capacity to fulfill the responsibilities of a particular Community in terms of its common life and apostolate. These criteria will be examined before you enter the Community and during the years before final vows. You will not be accepted for vows if you are incapable of living the life. But let that judgment come in its time. Just follow the Lord and trust in Him, and do not second-guess His call.

Jesus said, "I have told you this so that my joy might be in you, and your joy might be complete" (Jn. 15:11). Christ has come for joy; if He has given you a desire, He wants to fulfill it. He wants you to be happy. Do not be afraid!

In the inaugural homily of his papacy, Benedict XVI exclaimed, echoing a theme dear to Pope St. John Paul II:

> If we let Christ into our lives, we lose nothing, nothing, absolutely nothing of what makes life free, beautiful and great. No! Only in this friendship are the doors of life opened wide. Only in this friendship is the great potential of human existence truly revealed. Only in this friendship do we experience beauty and liberation.

And so, today, with great strength and great conviction, on the basis of long personal experience of life, I say to you, dear young people: Do not be afraid of Christ! He takes nothing away, and he gives you everything. When we give ourselves to him, we receive a hundredfold in return. Yes, open, open wide the doors to Christ—and you will find true life.[1]

This was something I knew intellectually but had a hard time believing. When I entered the Dominican Sisters of Mary, Mother of the Eucharist, on August 28, 2010, I knew exactly what I was leaving behind and very little about what the future held, except that God promises a hundred-fold to those who abandon everything for Him.

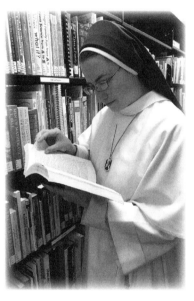

There were days when my whole being exulted for joy that He loved me in this way, and that He desired my complete self–gift in conformity to Him through the vows. There were days when the memory of that joy was ash in my mouth and lead in my heart, when only the conviction that He wished me to enter Religious Life kept me going.

But God does give a hundredfold. For me, this is true both in the personal and in the intellectual spheres. To me, an only child, He has given numerous sisters. And to my parents, numerous daughters. One of the greatest gifts of my Religious Life has been to see my parents welcomed into the various convents in which I have lived throughout the country. The Sisters describe their own projects and hopes and listen to those of my parents. They tell stories about me, just as siblings do; share recipes with my mother; enjoy my father's jokes and, beaming, absorb his appreciative comments. They witness to my parents "how good it is, how pleasant, where the people dwell as one!" (Ps. 133:1).

A deeper awareness of the communion between persons dawned in my heart as soon as I accepted my vocation in my junior year of college. Suddenly, my schoolwork was not the only thing that mattered. Upon entering and leaving the library, I chatted with the guards who check students' bags; eventually, they mentioned to me how I seemed less rushed and happier. I smiled and said, "I guess I am!" When finally the blissful secret grew too wonderful to conceal any longer, I confided to one of them that I would be entering a convent. He leaned back on his stool to absorb this atypical news and then said, "You know, my sister is a nun back home in Nigeria."

You will find that, as a Sister, you become the repository of surprisingly personal dreams and sorrows. It is a humbling experience, because you know that it is not to you personally that others reveal their stories but to God, whom they recognize, whether consciously or not, in you who are His alone. I was first privileged with these glimpses into others' lives when I started to share the news of my vocation. One professor, I learned, was educated by Franciscans. He seriously considered the priesthood and still travels a long distance each Sunday to attend a church staffed by priests of that order. Another emigrated with his family from England, not before his little brother joined a monastic Community at a very young age. "And," this world-renowned Shakespearean scholar murmured wistfully, "I have not seen him since that day."

ℬREAKING THE NEWS

Telling my friends and professors of my post-graduation choice did not always end well. Most often, the response was sadness and incomprehension. Those who loved me less or understood Religious Life less would usually end with a stoic, if doubtful, "Well, if it is going to make you happy..." Those who loved me more asked, "Why? Why are you doing this?" And I had to respond, "I think it is what God wants," realizing, with renewed discomfort each time, that I had never before mentioned His name in their presence.

One lunch with a dear English professor stands out as particularly memorable. This professor is as energetic in personality as she is diminutive in stature. No-nonsense and deeply beloved of colleagues and students alike, she had been my greatest ally at school. In her businesslike way, she had encouraged my writing and research. But I had not recognized how much she had looked forward to supporting my future academic career until this lunch meeting.

After a few minutes of awkward small talk, I worked up the nerve to volunteer, "You have probably guessed by this time, since I have not asked you for a recommendation for graduate school, that I am not applying."

"Yes," she replied drily, with a hint of disapproval. "May I ask why not?"

And then, again, I spoke of the convent, and God.

It seemed almost as if I had struck her. Was there any chance, she inquired, that my education would continue?

I hemmed and hawed, lacking the courage to tell her that, not only did I have no idea, but I could never enter the convent with any such hopes. I had to leave it all behind. Anything less would be a fabulously ungenerous response to God's generosity.

Was there an application for the convent? Would I need a recommendation for that? She would be willing to help in whatever way she could. And possibly my English and Classics background would be put to another use, in the service of theological studies, perhaps. She was grasping for anything that would soften the blow.

We walked back together to Widener Library, up the narrow cobbled streets flanked by the residential houses whose classic red brick buildings and august bell towers have captivated generations of students. As we were about to say good–bye, she stopped and, looking me straight in the eye, pronounced these astonishing words: "I want to give you a hug, because you have made a very big decision, and I admire you for it." And so, we solemnly embraced.

Grief and joy surged alternately in my heart. Never before had my loss seemed so real. And yet this professor had faith greater than mine. She was bowing to this reality more gracefully than I. While I tried to apologize for my vocation, she hoped there might be something greater in it than I could foresee, not only spiritually but intellectually.

It turned out that there was. Days before the date scheduled for first vows, our Mother Superior asked, "Would you like to study theology?"

"Of course!" I replied joyfully.

Each Sister who has been given the opportunity for further studies will tell you that it is a tremendous gift from the Community. Along with my gratitude, however,

I could not help wondering what theology would be like. I had never before studied it. Would it—could it, even—match what I had experienced at Harvard?

Within weeks of beginning theology classes, I recalled these doubts with some embarrassment. In theology, I was studying God's power and wisdom, not man's. All the linguistic beauty and narrative delicacy of Shakespeare and Tolstoy, all their mastery of the human psyche, all the cunning and humor of Cicero's rhetoric: all this is but a reflection of beauty, delicacy, creativity, wisdom Himself—of God. Theology alone, of all subjects, deals with the reality, rather than the reflection.

The tools I had honed in my study of texts and pursuit of languages were indeed that—tools. I used them to pick apart the meaning of biblical passages, to hear Aquinas speaking in his own precise Latin, to peruse secondary sources in their original languages. These tools serve theology, the *regina scientiarum*.

And my growing knowledge of God infused life with glory. As I sat at my small desk in our convent in Florida one day, the grackles screeching outside our lanai, and studied for my Triune God final, I found myself caught up in the grandeur of the mystery of the Trinity. Never again could I say the *Gloria Patri* during the Divine Office without bowing before that mystery with deep reverence.

Could I have imagined the splendor of theological studies? No. Would I ever have experienced it if God had not coaxed me to leave behind what seemed most intellectually fulfilling? No.

The professor who embraced me on that fateful day in Widener Library has continued a written correspondence that I treasure. Recently, I visited Harvard on a vocations trip with another Sister. The three of us shared a delightful conversation over lunch in the café nestled into the ground floor of the English department building, a place where I had often studied. None of the intellectual enthusiasm that drew us to one another has diminished, but to it has been added the sharing of something deeper, love of our God.

𝒯ALENTS, SEEDS, AND THE CROSS

The parable of the talents often comes up when young women are considering Religious Life, and it certainly did in my case, so I want to share with you an insight I received during my first year as a Sister.

Let me first outline the parable. A master goes off on a journey and entrusts three servants with gold talents, a kind of coin. Two of the servants invest their coins and earn interest; the last servant buries his coin in the ground. Upon the master's return, that last servant explains, "Master, I knew you were a demanding person, harvesting where you did not plant and gathering where you did not scatter, so out of fear I went off and buried your talent in the ground" (Mt. 25:24–25). What? This response does not make sense. A more comprehensible answer would have been, "Sir, I buried your coin in the ground for safekeeping because I was afraid that, by investing it, I would lose it entirely." But no. The servant acts as if fear of the master's expectations for further yield can explain an action intrinsically incapable of yielding further profit.

For years, this servant's words baffled me. And then, as I meditated upon them again during the fall of my postulant year, they resolved themselves into crystal clarity. "Dear God," I heard myself saying at the end of my life, "here are my talents. Frightened that they would not yield the fruit you expected, I shied away from investing them in Religious Life. In my fear of your expectations, I mistook investing for burying and burying for investing. Putting those talents at your service in Religious Life seemed like burying them, so I went on for further studies instead, pursued the professional career track. I should have realized that the 'burial' of Religious Life is actually the most lucrative investment, which places those talents in the hands of the Banker par excellence."

A fear of God's exaction makes us hoarders and buriers rather than givers and investors; it blinds us to His desire for our freedom and for the blossoming of our talents. The master in the parable wanted his servants to run the risks of investing, to act boldly. Instead, the third servant's paralyzing anxiety transformed the master's multipliable entrustment into a burden to be guarded.

"[M]an...cannot fully find himself except through a sincere gift of himself," reads a much-quoted line of *Gaudium et Spes*.[2] We must give ourselves away in order to find ourselves, hand over our talents to God in order to have them multiply. Here we have arrived at the foot of the Cross. A seed must fall into the ground and die in order to bear fruit. The talents have to be "thrown away" in order to multiply.

Religious Life is the fullest embodiment of the paradox articulated by St. Paul:

For Jews demand signs and Greeks look for wisdom, but we proclaim Christ crucified, a stumbling block to Jews and foolishness to Gentiles, but to those who are called, Jews and Greeks alike, Christ the power of God and the wisdom of God. For the foolishness of God is wiser than human wisdom, and the weakness of God is stronger than human strength. (1 Cor. 1:22–25)

In poverty, chastity, and obedience, the three vows that conform us, like three nails, to our crucified Spouse, we surrender the three greatest goods of human life and become participants in His own wealth, fruitfulness, and freedom.

Leaving my father's house

My mother and father are people of rare faith and magnanimity, and there are two perfectly understandable objections to my Religious vocation that they never made to me. In fact, the first time someone else threw them like icy water in my face, I realized with a shock what guilt my parents were sparing me. The first reproach: Who will take care of your parents when they are old? My parents refuse to let an uncertain future contingency dictate the present. They have faith that, somehow, any help they may need will be provided. And of course, the Community also desires their well-being. This does not mean that the sacrifice is not a great one for me. People often ask, "How could you have given up Harvard?" but there are other, greater sacrifices that each of our Sisters makes for her Spouse; remember the Cross and the hundredfold!

The second reproach: Your parents will never have grandchildren. Each time this topic has resurfaced in conversation with my parents, they have assured me, almost commanded me, "Do not let that hold you back." Perhaps it is their own difficult experience of twenty childless years of marriage that reminds them that even a married daughter might not provide them with a grandchild.

They also have, however, a beautiful respect for consecrated celibacy. An astounding conversation one day in the summer of 2010 brought home to me the radically supernatural and radically Christian nature of this commitment.

I grew up in a Jewish neighborhood. Our wing of our apartment building boasted two rabbis and their families. Perhaps my first conscious experience of Judaism occurred when, as a young child, I asked my father why our apartment door, alone of all the doors I had seen in our building, did not have a jeweled box affixed to its left.

"That is a mezuzah," my father explained. "It is a Jewish custom to place the Scriptures, written on a tiny scroll, at one's doorpost to remind one of God."

Each morning, as I used to walk the three blocks to 6:30 a.m. Mass at our local church, I would see an elderly gentleman making his shuffling way down the street, his prayer shawl grasped in his right hand, his cane in the other. "He is making *minyan*," my father said: "There must be ten men gathered for prayers to take place." This gentleman and I rarely crossed paths, but, when we did, a deep kindness shone in the eyes that he lifted toward mine. We were kindred spirits, each profoundly committed to God, although he was wending his way with much more difficulty than I.

In the summer of 2010, I, an almost total stranger, wrote him a note. I explained how my heart exulted each morning I saw him and how I would be entering a convent in Michigan and might not see him again. I wrote that he would always be in my prayers. It was not hard for me to catch up to him on the street and hand him the note, which he received with the unsurprised equanimity of the very old. The next time my father and I saw him, he was with his wife, and he stopped and introduced me to her as "the one who wrote that note." He gave us his name, Avraham; his age, ninety–eight; and some of the extraordinary history of his flight to America from the Netherlands during World War II. Until Avraham moved to Florida, my father would see him now and again and exchange pleasant words. He remains dear to my heart, and I trust that, wherever he is, whether on earth or in heaven, he prays for me.

Religious Life, you will find, opens your eyes to an invisible and magnificent network of like lovers of God, just as the morning dew settles like pearls to reveal thousands of delicate silken strands woven invisibly into our landscape.

All this is by way of preface to a conversation my father had with one of our Jewish neighbors in the lobby of our building. "You will never have grandchildren," Emanuel stated quietly. "Why would anyone want to give up marriage, one of the greatest gifts of life?" As my father tried to explain chastity as a radical availability to do God's will whenever and wherever He calls, he realized that, in the end, there is no satisfying explanation on the natural level for celibacy. Emanuel answered my father with a reworded version of his original question: "Marriage is God's greatest gift. Why would anyone give it up? Why would God want us to give it up?"

We have to reach for the supernatural to explain celibacy; we have to receive God's revelation in Jesus Christ: "Some...have renounced marriage for the sake of the kingdom of heaven" (Mt. 19:12). The Greek word usually translated "kingdom" in the Gospels could also be translated "kingship," and the broader term adds clarity. Consecrated persons forego marriage for the sake of Christ's kingship; they welcome, already here on earth, His exclusive reign in their hearts, the reign that will embrace all people in heaven. Marriage is a glorious means to the yet more glorious end of complete union with God. Religious persons begin this union before heaven, in this life.

The Jewish people possess a beautiful sense of sacramentality, of the numinous significance of places and objects—of bread, wine, blood, water. This sense of sacramentality prepared the Chosen People for the Sacraments instituted by Christ, in which all the old symbols become charged with new significance. Marriage itself is a Sacrament, because it allows the spouses to reach God through each other and because it models the union of Christ with His people. But in heaven we will no longer need Sacraments, because we will have God Himself; we will no longer need the signs and instruments of grace, because we will possess their Author.

Consecrated celibacy is not just availability for God's will; it is not that I give up a husband and children to be a perpetual FOCUS missionary or ACE teacher. I am not so much "giving up" marriage as choosing, in a positive sense, a fruitful spiritual maternity of a higher order, cooperating with God, in my own prayer and sacrifice and daily union with Him, to bring to birth His children in grace. These children are the students in my high school classroom, who sense the undivided attention I can give them, who ask prayers for recovery from an athletic injury, share their suffering at a loved one's death, explain hesitantly that they think they wish to become Catholic. These children are the father who approaches me in church to entrust his job search to the Sisters' prayers, the homeless person on the street who asks for a hug and whose "God bless you" reveals in its unusual intensity her knowledge that I, like she, know and love God.

CHOSEN FOR LOVE

The ability to live chastity—and poverty, and obedience—is a gift. Vocation is a gift. Even when sorrow at my parents' aloneness tears at my heart, I remain sure of this. Consider three scenarios related one after another in Luke 9:57–62. First, someone approaches Jesus and announces that he will follow Him. "Foxes have dens and birds of the sky have nests," Jesus answers, "but the Son of Man has nowhere to rest his head." This is the person who thinks she has a vocation and announces this to Christ. The answer comes, "How will you know where to follow Me? Following Me is difficult. There is no rest. You will not be strolling along a neat asphalt path; the way is harder than that of fox through forest and more unexpected than that of bird through air. Following Me is a grace, responded to, not initiated by you." Vocation is a one-way telephone line: We receive the call; we do not make it.

The next man in Luke's Gospel receives the call: "Follow me." The man replies, "Lord, let me go first and bury my father." A reasonable request, one would think. But Christ answers, "Let the dead bury their dead. But you, go and proclaim the kingdom of God." How can dead people bury dead people? Christ is referring to those who are spiritually dead, those whom He calls and who heed Him not. Apparently, the man is not spiritually dead, because he is not advised to go and bury his father. But he has lost the opportunity to live closely with Christ, because his new assignment is to "proclaim the kingdom of God."

It is possible to lose a Religious vocation. Because a vocation is a gift, if I purposefully ignore it and excuse myself from pursuing it, God has no obligation to continue offering it.

Last comes another man who seems to be responding to Christ's call: "I will follow you, Lord, but first let me say farewell to my family at home." To him Jesus said, "No one who sets a hand to the plow and looks to what was left behind is fit for the kingdom of God" (Lk. 9:61–62). Hopefully, this individual still has a chance at life with Christ, but he has surely been harshly warned: once you commit, you must throw yourself into the life wholeheartedly—no clutching dreams of other futures.

"It was not you who chose me, but I who chose you and appointed you to go and bear fruit that will remain" (Jn. 15:16). One morning recently, sitting with my Sisters before our Eucharistic Lord, whom we adore for an hour each day, I placed myself in the Holy Land during Jesus' time. What would I have wanted, once I heard Jesus speak in a field near my home? I think I would have come back again and again, to field after field, to drink in His extraordinary words, to gaze on this person clearly so close to God (not knowing, of course, at least at that point, that He is God). And, in my heart of hearts, I would have wanted to draw near to Him, to be not just one in the crowd but one who got the inside scoop after the crowds had dispersed. All my life, I have desired to draw close to beauty, to holiness, and it would have been the same in this instance.

And then, all of a sudden, I realized that He had asked me to do just that. He had asked me to draw near to Him, to spend my life with Him. At that moment, as I sat in Eucharistic adoration as a Sister, He was filling up to the full the desire He Himself had placed in my heart.

Will you let Him do the same for you?

"How beautiful on the mountains, are the feet of one who brings good news, who herald's peace, brings happiness" (Is. 52:7). The Church needs daughters of the Father and spouses of Jesus, His Son, to reflect and be a witness of God's immense love for us. In today's world, Sisters witness to this love through acts of mercy and by the solitude of prayer. This is the work of the Holy Spirit alive, active and living in us, expressed by our encounter with the living Christ who has changed our lives to be one with Him in this life and for eternity.
—Mother Loraine Marie, L.S.P., Provincial Superior of the Little Sisters of the Poor in Baltimore

Endnotes

[1] Benedict XVI, "Homily for Inaugural Mass, St. Peter's Square," Vatican. April 24, 2005, https://w2.vatican.va/content/benedict-xvi/en/homilies/2005/documents/hf_ben-xvi_m_20050424_inizio-pontificato.html.

[2] Second Vatican Council, *Gaudium et Spes: Pastoral Constitution on the Church in the Modern World*, 24, Vatican, December 7, 2965, http://www.vatican.va/archive/hist_councils/ii_vatican_council/documents/vat-ii_const_19651207_gaudium-et-spes_en.html.

Chapter 12

Wandering through the World, Looking for God...
Religious Life after Employment
—Sr. Amata Veritas Ellenbecker, O.P.

As I leaned back on my chalkboard in the back of my classroom and monitored the twenty–seven high school freshmen in front of me, I fingered the rosary I had in my pocket. I had graduated from college three years ago, and this was the second school in which I had taught. I was restless. I knew this was not all God had planned for me. I wanted more. I glanced around the room at those students hunching over their civics test and looking furtively at the clock, hoping the bell would ring soon. I shared their desire; I was also looking forward to the weekend. Time to go on a retreat, time to put the question to God one more time: What do you want from me?

That I had a rosary in my pocket was not unusual. I had grown up in a Catholic family, and my parents were very active in the Faith. They authentically lived what they believed. They were faithful witnesses to the Church's teachings on marriage and family. They were active in the pro-life movement, they took us to Confession regularly, and they passed on their love for the Church to their children. We grew up praying a family Rosary. Sometimes it was after dinner; sometimes it was just before bed. If we were traveling we prayed it in the car. Although it seems small, I know my devotion to Mary, nurtured by my parents, stirred the flame of my vocation. Like a true mother, Mother Mary steadily led me, with her hand on my shoulder, as I attempted to follow God's will.

The Catholic faith had always been a part of my life, and from a very early age I had a sense that God was calling me to "something," but that something was vague, cloudy, and never clear. I had been an active high school student. My life centered on basketball, cross country, track, band, and student council. By being so active in everything, I found myself "a jack-of-all-trades and master of none." I loved crafts, being with my family, being with my friends, and listening to music. As the fifth of six kids in my family, there was always something to do, always something to keep me busy. Yet I was always restless. That restlessness followed me through my college years, into my teaching career—right up to that moment fingering my rosary while willing the school bell to ring.

As I left school that weekend, I was heading to a vo-cation discernment retreat in Ann Arbor, Michigan. Other than a few emails sent out into the unknown the year be-fore, and my own searching on the Internet for information about Communities who were *avante garde* in even having a presence on the "World Wide Web" in the early 2000s, I hadn't ever done much about this vocational restlessness. I didn't have a strong sense of where God was calling me to Religious Life, if He was calling me at all.

Through my life I had intermittently "thought of a vocation," but never actually pursued it. Well, to be honest, I only thought about it when someone close to me would remark, "You should be a Sister," or "Have you ever thought of a Religious vocation?" My consideration of this vocation lasted a short time after my mom would suggest "I think you should discern Religious Life," every time we met a Sister. Maybe they could see something I couldn't. After each suggestion, I had quickly brushed off any consideration that this could be my call. Until that weekend in Ann Arbor.

I owe my own vocation to the good Religious Sisters who along the way taught me the meaning of "put out into the deep" (Luke 5:4) and how to give God everything without looking back. They embodied God's love and goodness in their service to the universal Church and our local church where their ministries permeated every fabric of our lives. They are at the forefront of it all: always seeking new ways to make the Gospel accessible to so many. The Religious, in their maternal way, are able to bring an incredible sense of the Divine to the people they serve. The life of a Religious is a total giving and complete abandonment to Divine Providence, so as to win souls for God. Thanks to these women, I discovered my own vocation as a priest—in other words, they gave birth to this priest. The life of a Religious is one of great love for the Church, and in return that love is made manifest in the many lives they touch, as through their various apostolates, they gently return souls back to God. Why would anyone not want to be a part of this awesome vocation where the Lord "takes away nothing and He gives you everything?" (Pope Benedict XVI). Say "yes" to a life of happiness and grace.
—Fr. Patrick Ike Nwokoye, Director of Vocation Promotion, Diocese of Springfield-Cape Girardeau

What had brought me this far? A convergence of providential meetings. My older sister was working for the diocese at the time and had introduced me to a young woman who was entering the Dominican Sisters of Mary, Mother of the Eucharist, the next fall. Up until that point I had never met anyone who was actively discerning a Religious vocation. Although I was not discerning yet, my curiosity and interest were piqued. She was the first example of someone who was pursuing Religious Life in whom I could recognize a little of myself. She was someone "like me" who had recently graduated from college, loved to laugh, and was interested in as many things in the popular culture as she was in "church things." I was intrigued, and the Holy Spirit had hooked me. My sister also prompted me, "Why don't you go on a retreat with the Sisters?" With the new image of her friend in my mind, suddenly the idea was not as far-fetched as I first thought.

What brought me to this point was a life that looked good to all appearances, but left me always searching for more. I had graduated from college. I was teaching, and I had recently been in a serious relationship in which marriage was a strong possibility. Still, even in all of this, I felt unsettled and restless for the "something" that had been in the back of my mind and in the silence of my heart for my whole life. I felt that I never was exactly where God wanted me. I liked teaching and truly desired marriage and raising a family, but somehow I knew this was not what God desired for me. For His part, however, God only invited; He never forced the issue. He wanted me to make the decision.

I realized that I needed to make a space for God to speak, and I needed to slow down enough to listen. My family had another practice that deeply formed my vocation: Eucharistic adoration. As long as I can remember, my parents committed to an hour of adoration each week. When I was young they would sometimes take all of us.

When I was older I would sometimes ask to go. And when I was on my own, alone in an unfamiliar city and uncertain of God's plan for my life, it was where I took refuge; it was where I sought answers; it was where I could see Jesus face-to-face. I knew it was here I could listen to that still, small voice that grew steadily louder and began to clamor in my heart.

When I arrived at the airport for the retreat, I was met by the Sisters. Their youthfulness and joy struck me to the heart. I was particularly shocked that they seemed just like me. They too, had wandered through the world looking for God, knowing there was "something else," before realizing it was really "Someone" else! They had found Him here. I watched them the whole weekend. Now I was not only intrigued, but almost envious. They had what I wanted. They seemed to embody the "feeling" I couldn't put into words. Although I had no expectations for the weekend other than just a quiet time of prayer, my heart became attuned to the joy of a life given to God, a life these Sisters seemed to embody.

As the other girls either flew or drove in for the retreat, I was also amazed to meet the variety of young ladies God had gathered together for the weekend. Each young woman had her own story, her own journey, and her own unique way. God was working in each of our souls. We were all different ages; some of the youngest were still in high school, some were in the work world like me. Yet here I immediately felt that age did not matter; in fact, I was deeply humbled by the teens who had the courage to seriously consider taking the life-changing step of entering the convent. Some of these women were young enough to be my students! I could have been correcting their papers! But the wisdom of the "little ones" often leads the way, and in this case I was humbled and inspired by their youthful courage and certainty. I was especially intrigued by a young woman who was entering a cloistered Carmelite Community the following fall. Though I only talked to her briefly, I could see her peace with her decision and her excitement. This was also a glimmer of the "something" in my heart for which I had been looking. She provided a mirror for my deepest desire: resting in Him, giving everything to Him.

All weekend I was again and again astounded by how much I "fit in." In fact, I began to sense that I was made for Dominican life. I loved the prayer, community spirit, and communion with other people whose goal was to love God more. I loved that one minute we were laughing uproariously at the banter between the Sisters, and the next we were in silence at the feet of our Eucharistic Lord. This, I discovered, was the secret that was tucked into my heart. It was the secret I wanted to pursue further. I wanted to love God more; I desired to love God more. I came to know that I would never be happy unless I was single-heartedly devoted to loving God more and receiving His love. It didn't come to me in a flash, or even a moment of conviction, but that mysterious "something" of my entire lifetime was being unwrapped like a gift. I knew I was called to give God everything. I knew the invitation was there, and I knew what God was asking.

The retreat concluded, and I returned to my normal life: teaching and grading homework. But now my eyes and my heart were opened to the possibility of a vocation, and I wanted to respond.

Through another couple months of sure and steady steps forward toward the convent (interspersed with a couple of moments of sitting down and stubbornly refusing to move anywhere) God's grace and the guiding hand of Mary, continued to lead me. Although I knew where God was calling me, years of not having any clear goal had shaped me; it was difficult for me to simply "do it." The months between God's invitation and my entrance into the convent were unsure. But I had faith that God would provide what I needed, both in the assurance that this was His will for me and in the strength to do it.

The day of my entrance arrived, and my parents accompanied me to the convent. It was as much of a new adventure for them as it was for me. As we walked through the front door of the convent, I didn't know what the future would hold. I didn't know what the formation would be like. I didn't know the process of becoming a Sister and didn't really even understand the Dominican charism. What I did know was that God had led me to this point. Though it had been an emotional couple of weeks as I said good-bye to my friends and family, I had peace as I walked through those front doors. I had peace as I donned the postulant outfit of a white oxford shirt, blue polyester skirt, and blue knee-high socks. I had peace as I tearfully said good-bye to my parents. I had peace as I sat at dinner that night in the midst of my new Community. For the first time in my life, there was peace; my lifelong restlessness had diminished.

The peace of my postulant year continued. In my prior life I had often felt directionless and undecided. When it came time for me to pick a college, I just could not decide. When it came time for me to pick a major (after being "undecided" for my freshman year and half of my sophomore year!), I finally settled on teaching. Even after graduation, I didn't have much preference on where I wanted to teach. Although I knew that each person's purpose was "to know [God], to love Him, and to serve Him,"[1] I never quite knew for what purpose God had made me. After I entered the convent, it was as if my whole life coalesced in clarity:

- Consecrated to God. This is why God made me.
- A life dedicated to prayer and zeal for souls.
  This is why God made me.
- The serious pursuit of holiness, surrounded by others
  who share this goal. This is why God made me.

The challenges of adjusting to Religious Life paled in comparison with the peace and joy that came from finally knowing God's will in my life. In embracing a life of poverty, I desired to possess nothing and only to be possessed by God. In embracing chastity, I desired to give God my heart completely, totally, and single-heartedly in order to become a spiritual mother. As I let go of my plan for my life, I embraced firmly and completely God's will through obedience.

Endnotes

[1] Third Plenary Council of Baltimore. *A Catechism of Christian Doctrine*, q. 6. (New York, 1885), e-book, https://archive.org/stream/baltimorecatechi14551gut/14551.txt.

Chapter 13

Making It Big Only to Feel Small...
Life Beyond Three Car Dealerships
—*Sr. Maria Silva, O.P.*

THE FIRST CALL

I will never forget the first time that I felt I was being called to Religious Life. Fr. Larry, my spiritual director, had asked if I could help lead an Emmaus retreat, and I had agreed. Knowing how important the retreats had been for me when I was a student at Cardinal Spellman High School in the Bronx, I was thrilled to be a part of it. I had graduated the year before and had just started at Courtesy Car Dealership when Fr. Larry called me.

We were all sitting in the living room of Blair Lodge Retreat House in Putnam County, New York. A fire was blazing in the brick hearth, and the Blessed Sacrament was exposed in the monstrance on a table before the fireplace. The soft candlelight around the monstrance bounced off the wood paneled walls, shadowed by the retreatants in adoration. Suddenly, as my eyes were fixed on the monstrance, the strangest thing happened. Everything around the Sacred Host went gray. My eyes seemed to undergo some weird kind of movie effect, but as soon as I noticed this strange haze, it was gone. In that moment I felt as though a switch had been turned on. The thought immediately popped into my head: I think I have a Religious vocation.

A flood of emotion overwhelmed me, and I was filled with a joy and a peace that I had never experienced before. When a friend of mine had entered a Carmelite monastery the year before, there was something beautifully appealing to me about it. At the time, I shrugged it off, because I thought there was no way that I was actually called to Religious Life. What I could not understand this night was that I had fallen in love with my Lord in a very different way than I ever had before. However, when the thrill of the moment passed, and I gave the possibility serious thought, I suddenly became afraid. I thought my life would be over, and I would have to give up so many things. I also knew that my Brazilian mother would not be pleased.

A few years later, when I told Fr. Larry about my experience, he recommended that I contact the Dominican Sisters of Mary, Mother of the Eucharist. I thanked him for the suggestion but put it in the back of my mind, because the prospect of entering a convent was almost terrifying. What would my family say? What if I was just inventing all of this, and I did not really have a vocation? Then I would have to start all over. Nevertheless, the question in my heart only grew louder and the tug stronger.

THE DISCERNMENT SAGA

I tried to feel out my mom on this idea. She was one of those people who had very strong opinions and was not afraid to express them. Sometimes it was actually funny, because she had a heavy accent, and she was so direct, a little too direct at times. I casually asked her how she would feel about my becoming a Sister. She looked me square in the face and said, "Why you so stupid-a? Why you no have-a kids and gett-a married?" I guess maybe I was hoping that her reaction would have been milder, but I should have known better. I can laugh now about it, but I was not laughing then. I suppose her response could have been worse, but from then on I did not bring it up with her again. I knew that it would be too hard for her to deal with, too hard for her to let me go.

At least that is what I told myself, but it was actually the reverse. I was the one who was too afraid to let go. So I simply tried to ignore my fear. The more Religious Life seemed like a reality for me, the more I would come up with ways to distract myself from the thought. The unknown, even if it appears attractive at first, can become very scary, even when you know it is the right and best thing for you. Thus began my chronic discernment problem. I would discern, and then, when it got too scary, I would put it back on the shelf for a while.

In the winter of 1996 my discernment had to be put on hold for reasons other than my own fear. My dad became ill and had to go on disability. This meant he could not work and could not support our family. My mom asked me to take time off from Fordham University's night school so that I could help support the family. I had already been working as a salesperson in the car business and was making decent money for a nineteen-year-old from the Bronx. Supporting the family did not seem as though it would be so hard.

The first three months were not too bad. School was on hold only temporarily; it would still be there when things were back to normal. All the bills were paid, and there was always an abundance of food. I was still able to shop, and I did—with gusto! Then, by the sixth month, I started to feel the financial pinch. Assuring myself that my dad would be back to work any day, I continued to spend money needlessly, relying on credit cards to make purchases.

After a year, I stopped spending money on myself, but by then it was too late. I was twenty thousand dollars in debt, and I had very little to show for it. Once I had started borrowing money from credit cards to pay the bills, they had me under their control. My plans, including discerning Religious Life, would just have to be put on hold for a while...again. I told myself that I was still young and had plenty of time. Besides, I could not enter a convent with twenty thousand dollars' worth of debt.

A year and a half after he fell ill, my dad was finally getting back on his feet. He would need more months to get back to normal, so my help was still needed. But knowing that the end of my financial obligation to my family was in sight, I breathed a sigh of relief, hoping to recover from the financial damage of the past year and a half. But the longer I stayed away from school, and the more I was promoted at the car dealership, the more I was able to justify not going back

$\mathcal{M}$OVING OUT: A BREAK WITH TRADITION

Several months passed, and my father went back to work, but my parents were still looking to me to pay the bills. My sense of duty slowly turned into resentment, and I stayed away from the house more and more. Confused about what to do next, I decided to talk to Fr. Larry about the whole mess. I knew I had to take a step back from the household affairs, or I would end up in further debt and unable to move on with my life. Fr. Larry always had practical answers to problems, even if his solutions were not the ones I wanted to hear.

I left our meeting afraid and uncertain. Father suggested that I move out of the house as soon as possible. My heart sank. There has to be another way. He had no idea what the Brazilian and Portuguese cultures were like. You did not just leave your home before you got married! No one in my family had ever moved out on her own. However, knowing that Fr. Larry would never steer me wrong, I decided to take it to prayer and to give the possibility serious thought. After a week of prayer, I knew what I had to do.

My mother did not take my moving out of the house well. She refused to talk to me, saying, "You should-a be shame-a youself, fo leave-a da house befo you gett-a married." For the first time in my life, my mother gave me the silent treatment. Guilt consumed me, and I almost broke down in tears, hoping to win back her approval. But God gave me the strength to remain steadfast.

After the second week of silence, I showed up at the house, and three huge cardboard boxes lined the hallway. My brow wrinkled in confusion as my mother approached me from the kitchen.

"I put-a some tings together fo you to take-a to you house."

My eyes welled with tears, knowing how difficult it must have been for her to do that. I had always had a great relationship with my mother: we could talk about anything. But in the last few years we had become real friends. Knowing from her pained expression that she thought she was losing not only her daughter but also her friend, I grabbed her and wrapped my arms around her round little figure.

"Mommy, you know I'll come over all the time and talk to you on the phone every day. We'll probably talk more when I'm away than we do now." Tears formed in her dark brown, almond-shaped eyes, and she said, "Yeah, sho."

I pursed my lips at her obstinacy. "Ma, I promise, OK?" We stared at each other, laughed at our shared stubbornness, and held each other again. I saw in my mother's eyes the sword that pierced her tender heart, allowing me a glimpse of my Blessed Mother's sorrow, but that was too much for me to bear. My heart felt as though it was being torn from me, but that could not compare to what my mother must have been experiencing. The love of a mother for her children is utterly unique and special, a true reflection of the love God has for each of us.

How difficult it must have been for my mother to let me go that day, but she did. Not only did she let me go, but she had given me her blessing and enough china, pots and pans, linens, and pot holders to last me a lifetime. How could God have blessed me with such a wonderful mother?

The "successful" years

I do not know how it happened, but time seemed to slip past me without my realizing it. It had now been eight years since I had that moment in front of the Blessed Sacrament at Blair Lodge Retreat Center. I had been hopping on and off the discernment fence for so many years that it almost seemed normal.

One day, as I was looking at want ads after leaving a bad situation at a dealership, I noticed a peculiar solicitation: "Do you want to spend the next twenty years together? Are you looking for a position as a controller at a dealership you can call home until you retire?" I kept reading, laughing at the banality of the ad but intrigued by its sentiment. If I was not called to Religious Life, this would be the perfect place to make a career. If I was called to Religious Life, with ads like that, the manager certainly would not have a hard time finding someone to replace me. I called the number and scheduled an interview with "Mr. P." in Long Island City. He and his son James hired me within a week.

Mr. P.'s dealership gave me one of the best experiences I ever had in the car business. The transition was seamless and I was again making more money than a low-income kid from the Bronx could ever dream of making. So, of course, I continued to spend money as I saw fit, as if I were printing stacks of it in my basement.

The thought began to cross my mind that perhaps I was not called to Religious Life. Maybe I had found my niche. Would it be so wrong for me to be a good Catholic in the workplace? Do we not need a strong Catholic witness among lay people? So the discernment question once again ended up on hold. The next two years hummed along smoothly.

One cool, bright Monday morning, Mr. P. asked me into his office. He stared at me and said, "I've had to make a tough decision. Over Christmas, James told me he doesn't want to take over the business. I've been in negotiations with General Motors to sell them the three stores. This isn't what you signed up for; I know I promised you the next twenty years together, but I'm getting too old for this. I told General Motors that the deal is predicated on a couple of things. One of these is that they hire you as the CFO of the three stores. What do you think?"

Overwhelmed by the sudden news, I tried to process what was happening. This was the last thing I had expected.

"I'll do it," I finally said.

Mr. P. smiled: "I was hoping you would say that."

At about this time my friend Charles asked if I was interested in renting a lake house he had been renting. He would be leaving soon, and his landlady said she would give preference to anyone he recommended.

As I followed Charles over the wooden bridge into the "Sedgewood Club," I was engulfed by trees of every imaginable shade of green. The water sparkled in front of me, trees lining the water's edge. The wind kissed the water and momentarily distorted the painting created on the surface of the lake. I thought that I had just found heaven.

Stepping inside the house, I was so jealous of the glass sliding doors over the gray carpeted living room which housed a wood-burning stove. I walked about a mile to get to the kitchen—perfect for entertaining. The double-door entrance led into an expansive room with a bay window overlooking the lake. This house was what I had dreamed about as a girl. I decided that if I ever left this place, it would have to be for the convent, because it was the only place I could think of that could be closer to heaven.

I moved in, and I was living the "good life." I entertained almost every weekend and had everything I wanted.

STRANGE PRAYERS ANSWERED

Then the rug was pulled out from under me. Within three years after General Motors took over the business, each of the dealerships I worked for had to be shut down. I was almost unsurprised. In a moment of grace, two years previous, I had prayed that if the Lord wanted me to be all His, I would need Him to take away my distractions: the six-digit salary, the demo cars, the designer clothes and shoes. So, when it actually happened, I was somewhat relieved. God has always had to speak with me in big ways to get me to listen. Even then, I am sometimes quite deaf.

Eventually, I had to work with the liquidator to close out the books. The thought occurred to me that perhaps God was trying to tell me something in a Book-of-Job way, but I was not ready to say, "The Lord gave and the Lord has taken away; blessed be the name of the Lord!" (Job 1:21). That sounded so extreme. After all, He had not taken everything away. I was back to the want ads, not knowing what was next.

To distract myself, I threw myself into decorating my lake house. Finally, my last task was to set up my bedroom's home theater. Sitting down on the couch in front of my huge sleigh bed, I glanced around the room and felt a sense of accomplishment. But there was still a strange emptiness. I looked at my reflection on the dark TV screen and then out the bay window to the lake. I sighed heavily and said, "I could give it all up tomorrow and it wouldn't amount to a hill o' beans." Surprised at myself for speaking aloud and embarrassed for using such a cheesy phrase, I slumped into the soft cushions.

What had my life amounted to up until then? I was twenty-nine years old, and all I had to show was a closet full of shoes, handbags, and designer perfumes. Yes, I did "good" things for the Church: I was an Extraordinary Minister of Holy Communion, a reader at Mass, a youth ministry assistant, and a religious education teacher. But none of it seemed enough. I wanted more, and for a long time I had thought that meant more "stuff." I was successful by the world's standards: possessing the nice car, fancy clothes, and beautiful home, with money at my disposal. I had worked hard for these things, and yet I felt empty. God heard my strange prayer, and in response He brought my worldly success to a screeching halt.

Getting up, I walked into my closet and turned on the light. I was worth more than the contents of my closet, infinitely more. My Lord loved me so much that He helped me to see what it was that I truly desired, and I was filled with a new joy, a real joy. My head cleared. I knew that throughout life I had been focused on one thing: myself. I had never truly been resigned to God's will and had worried needlessly all these years.

"Therefore I tell you, do not worry about your life, what you will eat [or drink], or about your body, what you will wear. Is not life more than food and the body more than clothing? Look at the birds in the sky; they do not sow or reap, they gather nothing into barns, yet your heavenly Father feeds them. Are not you more important than they" (Mt. 6:25–26)?

Upon reflecting on the life of the Church, we can clearly feel and see how important is the presence and work of the Religious women and men serving the Lord with Joy and Humility. To be a nun is to give beauty to Religious Life, consecrating herself to pray, work and witness on a daily basis. In other words, nuns are the lungs that provide oxygen to the body, the Church, whose head is Jesus Christ.
—Fr. John Paul Bassil, O.M.M., Maronite priest and Director of the Center for Digitization and Preservation at Notre Dame University in Lebanon

$\mathcal{B}$ACK TO DISCERNMENT

Finally, nine years after first hearing about the Community, I signed up for the Dominican Sisters of Mary's November retreat; it was three months away. I felt like a zombie: walking around, doing what needed to be done, but lacking fulfillment. I remember going to work at my new job at an accounting firm and thinking, What is the point? This isn't what I'm supposed to be doing. Nothing seemed real any more except the upcoming retreat.

When I got to the Motherhouse, I met Sr. Joseph Andrew, the Vocation Directress. I had thought I had a big personality! She talked loudly, laughed loudly, lived loudly. I came to know later that she loves loudly, too.

She ushered the retreatants into the chapel and told us that we would have dinner after prayers. I knelt down in a back pew and stared at the monstrance holding the Eucharist, the Real Presence of Christ, framed by the golden reredos nestled in the center of the sanctuary. I felt absolutely nothing. My heart should have ascended into the heights, but instead it remained firmly planted in that pew. I generally appreciate art naturally, instinctively, but in that moment I felt numb to my surroundings. Only later did it strike me that there had been a strange sense of being at home. Prayers with the Sisters seemed to go by too quickly. Soon, we were whisked away by a Sister into a guest dining room.

The room was filled with polite, frivolous chatter as we all awkwardly chose seats. After praying grace, we met with that uncomfortable silence all too common among people who have just met. Knowing someone had to break the ice, I said, "So, why don't we go around the room and say our name, age, where we're from and whatever else you might want to share? I can start..."

Everyone took turns going through their introductions, and soon the room relaxed into easy conversations. Sr. Joseph Andrew came in amidst the chatter and sat down at the table opposite me. I sat up a little straighter, trying to be on my best behavior. Then all of a sudden she looked at me and said, "Why don't you just let loose!"

The look on my face must have been priceless! How on earth did she figure me out? I was really trying to "lie low." Smiling, I said, "You don't even know me. What makes you think I have to let loose?"

She laughed warmly again. "Oh, I see fire in you!"

I looked right at her and asked, "How can you possibly have me pegged so easily?"

She just gave her full laugh again, and everyone else joined in but me. Shaking my head in disbelief, I could only smile and wonder what was happening. My plan had backfired, and it had served me right. How could I possibly expect to make the most important decision of my life and not be "me" when I was trying to make it? How could I possibly lie to the very people with whom I could very well spend the rest of my life? If they did not like me for who I really was, then obviously I would not belong here.

The rest of the evening seemed a blur; all I wanted was to spend time with the Blessed Sacrament. I felt as though I was being pulled, as though I had forgotten something that was waiting for me there; but I would have to wait.

During one of the retreat activities, Sr. Joseph Andrew passed around a manila envelope full of Marian litany titles. We were instructed to take one, meditate on it during our

Holy Hour that night, and then discuss on Sunday afternoon why we had received that title. I reached in and pulled out "Mary, Mother of Jesus." Well, that's boring. I looked at the people around me, wondering if they would notice if I quickly switched it. No, that would be bad. I passed the envelope to the person in the next row... I did not have to worry about it now. I could think about it that night during my Holy Hour.

My Holy Hour was scheduled for midnight, and I looked forward all day to my "date" with Jesus. Making my way to the chapel, I pulled out my litany title and stared at it. I started thinking about Mary in Egypt with the infant Jesus. I thought about her as a mom, playing with her little boy, making Him smile. She probably kissed His little hands and feet, as mothers often do. She must have played games with Him, like peek–a–boo. She would cover her eyes and say in baby talk, "Where did the Messiah go?" And then removing her hands she would exclaim, "There He is!" much to the little Infant's delight. I could just see her holding Jesus up in the air, jostling Him gently, to and fro, as many adults do with babies, risking them spitting up directly into their faces or, worse still, their mouths! I could picture Mary holding Jesus the way she holds Him in the medal worn by all the Dominican Sisters of Mary, cooing "Who's the Son of God? Yes, you are!" I chuckled softly to myself, but since I was having a little fun, I kept going with my meditation. Then I saw Our Lady pull up Jesus' little tunic and give Him a raspberry on His belly.

If you have ever given a baby a raspberry, you have heard pure laughter, a laughter that echoes every ounce of joy contained in his tiny body. He laughs so intensely, so hard, that he looks like he is struggling to breathe, but instinctively you know that he has not breathed life in fully until this moment. You cannot help but laugh with him and revel in his joy. Not only was our Lady the one to hear her Son's giggling, but she was the one to cause it. Did it bring tears of joy to her eyes too? Did she know that she was bringing joy to the heart of God? How she must have relished holding Him in her arms and breathing in that sweet baby smell, feeling the softness of His little curls against her lips. When He fell asleep in her arms, she must have nestled His head against the nape of her neck, His pudgy little arms wrapped around her shoulders, His warm breath kissing her skin ever so lightly.

Suddenly, my eyes opened. I remembered a list I had made of criteria I wanted in a Religious Community, and I almost gasped aloud! I went through the list mentally. First, they were completely Marian. They made their consecration to Mary as a Community and prayed the Rosary together daily. If I entered here there would be no question of my devotion to the holy Mother of God. I knew that if I found a Community that was devoted to Mary, they would also be devoted to the Eucharist. So, the second requirement on my list was fulfilled as well. They were very devoted to Jesus in the Blessed Sacrament. They had a Eucharistic Holy Hour daily as a Community, and their name was just priceless: Mary, Mother of the Eucharist.

Third, they were traditional. I wanted authentic Religious Life, the whole thing: fifteen-decade rosaries, veils, and a long, flowing habit. The world needs visible signs of virtue and of sacrifice for the sake of love. The great Poope St. John Paul II said that the world needs saints for today, and I knew that the only way for me to be a saint was to live authentic Religious Life.

Fourth, I wanted a Community that was going to challenge me intellectually. I always thought that if I got married, I wanted a husband with whom I could debate intelligently and who could even prove me wrong once in a while. I knew that Dominicans would have no trouble in this arena with world-renowned theologians, like St. Thomas Aquinas and St. Albert the Great.

Fifth, I needed a Community that had a sense of humor. I needed to be able to express myself in a light-hearted way, or else I would never make it as a Religious. Everyone needs balance in life, and I have found that laughter is the best way to keep things in perspective, especially as a Religious. I remembered Sr. Joseph Andrew's full laugh and the smiles on the Sisters' faces that showed the joy in their hearts. Jesus, I think I just found our new home.

I received an application from Sr. Joseph Andrew at the end of the retreat. Undaunted by the massive stack of forms, I started counting down the days until August 28, 2007. After my last doctor's appointment in January, I put the required forms into a FedEx envelope and sent it for "next-day" delivery. Now the Community had to decide whether they agreed that this was my home.

On March 3, while at work, I went through my normal routine. Sitting at my desk, I started the computer and logged my email account. I noticed an e-mail with an attachment from Sr. Joseph Andrew. I clicked on it, opened the attachment and there, under my name, the "Accepted?" box was checked: "Yes." I stared in disbelief. When I came to my senses, I spun around in my chair, threw my hands up in the air and mouthed, "Woo-hoo!" Margaret, my secretary, who happened to be in the room, looked at me, confused.

I did not want the others in the office to know yet, so I mouthed to her, "I got accepted!" She had a big smile on her face and whispered, "I knew you would. We're really going to miss you." I floated into the hallway to call Sr. Joseph Andrew and thank her.

$\mathscr{B}$EFORE ENTRANCE

All it takes is three seconds. Three seconds, and your life can change completely.

Ten days later I was at St. Augustine's in Highland, Fr. Larry's parish, helping my friend Esther with the week-long Family Lenten Mission. Esther and I were ready with our "ice-breaker" skit. I was supposed to play a very excited little boy who was trying to make some extra cash by selling pencils. Well, I thought it would be really funny and dramatic if I slid across the stage on my knees at a key moment of the performance. When I was done the audience would never have seen a performance quite like the one I was going to give them.

The moment arrived, and I prepared for my big "stunt." I took a few quick steps and planted my knees on the hard wooden stage, anticipating that I would slide across the length of it. Much to my chagrin my boot got caught in my pant leg and my ankle was no longer behind me but parallel to my knee. I sucked in air, because the pain that shot through my leg was incredible. I almost passed out but tried to pull myself together with the thought, "Just get up and get through the skit." I took one step and fell over from the pain. Sweat beaded on my brow; my hands and feet went cold. Esther whispered, "Are you okay?" I went white and said nothing. I learned that day that I might be dramatic, but I am not agile.

My friend Maureen took me to the emergency room. As I hobbled through St Joseph's Hospital with a crutch under each arm, I was angry for doing something so stupid. Tears formed as I felt entrance to the convent slipping away! The X-rays came back negative, so my worst fears were starting to materialize. The damage was probably to cartilage and ligaments, but I would not know what kind of recovery time I was looking at until I had an MRI.

I really did not want to call Sister and tell her, but I could not avoid it. I had to let her know what was going on, so that she would not be surprised after I got the results from the MRI. Actually, the call went better than I thought it would. She asked that I keep her informed and assured me that she and all the Sisters would be praying. She then issued the challenge: in order to enter the convent I had to be at one hundred percent. I had five months to recover.

The MRI news was grim. I had sustained three major sports injuries in one. I would need surgery as soon as the swelling was gone. There was a choice regarding using my own tissue for the ACL repair or that of a cadaver. I called Sister to discuss my options with her, but she told me that ultimately I had to make the decision. I was back where I had started. No one was going to tell me what to do; I had to figure it out on my own.

You never realize how much something means to you until you are in danger of losing it. Whenever I thought that perhaps I would not enter in August, I felt physically ill. My stomach would turn, I would get migraines, and my nerves would be on edge. So I really had only one choice; I would have the cadaver tissue surgery—which would shorten the recovery time tremendously—and pray that it was successful. I did my research, and the odds were in my favor.

You know the saying, "A watched pot never boils?" Well, I think there should be one that goes like this, "A watched swollen knee never goes down." Nothing seemed to work: elevation, icing, compression, and tons of prayers! After a month and a half, I was getting desperate; I needed to have the surgery so I could start the three-month recovery period.

My heart pined for Christ and for our new home. I longed to be completely His, so I did the only thing I could do: pray. I prayed more than I had ever prayed before, and slowly my heart was becoming resigned to God's will. My heart found peace, and I learned that patience means to be resigned to God's will at every moment and to "take it as God sends it" (Venerable Pierre Toussaint). I had made my Beloved wait for over ten years, and if it was His will, I would wait for Him as long as He deemed necessary.

Two weeks went by, and I did not pay too much attention to my knee. If the good Lord wanted me to enter in August, He would make it work. The doctor measured my knee's range of motion, looked up at me, and said: "I think you're ready for surgery." He knew my future plans, so he smiled at me and said, "I think we might just get you to the convent by August. Just stay on top of the physical therapy and take it easy. No more crazy stunts, OK?"

I laughed. "Very funny."

The next available surgical slot was, wouldn't you know it, May 22, feast of Saint Rita, patroness of impossible causes. That would give me three months and one week for rehab before entrance day. Those three months were a challenge, but also a tremendous blessing. Sometimes it got frustrating because I did not see results from day to day. The only thing that kept me going was knowing that

I had to be ready for August 28. I have never been more vigilant in my life about a doctor's orders. The thought that I might have to wait another year to enter the convent was too excruciating to bear. I physically ached to be with Him, and I knew that that pain would not subside until I was in Ann Arbor.

Those last three months were a time of pure grace. I settled my affairs, spent time with my loved ones, and organized an estate sale, assisted by my family and friends. They showed me that accepting generosity from the ones you love is not only the humble but the right and loving thing to do. In his book *The Four Loves*, C.S. Lewis talks about the different kinds of loves. The one he says is most important is not "gift love" but "need love." "We love because He first loved us" (1 Jn. 4:19). If we do not need love then we are lost, and it is only because we need love that we can give it in return. I needed to "need" my family and friends so that they knew that I loved them, too, and so that I could love them better.

REDEFINING "SUCCESS"

Sanctity is what it all comes down to. God will not ask you how much money you had in the bank, or how many pairs of designer shoes you owned, or how many friends you made. He will not ask you if you were successful in life but whether or not you were holy. He will ask you, "Did you love Me?" That is not a question I want to leave to chance.

Life in the convent was not an easy transition, but every night as I put my head on my pillow, I was happy. At five o'clock in the morning when the bell rang, I did not want to press the "snooze button" (well, maybe once or twice I would have liked to), because when I woke up, I was still happy. I had found the life I loved, and I loved living it. Of course, I had bad days just like anyone else, but a lingering sense of peace and joy colored the weeks and months as I transitioned from a lay person into a Sister.

My mom came to visit with my sister when I was a postulant. My sister, Clarissa, was always supportive of my vocation and was excited to meet the other Sisters. When I was walking around with my mom, I ran into Sr. Mary Samuel (one of our founding Sisters). Sister greeted my mom and asked her, "Mrs. Silva, aren't you glad your daughter is here?"

My mother responded without missing a beat, "No, I no wanna my daughta ta be here no mo." I was mortified, but fortunately Sr. Mary Samuel laughed and took it in stride.

When my mom came back to visit the following year, she was more herself. She even walked into the kitchen and offered to help the Sisters making cookies. She was always seeking to help others. Love wishes to serve. I think that was when my mom realized that my decision had been strongly influenced by what she taught me and how I had been raised. Love demands a response. My mother's response was to love the Lord in her children in her family. My response was to love the Lord in His children.

Three years after I entered the convent, I decided to get married. I even invited Oprah (which is a whole different story) and, wouldn't you know, she sent her crew to tape the ceremony for her. That is, on Friday, August 6, in the year of our Lord 2010, I professed vows of chastity, poverty, and obedience to the Eternal Bridegroom, and He took me for His spouse. I will not attempt to put that moment into words; how can I possibly describe a moment that transcends the natural? How could I describe a moment when heaven and earth met, and Love Himself enraptured my heart?

During the vows ceremony, the Sisters who profess their vows lie prostrate on the floor as an act of renunciation of the world and of their old selves. As I lay on the floor, I could not help but think of what I had given up. I was not concerned with what I no longer had, but instead I marveled that I had actually left everything I had behind. I remember thinking: How powerful is your grace, O Lord! By my own merits, I should not be here. I should still be at the lake house, living excessively, deluding myself into believing that I am living a life of virtue. But there I was, flat on the floor at my Savior's feet and resigned to whatever He had in store for me, because I knew that I had finally given everything to Him. I vowed to Him the unknown, the future, because I trusted that He would take care of me, His bride, and that He would lead me where I needed to go. Indubitably, if He could get me to a convent, He can do anything. I used to be living "the good life," which by the world's standards should have made me content. But now I am living the best life, and the world simply cannot comprehend how that is possible. My life is truly a miracle. He got me here.

Five years after my first vows, I gave my heart to Christ forever; I professed my final vows on July 29, 2015. I have never known that such love—such success—could exist until now. The great paradox of my life has been that because I have nothing, I now have everything. I have found the pearl of great price, my treasure. It is the Heart of Jesus, and, in the end, that is eternally more than enough for me.

Chapter 14

Finding God through the Shadows...
From Convert to Convent
—*Sr. Maria Catherine Toon, O.P.*

AN EARLY LOSS

In *Surprised by Joy*, C.S. Lewis writes, "With my mother's death all settled happiness...disappeared from my life ...no more of the old security. It was sea and islands now; the great continent had sunk like Atlantis."

I have no memory of my mother. When breast cancer suddenly took her from our family, I was three. My grandmother would look at me helplessly as I asked, "Can Mommy come back today?" It was like my heart had been ripped out of the world.

As a child, this early loss made me think that we had struck a sour deal with God. If only we could renegotiate, she could come back, I thought. It seemed like she was still alive, she had just abandoned me for another world. The burning hole in my heart made me wonder where she had gone.

There was never a question of God's existence. I knew that the whole of creation pulsed with His presence and His permanence. I also mysteriously knew that my mother was with God. I cultivated a void that took root in my heart; closeness and intimacy became more and more distant. For as long as I can remember, I would "check in" with God before I fell asleep. God was someone to be reminded of what I needed, and He rarely gave it to me. Despite this, people around me repeatedly told me that He loved me. So, why did He take my mother away? How could He love me and take away the most important person in my life? In a confused sort of compromise, I did try to talk to Him a little. I thought I would string Him along, hoping that these attempts at communication would be a trump card in any battles when I really wanted to get my way. If God loves me, He would give me what I want, right?

Many times while I was falling asleep, I could feel God's closeness, and I would even cry thinking about His agony on the cross. But these feelings amounted to amorphous fuzziness. I was not sure what God was really like and my earliest memories are marked by a kind of disconnectedness, loneliness, and isolation.

Life as a young Presbyterian

My stepmother, Jean, was enamored with my father and his two daughters. Jean and Dad knew that the right thing to do was to "take the girls to church." My father was rather apathetic about organized religion, and Jean had grown up Presbyterian. So, it was decided that we would be Presbyterian.

Jean, Dad, my older sister Barbara and I would all go to church together. Over time, I began to love church. It was the friends, the summer trips, and the charismatic youth leader that were all my joy. For a few brief years, there was real tangible communion that had been missing in our family, and that covered the wound from my mother's death and her following absence. God's presence was spotty, but it was there, and I began to recognize it. A friend from that church, who was in my department in college, said years later, "Don't you remember, we would go up to church just to see who was there?" She had felt it too.

I remember being about seven and standing on the pew next to Jean while reciting the Apostles' Creed from page fourteen of the mauve hymnals that dotted each row. As the congregation recited the Creed in a steady modulated tone, I could smell her perfume, and watched her polished, manicured finger follow each of the words. To this day, I always remember the maternal comfort that this prayer offers because of this memory.

On those mornings, I would look up at the fourteen-foot wooden cross, the sole ornamentation in the sanctuary. God is everywhere, I thought. I could feel Him. A little flame rose up in my heart. I wished I knew exactly where He was. I wished silently that God was in one place, so I would know where to worship Him. It was overwhelming to picture how God could be everywhere. I scrunched my eyes shut and tried: a mild headache followed. I badly wanted to give Him everything, but I was not sure how to go about it.

A few years later, when I was ten, I approached a Presbyterian Elder, mostly because I thought he was the handsomest Elder (admittedly not the surest measure of wisdom) and questioned him: "If God says that we should all be one, how do we know we are in the right denomination?" He seemed embarrassed at my question. I forgot his answer a few minutes later.

When we came home from church on Sundays late in the morning, I was relieved to peel off my white opaque tights and tight leather flats that always squeezed my toes. It was so refreshing to just sit in the cool quiet of my upstairs room and stare out the windows overlooking our driveway. During this weekly routine, I stealthily removed the NIV Bible from Dad's downstairs bookshelf and began reading the Book of Revelation. The thin pages made this particular book solemn and professional. Only serious people who were serious about life would read a book like this, I thought. It became a hallowed pattern enkindling the flame in my heart a little more. Leafing through those pages was a source of comfort whenever I was feeling lonely on those early Sunday afternoons. The letters to the seven churches (Rev. 2–3) both terrified and gripped me. I loved the cataclysmic episodes in this book of Scripture; it was like an epic movie that possessed a reliable narrator and a grand sweeping story with a happy ending that filled me with hope. But Revelation was also abundantly clear about the danger and risk of the faith. The Bible made the Christian faith seem like a wild adventure.

As a Presbyterian, there was no obligation to go to church on Sundays, and my friends had all chosen to attend different high schools. The increasing demands of rehearsals from the magnet high school for the performing arts that I began attending my freshman year made it more difficult to justify taking the time for church. My parents and I gave it up as a matter of course. But I still longed for answers about who God was, where He was, and how to worship Him.

While in a local public library, I stumbled across a handbook on how to become Wiccan. I found it fascinating. I was desperately seeking some kind of confirmation of what I understood about the spiritual dimension of my life. I wanted to feed the flame inside of me. Reading about Wicca led to a deeper curiosity about New Age spirituality and the occult, which I began to integrate into my life. I wanted more control over social anxieties and these practices, at least temporarily, seemed like a valid answer. I wanted to design my own spiritual life with the haphazard mantras, superstitions, and curiosities that I found attractive. In short, without a true tabernacle in my life, I wanted to build my own tabernacle without God. However, the more I pursued these things the emptier I felt, and the fewer answers I had.

It seemed to me that, as a Protestant, there weren't really consequences for sin, nor were there really concrete rewards for being faithful. Therefore, I thought, Christianity could not possibly have any answers to my desire for purpose and community. A tangible experience with the spiritual world would have to be found elsewhere. A high school classmate of mine was Bengali and a Hindu. I relished dressing up in her mother's saris and attending pujas with her and her family. There is something very womanly about wearing a sari. It was so foreign but it seemed to grasp at the spiritual realm more earnestly than the WASP (white anglo-saxon Protestant) culture in which I was steeped. I feverishly read anything I could about other cultures and religions.

CATHOLICISM TAKES ROOT

For my eighteenth birthday, my Aunt Gertie gave me a rosary. It was deep, fiery red. She gave it to me, she said, because my mother loved to pray the Rosary. Although I never prayed it, it remained special to me as a connection—however small and frail—to Mom's Catholicism. Aunt

Gertie was the only practicing Catholic in my family, and she was my Godmother. I knew that she and her family went to Mass every Sunday, but she never talked about it. Hoping that the rosary would unlock something about my own womanhood and my identity, I hung it on the mirror of my closet door and would look at it every day.

By the time I attended college, I had no idea what to believe in, but I wanted to believe in something. Something in me knew that my life was important, and that I needed to spend it well, but internally I had no direction. It was important to my parents that I be free to choose whatever career path I wanted, and they consistently gave me their support. But whenever I thought about making big decisions, there was a constant sense of grief and mourning that frequently threatened to present itself. My mom had died over fifteen years ago—why did I always want to cry? Why was I not able to trust anyone or make significant decisions about what I wanted to do with my life?

Between my last year of high school and first year of college, I became depressed, but tried to hide this from my family and friends. Ever the utilitarian, I decided the answer was a summer job. Salsa dancing was beginning to crop up as a craze all around U.S. college campuses and I wanted to give it a shot. Downtown, there was a combination restaurant and salsa club. I landed a job as a hostess for the restaurant with free dance lessons thrown in.

One man, David, came to the club several times a week and frequently took lessons. He was a disciplined dancer, and proved to be a strong and frequent dance partner. He was at least eight years older than me, and, like an older brother, he took an interest in my studies. He had taught himself two languages, had serious training in martial arts, and was a committed Catholic. Although I was not interested in him romantically, I was a little intrigued.

Slowly, David's personal philosophy began to trickle through the things he would tell me about life. He explained the Book of Tobit one day while we were waiting for practice to start. Since this Old Testament story is in the Catholic Bible but not present in the Protestant one, it was entirely new to me. Tobit's family is ripped apart by misfortune and sickness. Through the narrative God orchestrates healing and many spiritual blessings for Tobit's family because of Tobit's faithfulness. God even heals Sarah, who has a seemingly impossible case of demonic oppression.

At the climax of the story, Tobias, Tobit's son, prays to God on his wedding night with Sarah. Tobias' sincere words and purity of intention provide the source of healing for their marriage. This biblical story illustrated how integrated God's healing is meant to be: Tobit's blindness is healed, Tobias matures as the head of his family, and Sarah fully embraces her identity as wife. Hearing the story gave me a new and profound hope for a kind of healing I didn't even know I was looking for. Tobit even speaks of a tangible presence of God "be[ing] rebuilt in you with joy" (Tob. 13:10).

I felt an immediate connection with Sarah because of my background in New Age spirituality. David made the case that if I was using Wicca practices to try to control my life, I was actually opening doorways to the devil, who was disguising himself through what I had thought were inno-cent practices. It was dawning on me that the books I was reading were not bringing the blessings I had hoped but were exposing me to spiritual dangers that could account for my depression. He was able to explain definitively why the occult and New Age were so dangerous and not a path to the truth.

As I embarked on my Christmas vacation that year, I was really missing my mother. Would she have given me the guidance that I wanted? Desiring to get as close as possible to my mom, I called Aunt Gertie, and casually asked, "Can I go to Mass with you?" Maybe if I went to a Catholic Mass I would have some chance to be closer to her.

Mass was a makeshift affair—held in the parish hall, complete with scaffolding for a remodeling project—but I didn't notice. God had begun rebuilding me. From the moment we walked into the building, I knew I was going to cry. It wasn't just the gentle tearing up that could be dabbed away with a tissue; something in me needed a full-out sob. I sobbed through the whole Mass. This was the place where Mom had been. My aunt had told me she had seen me at daily Mass as a very small child with my mom. My two-year-old body would scramble over the pews. So Mom had been here. And I had been here with her.

Returning to school, I called David and we agreed to meet for coffee. The fact that he was a practicing Catholic had been lost on me when I first met him. Going to Mass and experiencing a connection with my mother made me more curious about Catholicism.

After shooting the breeze for fifteen minutes or so, I broached the subject of the Catholic Church. Quickly we got down to the tough questions: abortion, homosexuality, and the role of women in the Church. Truthfully, I had been conditioned by our culture. I had never known anyone who openly professed that abortion was a sin. David had clear and logical answers for everything. Even what I had learned from Wicca and Hinduism, David quickly integrated into the Catholic Church's understanding of man's desire for truth and wisdom.

But what really impressed me was how David spoke about Scripture and his faith in an intelligent manner. His commitment to Catholicism made him seem trustworthy. Here was someone who actually believed that Jesus' presence in the Eucharist is truly the key to human flourishing. Every inch of his life evinced that all of creation is ordered towards being possessed by Christ and adoring him in the tabernacle.

As David fielded more of my questions, he told me openly, "You are smart. Do the research. Keep asking these questions until you find the truth." His implicit confidence was just the boost I needed. Later that week, I scoured the Vatican website looking over Church documents, wanting to read the Church's teaching from the Church herself. I found things just as David had described. The Catholic faith is not opaque; it is meant to be discovered, studied, and enjoyed. God does not hide in the shadows; He wants to be known and loved.

Over the next few weeks, we met for coffee again. My attention turned from my burning questions to the freedom that my friend possessed. His demeanor, intelligent but uncomplicated, communicated to me that part of being a Christian meant that the faith is logical enough to discover, and that I could learn from others like him who were living it in a freedom I had never seen. I wanted that freedom.

Although my family, friends, and college classmates assured me that I was clever and able to do whatever I wanted, unbridled by any convention, I had tried most of what that entailed and still felt lonely and unsatisfied. Yet here was David, who seemed to have received less support than I and yet was deeply content with life. He was a man who had carved his character and integrity with discipline and reaped a rich reward in prudence and wisdom. That inspired me to seek what he had found.

𝒯HE MOMENT OF CONVERSION

One crisp Tuesday in January, I woke up at 8:00 a.m. and sat straight up in bed. Eight in the morning is too early for any college student to think, but memories began to flood my mind. My mother's death. The childhood longing to belong and the rare moments when I felt like I did belong. My desires to give myself freely, to be loved and certain that love would be returned. All of them were dragged out before me.

As I sat there in bed, I remembered having visited an adoration chapel at David's church weeks earlier. The soft, yellow glow of the candles made the small chapel warm and inviting. The Blessed Sacrament, the true presence

of Christ in the Eucharist, was housed in a gold monstrance in the middle of the altar. There was Jesus right in a spot where I could worship Him. There in His house, I could be certain of His presence in my life.

Those weeks of meeting with David reminded me of what I had wanted as a child. It had been years since I had remembered that I used to fall asleep crying over Christ's crucifixion and would read the Book of Revelation over and over again. David made it seem like Christ was real again, and that everything I had believed before was true. Jesus had not been an impartial observer to all my suffering; He had been there and had suffered with me. Going to Hindu pujas, reading about witchcraft, and crying during the Mass, were all signs that I was deeply longing for Christ's real presence, a presence that is really efficacious and meaningful. I had been trying so hard to create my own religion. It never occurred to me that maybe God was trying to save me the trouble.

The words I had read as a girl came through to me very clearly and rang through my mind as I lay there: "Behold, I stand at the door and knock. If anyone hears my voice and opens the door [then] I will come enter his house..." (Rev. 3:20). I recalled that former flame in my heart that had been unlit for so many years. The choice lay before me: I could continue the life I was living, being happy in a mediocre sense. Or, I could become a Catholic. Conversion would demand great sacrifices and suffering. It would mean breaking down my way of life and building a whole new understanding of the world. But it would also mean that I could have a shot at real happiness...a happiness that this world couldn't give. I wanted the 'rebuilding' that Tobit spoke about.

That morning, I called David. "I want to become a Catholic. What do I need to do?"

$\mathcal{E}$ARLY LIFE IN THE CHURCH

After I completed RCIA and was received into the Church, David and his friends continued to walk me through living the faith. David introduced me to Nicole, who was fashionable, put together, and also a convert. She was a perfect role model for me, and quickly became a close friend. She accompanied me to RCIA classes, and we often chatted about what I was learning.

David and Nicole were also friends with a married couple, Frank and Gwen. The five of us formed a unique close-knit group. Their freedom of living in Christ showed me that God's grace is meant to be enjoyed. I remember leaning back on the roof of their car one July 4th and just delighting in the fireworks without anxiety about who I was with, or what came next. Being with my new friends meant we savored being together. I actually started to crack jokes without worrying that no one would understand my sense of humor. We were all able to relax together in Frank and Gwen's house and talk about problems we experienced at work.

Nicole and Gwen were true friends who helped me make prudent decisions. They never feared telling me when I was at fault. I'll never forget the day they pulled me aside after Mass and shared with me that my tank top, flip flops, and cut-off shorts were not appropriate for daily Mass. They communicated these corrections charitably, and their friendship enabled me to take these episodes in stride and see them as opportunities for growth. In a very real way they showed me how to build the fire in my heart and fan its flame. I will be forever grateful for their vigilance over my fledgling faith and their real love for me.

My new friends had a special relationship with the Virgin Mary. When difficulties arose, they all flew to Our Lady. I started to notice that not all Catholics seemed to have this love for her. But the ones who did seemed more at peace and weathered sufferings more easily, and help came to them at just the moment they needed it. When someone gave me St. Louis de Montfort's *Way of Total Consecration to Jesus through Mary*, it seemed like the right thing to do. After all my years as a Protestant, devotion and prayer to Our Lady was a little foreign. But I remembered keenly the day Aunt Gertie had given me that red rosary. This is what Mom had done when she needed help, I thought. I realized I needed a spiritual mother. Our Lady became an indispensable help in my own spiritual life.

DISCERNMENT ON THE HORIZON

When I was helping Frank and Gwen with their move out to the country, Frank and I were in his pickup hauling a load out to their new house. "Have you discerned your vocation yet?" he asked as he gently maneuvered the steering wheel of his pickup. I was puzzled by the question. He looked over when I was silent. "It means: have you thought about if God is calling you to either marriage or Religious Life?"

Although from my earliest memories I had always pictured myself married, there seemed to be something wrong with that picture in my head. Truthfully, as I looked around my life, there were a lot of marriages that seemed unhappy. Despite this, I thought I desired the married vocation. Besides the companionship and physical pleasure that marriage would bring, I also loved the thought that I would be a wife, and that I would belong to someone else and he would belong to me. The rich connotations of the word "wife" would come to mind when I thought of my stepmother (and recalled the smell of her perfume) and when

I met married women in the grocery store. I would catch a glimpse of a golden–banded left hand resting on a grocery cart, while her right hand fingered cereal boxes and fruit. In the deepest sense, wives are women who belong to someone, and someone belongs to them. "My lover belongs to me and I to him..." (Song 2:16).

For wives, their bodies have been physically and spiritually given over to their husbands and children. Their spirits are molded to the shape of love through daily routines of making a home. Their lives are ones of shared holocausts and true communion in a family. As I grew in my newfound faith, I started to watch my friends and acquaintances forge examples of true, authentic marriage. In my mind, it was settled: I definitely wanted to be a wife.

One of my mentors, who had married in college, told me about his wife. "When I met her I knew she had 'wifeness'," he said.

"Wifeness?" I asked.

"There was just something in the air around her that told me she had all the qualities to be a good wife," he explained. "My wife."

Thinking about my own vocation, I started to ask myself, "Do I have wifeness?" I immediately would answer myself, "Yes! But in what sense?"

That fall I was in my last semester of college. I was walking across the quad of my university when it hit me: I realized that all the men I was dating looked like Jesus. Not only that, but now that I was a Catholic, it meant that marrying Jesus, as a Religious Sister, was actually...possible.

Oh no, I moaned inwardly. This was not a good sign!

When I got home, I started to panic a little. Hyperventilating, I called Gwen and told her of my fears. "Relax," she said, "What makes you think you might be called to Religious Life?" I had always sensed a closeness to the Lord and that He was always watching over me. But that did not mean I had to give up having my own family, right?

I pointed out to her that I was new to being Catholic and I wanted to be a good one. I decided that good Catholic girls are supposed to discern their vocations. She and I had talked a lot about the Second Vatican Council and the meaning of Religious consecration. According to the Fathers of the Council, the charism of the Community is what holds it together and gives its members their shared mission. To lose the charism through a desire to remake Religious Life in our image, would sound the death knell to any Community.

So there was nothing to be done but to go to the closest Carmelite monastery and "discern" with them. The Discalced Carmelites had struck me as having preserved the charism of their Community. From my rudimentary knowledge and judgment, they seemed to be living an authentic Religious Life.

As I pulled up to the monastery, all the lies charged in: I'm not really free to do what I want. God does not want me to be happy. He wants to punish me for my past sins. I visualized two models of Religious Life, both of which were painful: wearing a pantsuit and bangs for the rest of my life or wearing a beautiful, feminine habit and being stuck praying somewhere and never being able to see other people, on the other. These two disparate and acute fears characterized my discernment. If God was calling me to Religious Life, it must be some form of punishment. And I would never be a wife.

I parked my car, dust from the unpaved road clinging to it, and walked into the monastery chapel. My shoes clicked on the Spanish tile floor, and I slipped into a cool, wooden pew. The Sisters chanted the Divine Office unseen, and led all of us in the Rosary. They were so happy and at peace. I was not.

I sped out of there so fast that the tread marks from my tires probably still mark their driveway. Their steady way of life genuinely called to me, but I had a terrible feeling in the pit of my stomach that told me something wasn't right. So, I pushed that calling deep, deep down, checked discernment off my list, and moved on.

For the next five years, I tried to tell myself that I had been responsible about discerning my vocation: I had visited the only Community I would have considered joining, and it wasn't for me.

Putting these parameters on God made praying hard. How could I trust God when it seemed like He was not showing me my vocation to marriage? Nevertheless, I was going to confession regularly, striving to pray a daily Rosary, and going to daily Mass several times a week.

I was also dating a man who I felt had real potential. Ethan and I had gone to college together. A couple of years later, we saw each other at a pro-life event, and I invited him to pray the Rosary at my house with some friends. He was the only one who showed up. Ethan broke through a barrier that most people did not get past: he was probably the first man I really trusted. All his actions in our relationship demonstrated to me that he was disciplined and ready to sacrifice in a way that a husband and father should.

There were signs, though, that Ethan and I were not made for each other. One day when we were in the car, he cautiously told me, "I really don't need to go to adoration as much as you do. I'd actually rather be with my friends."

His comment was a reminder that most lay people don't need to go to adoration multiple times a week to feel complete. It was a sticking point that reminded me I might not be called to marriage. As time went on, it became clear to me that God could be calling him to the priesthood. So, it seemed like the best thing to do was to break it off. Nine months later when he packed his car and drove to the seminary, I was both relieved and excited for him.

Over these next few months, I would often spend my days sitting at an extremely underachieving job shuffling paperwork, running off copies, and staring out the window, wanting my life to be...something else. Dreaming up all kinds of schemes during the work day, I would come home and fall into my routine of watching movies or going out with my friends, but I wouldn't really pursue anything. The gnawing in the pit of my stomach was growing. Where was I supposed to direct the blaze that was growing in my heart?

One of my last stalling tactics was to move into my grandmother's house. All the cousins and I affectionately called her "Gromie." She was a great source of information about my mom. She seemed to remember everything. Not only that, but she possessed a great sense of humor and a steady daily routine that I badly needed in order to see clearly. The steadiness of her life helped me to build a regular schedule. Even though my grandfather had passed away, she shared a lot that gave me deeper insights into the love and sacrifices that made up their marriage. After spending all day working for a bank in a skyscraper downtown, it was easy to come home to Gromie.

After six months, my steady bank job became the casualty of a merger, and I received three months' notice that I would be laid off. March 31 would be my last day. Later the same week, Gromie informed me that after a lot of deliberation, she would be selling her house to go to the "old folks' high rise" (as she called it) and planned to move out March 31. Although for most people this situation should have felt like my world was caving in, for me it was actually a sign that "Aslan was on the move," so to speak. I knew that the Lord was on the verge of showing me His will—and that was exciting.

By the last week of March, I had landed an ideal job and was happily moving in with a friend who had a spare room. My situation was perfect! I lived within a 15-minute drive of my parish, my job, and my new roommate. My job was doing marketing and branding for an academic think-tank, which required a lot of reading. I love to read! Working for this non-profit introduced me to intellectual vistas I had never been exposed to: political theory, ancient philosophy, and Catholic social teaching. I was actually being paid to study and talk about what I was studying. I thought I was finally primed to shape a life and a career for myself.

Abruptly, Ethan showed up in my life again. He had left the seminary. We went to dinner. He was living in another city and had accepted a position similar to mine near the capital city of our state. We had a wonderful time, and I remembered what a genuine friend he had been to me. But pretty soon, he was coming into town a lot.

On one of these visits, he was at my house, and we were sitting on the couch talking. As I looked at him, I could feel Jesus standing behind him, and it seemed as though I had a choice before me: Ethan or Jesus. Ethan's affection was pleasantly overwhelming. Whom was I going to choose? It seemed like I could not commit to both Jesus and Ethan. I had finally found someone serious and mature enough with whom I could build a life. Couldn't I embody "wifeness" for Ethan?

After he left, I sat alone, staring at an icon of Christ in my bedroom corner. He gazed back at me, silent but available. I was just starting to love my life. I finally had a job that challenged me intellectually and professionally and a shot at an authentic relationship that would be permanent, stable, and rewarding. Why did I still have this feeling that I was avoiding Religious Life?

"It was worth it to Me to wait for you," Jesus said to me in my thoughts. Even the messed-up parts of my heart— He wanted it all. He told me clearly, as I sat there, that everything that I had been afraid of, or botched in the past, did not matter. I could still be the wife that I was wanting to be. His wife.

> The Church needs more Sisters to bear joyful witness to the graces the Lord presents to us, and to pray for increased graces throughout the world! I am constantly hearing wonderful stories about how Sisters educated, cared for, and guided some of the best Catholics around the world. However, there are fewer and fewer young Catholics with these amazing stories because there are fewer and fewer Sisters to make a positive impact on their lives and faith formation. This is a troubling trend which needs to be reversed immediately!
> —John Liston, Executive Director, Serra International

As I came to this realization, I started to recognize that the only time I was at peace was before the Blessed Sacrament. I felt a deep call from Jesus to spend an hour with Him in adoration every day. This was where He wanted to build my spiritual house. But I still wanted to stall.

Through Holy Hours with the Missionaries of Charity, I met the woman who would become Sr. Catherine Thomas. She was a few years younger than I and was enthusiastic about joining the Dominican Sisters of Mary, Mother of the Eucharist as a postulant. After running into one another at daily Mass, we decided to have lunch. "You should really call Sr. Joseph Andrew in Ann Arbor," she said after hearing my story. "She could help you sort this out." Her suggestion was friendly, but I did not feel inspired to act.

$\mathcal{A}$ WIFE TO GOD

The next week when I walked into work, my boss informed me, "We're going to Michigan for a week next month. Mark your calendar." This was not a good sign. Remembering that talk last week after Mass about the Dominican Sisters in Ann Arbor, I took a deep breath and asked for an extra day off when we were up north.

That week in Michigan turned into an extremely challenging one in terms of work. I practically collapsed at the door of the Motherhouse of the Dominican Sisters in Ann Arbor, sleep–and prayer–deprived. The truth is, too, that I really did not want to be there. I did not want to discern my vocation. But there I was in my jeans, with my chocolate sweater and my blonde curls, hoping that I could keep running away.

Sr. Joseph Andrew met me at the door of the convent in her swooshing habit and airy southern lilt. Walking into the cavernous chapel with the two–story gold Spanish reredos, I touched my right knee to the cold marble floor. The coolness and the silence quenched the fire and quieted the noise in my heart. I took that feeling with me when Sister led me to a parlor.

A postulant, who had entered a few weeks before, giggled as she happily explained to me several parts of her daily schedule while I tried not to distract myself. She was so happy. Really happy. Is God calling me to be this happy?

Sr. Joseph Andrew and I had dinner. "What are you looking for in a Community?" she asked. I explained that I loved Our Lady, wanted daily Eucharistic adoration, and wanted to be committed to the life of the mind.

"Sounds like you found it, hon. We have all those things." Uh-oh. I gulped. She looked me straight in the eye. "Maybe you should come on our retreat next February."

"Hmmmm..." I responded noncommittally and gazed into the garden adjacent to the window.

After our plates were whisked away by a bright-eyed young Sister, several other Sisters in their white habits and black veils joined us in a parlor for a board game. They were so welcoming! "Have you thought about coming on retreat?" they asked. I looked at Sr. Joseph Andrew. "Maybe you should come in November." She looked at me hard again but not unpleasantly, as if she was deciding something. When the bell rang for Compline, the Night Prayer of the Church, Sr. Joseph Andrew pulled me into an adjoining parlor.

"How tall are you?" she asked hurriedly. "I'm 5'4 ½," I said, emphasizing the half.

Sister replied, "There was a Postulant who was scheduled to enter this year, but couldn't." Her postulant outfits were unused, looking for a body to fill them. "They're for someone who is 5'4"." She looked at me steadily. "How soon could you be here?"

I was almost afraid to think, but I felt myself moving slowly towards this possibility. What if I just entered? Just like that. What if I just left everything behind, and just tried this?

"We're going into Compline now. Why don't you just ask Jesus what He wants for you? You can let me know afterwards," she said, patting my arm assuredly.

As I walked into the Chapel, the first sound I heard was the soft click of the Sisters' rosaries as the metal hit the marble when they genuflected. Their silent footfalls took them into the one hundred wooden stalls specially carved for a life of prayer. All these beautiful and serene women were dedicated to God. They were brides. They were each a "wife" of Jesus.

When Sr. Joseph Andrew came to get me after Compline, she asked, "Well, what did He say to you?"

I was ready to tell her I needed to think about it. I was ready to tell her I had not slept in four days. I was ready to tell her that I would talk to my spiritual director. Anything to put it off, one more time.

In a swift moment, however, I assessed my situation: I was twenty-seven years old. I was running out of reasons to run, and I did not feel free to give myself to marriage until the question of a possible vocation was answered. What was I waiting for?

"I don't see why not," I articulated slowly but with commitment. After all, how many in this world can be a wife to God?

Now when I look back, years after making final vows, I am so grateful to Jesus for all the topsy-turvy questions, longings, sufferings, and joys that tunneled their ways into my heart, so that He could build a real blaze in me, the blaze of His love. I needed all those things to know that He is my answer.

Endnotes

[1] C.S. Lewis, Surprised by Joy: *The Shape of My Early Life*, (New York, NY: Harcourt, Brace), 21.

Chapter 15

Reading, Writing, Arithmetic... and Religion...
Sisters Teaching in Elementary Schools
—Sr. Mary John Kramer, O.P.

UNLESS YOU BECOME A LITTLE CHILD... (MT. 18:3)

THE APOSTOLATE AS A RESPONSE OF LOVE

The call to Religious Life is, more than anything else, a sublime invitation from Jesus Christ to be His bride. When a woman enters a Religious Community, she does not do so with the intention of being a pious nurse or a saintly teacher; she enters to be Jesus' alone through her vows of poverty, chastity, and obedience. However, many Sisters are, in fact, pious nurses and saintly teachers. Some work with the poor, while others minister to the needs of a diocese or of individual parishes. Still other women devote their entire lives to praying for the needs of the Church and the world as cloistered contemplative nuns. The particular role undertaken by Religious Communities is called their apostolate. The apostolate in Religious Life flows from the charism (a gift of the Holy Spirit at work in the Church) of a particular Community—usually exemplified in the Community's founder—and the spousal union of the individual consecrated woman with Christ.

When a woman begins her discernment, she should not try to decide what occupation she would excel in and then limit her exploration of Communities to those whose apostolate fits her criteria. Her first question is, "Is Jesus calling me to be His bride?" If the answer is "yes," she makes a total surrender of her heart into Jesus' pierced hands and asks Him to guide her where she will be able to respond best to His love.

In any Community, the apostolate is the concrete expression of the consecrated woman's spiritual motherhood. This is the "place" where her love for her Divine Bridegroom manifests itself through her actions. If it is the life of prayer in a cloistered Community, she is like the heart or lungs that support the outward actions of the Body of Christ, the Church. She is like Mary at Ephesus, supporting the work of the apostles by silent adoration of her Son. If she is an active Sister working in a hospital, feeding the poor, or teaching, she expresses her love for Jesus by becoming an icon of Mary in the world, tending to the Body of Christ. Whatever she does, she seeks the face of Jesus her Spouse in the spiritual children He has placed in her care through the apostolate of the Community where He has called her to be His own.

THE APOSTOLATE OF PARTICULAR COMMUNITIES

In any given Community of consecrated women, you will find Sisters who always felt drawn to that Community's particular expression of love. You will also find Sisters who were surprised by the new path the Lord laid out for them as they discerned His will.

Sometimes God the Father places a desire in a woman's heart as a means of helping her find the expression of her love. For example, a woman may deeply desire to give spiritual and temporal nourishment to the Lord's children through a Community that ministers to the homeless. But it also often happens that her desires are surrendered at the foot of the cross as a wedding gift to her Beloved. We discover that we can find happiness most easily when we lay our own expectations and desires aside and focus only on Him.

I grew up with Religious Sisters as part of my life. They taught me catechism, prepared me for Confirmation and turned my life back to the Church, after my parents went their own separate ways, with all with the gentle love and understanding only a woman can provide to a young boy. My paternal grandmother's sister, a Sister of St. Martha of Antigonish, Sr. Mary Celine, told me to "go to church and listen to the Sacred Scripture [because] there is too much evil in the world that must be fought against by young good people." I actually listened to her...and became a daily communicant like many others in my family. She led me to my vocation in the Society of Jesus. She was also my first funeral.
—Fr. Alan J. Fogarty, S.J., President of the Gregorian University

A woman's journey through discernment begins with this question: "Am I called to Religious Life?" Then, she will seek out the Community to which she is called. It can be tempting during discernment to look at the apostolate of a Community first, but she cannot be sure what work she will be assigned to do. The apostolate flows from the life of the Community, and the young woman will find her peace in the will of God, whatever her assignment may be. Individual assignments often come with challenges, but there is an abiding peace in knowing that this is the place and way Jesus wants to meet His bride.

$\mathcal{E}$LEMENTARY TEACHING APOSTOLATE

My own experience of an elementary teaching apostolate was something of a surprise. When I discerned Religious Life, I focused on the contemplative aspects of our life as Dominicans. Since there were only two Sisters of the Community actually teaching at the time of my initial discernment, I did not have a clear image of what my life would look like as a teaching Sister in the Community. I knew that we were teachers and that the logical result of my entrance was that I would eventually teach, but my desire was set only upon giving myself entirely to the Lord—as soon as possible! Only in Heaven will I really understand why the Lord wanted me to serve Him as a teacher. But, over the years, He has given me some clues as to what He may be doing.

The apostolate is the place for fruitful spiritual motherhood. One way a natural mother shows her love for her husband is by caring for the children God entrusts to them through their union. She loves each child individually and for his own sake, but she also sees the image of her husband in him. Her children are concrete expressions of their mutual love. As she cares for the children, she is continuously making her love for her spouse fruitful. In a similar way, as the Religious woman cares for the "little ones" of the kingdom, she also seeks the face of her Beloved. At times, He will peer through the lattice of her classroom, showing up in the least likely places (cf. Song 2:9).

There is also a very real dimension to elementary teaching which is formative for the Religious, even as she helps to form the young people in her charge. Each of the vows—poverty, chastity, and obedience—that bind her to the Divine Bridegroom is expressed in the classroom, and He is continuously drawing His bride to Himself in and through the apostolate.

$\mathcal{P}$OVERTY: TRUST IN ACTION

I have often heard it said that God doesn't give us anything we can't handle. I disagree with this, at least on the surface. It seems to me that He gives us things all the time that we can't handle on our own. Every day. It is one of the many ways He draws us to Himself. If we are not tested in trust, the prayer, "Jesus, I trust in you!" means very little.

It is in the apostolate that I feel my vow of poverty most strongly. We often live out our material poverty in the classroom because we cannot provide everything we would love to give our students, like extra books or colorful stickers. Many other teachers, who do not live under a vow of poverty, go out of their way to provide some of these extra goodies and resources from their own pockets. But for us, this is not an option.

Other times it is our spiritual poverty that cuts to the heart. So often the children we teach have clear needs that go beyond what one teacher can provide or what one human being can do. In addition to being a teacher, I would need to be a seasoned psychologist and perhaps a few other things to meet every need of the children entrusted to me in my classroom. There are few realizations more humbling than recognizing the needs of the children before you and knowing that you simply cannot meet all of them, or even most of them. In these moments, it is helpful to remember that the Lord did not teach the apostles everything in the three years He walked with them. He sent the Holy Spirit to continue His work in them. The apostolate is a constant reminder that we must live a supernatural life.

But, from our poverty, there are deep and wonderful gifts that we can give our students. Our monastic formation allows us to keep a deeper silence, the better to listen to a child. We listen to the heart of the child—his hopes and desires, his questions— and thus, we become attentive to the heart of God. We can help shape the child into what God created this student to be, what will help him or her reach the fullness of life both in nature and grace. Finally, we can fortify the child for the world outside the safety of the classroom.

We also offer our students the gift of our prayers before the Eucharist every day. There are many questions to pray and ponder over before the Eucharistic Lord every evening, as the to-do list lies unheeded on the pile of ungraded papers. Eventually, all these concerns become an oblation at the feet of the Lord because, in the end, the children are His, and so are we. It is time to give the worries of the day to Him and let tomorrow bring its own worries (see Mt. 6:34).

Chastity: Spiritual motherhood with open arms

When the world looks at our vow of chastity, it often sees only abstinence from sexual pleasure. But the vow of chastity, while it includes this very integral aspect, is not simply a "no." It is a "yes" to a love without limits. Chastity is what makes our love for our Spouse fruitful, and it is what allows our students to be our spiritual children. Unlike natural mothers who can claim something of the heart of their children, for they are indeed flesh of their flesh, the Sister can only love the child as he or she is—pouring herself out, while never actually claiming any part of the heart of the child. She loves with the intention of leading to a higher Love. She sees her Beloved's resemblance in the soul of each baptized child and the beautiful potential of being a beloved child of God in those who are not yet baptized.

The Sister's zeal for souls grows as the relationship of love between her and Jesus grows. The Sister sees a beloved child of God; the child sees, through her, the loving heart of the Church, personi-fied above all in Mary. It is not unusual for a traveling Sister to walk through an airport or a grocery store, or down the street, and overhear a young child referring to her as "Mary." Our students rarely say such things publicly, but when they think we are not watching, they sometimes voice similar sweet sentiments.

When I read to my class or tell them saint stories, I

usually have at least two girls hanging on to my rosary, and occasionally, my scapular. One time, after sharing with the children the gift of wearing Our Lady's scapular and the indulgence attached to my kissing it after I genuflect before the tabernacle, I caught a little girl sheepishly taking a corner of my scapular and kissing it. My scapular has also become the first veil of many students. At recess, vocations are already blossoming: while one group of girls plays "family," another group plays "Sisters." Priestly and Religious vocations in boys are also fostered quite naturally as boys play "Brothers" or "Monks." Religious Brothers are a rarer sight in some of our schools, so sometimes I have to tell the boys that they do not need to use their sweaters as veils, since Dominicans friars have hoods instead of veils. On occasion, the Sisters have had to disband a newly formed "Religious community" when misplaced zeal has resurrected a military order: "Brothers" building shrines and guarding them jealously with sticks. I affectionately called this group the Little Brothers of St. Joseph, Terror of Demons.

OBEDIENCE: RESTING ON THE HEART OF JESUS

Jesus came to serve, not to be served. He did not do His own will but His Father's. Each of the vows—poverty, chastity, and obedience—is a "yes" to the life of our Spouse. Through our vow of obedience, we renounce our will so that Christ can live and work in and through us. This reality manifests itself powerfully on "assignment day." Every spring, often around Easter, the Sisters of our Community are given their assignment for the following year. Usually, each Mission Superior receives the list from the Motherhouse and reads it out loud to her Sisters. We hear the list of assignments with nearly every emotion in our hearts. We try to take in all the other Sisters' assignments while still listening for our own names in the ever-lengthening list. There may be new missions, new grades, new Sisters added to smaller communities, or you may be surprised to find yourself staying just where you have been with exactly the same people.

Assignment time is always full of grace. Underneath the roller coaster of emotions, I have a peaceful sense that really, this is God's will, and I would not have it any other way. He knows what He is doing, and all I have to do is to be obedient to His graces. When Sisters are moved, the goodbyes are difficult. There may be an aspect of "shaking the dust" from time to time (cf. Mt. 10:14), but each location brings special graces offered from Jesus' Heart, and, in this way, each assignment is dear. Each new assignment brings with it a new set of spiritual children and a new openness of heart to what the Lord is doing in me, in those I have grown to love, and in those I will love in the future. The change, though hard, gives new opportunities to let the Lord move in new ways.

Teaching as a Pathway to Holiness

The Liturgy of the Hours— the prayer of the Church that all priests and Religious pray every day—contains a whole set of prayers devoted to saints who were teachers. Teaching is surely a path to holiness! Many teachers, and certainly teaching Sisters, will tell you that managing a classroom provides plenty of opportunities to practice and grow in virtue every day. I remind myself of this often as

I ask eight–year–olds, for the 152nd time that day, to pick up pencils. And this constant growth in virtue is important for the good not only of the Sister but also of the students. If the children are really going to learn anything, it must be conveyed through that greatest virtue, love (cf. 1 Cor. 13:13). The pathway to holiness in the classroom may not be as glorious as the martyrs' journey to the Roman amphitheater, but it does require the same sort of fidelity to lay down your life daily. My greatest moments of teaching come when I am able to step aside interiorly from my own projects and plans and let the Lord and Our Lady teach through me. They know how to care for their little ones far better than I do.

SELF–KNOWLEDGE

Certainly self-knowledge plays an important role in the classroom, where virtues can tested to the breaking point. I used to think I was a patient person. Now I realize I have a long way to go in this virtue. It is a daily struggle in which I am constantly tested. The 3:00 p.m. Hour of Mercy has all sorts of meaning to a teacher, since we both rely on God's mercy in a special way and try to show it to our students. 3:00 p.m. usually falls near the end of the school day—a moment when we most need to remember mercy! This is not the only form of self-knowledge, though. Self-knowledge comes when I notice that all my children need to work on humility...and then realize my own humility could use some work. "You spot it, you got it," as the saying goes. There are also the uncanny ways that children can point out faults. They examine their consciences with greater detail and care than adults generally do, and can, at times, take up examining yours—with surprisingly accurate results!

*I*LLUMINATIVE

The path to holiness through teaching is not all purgation, however. Children can offer magnificent insights into parables and Scripture stories that may have grown stale in their teachers' hearts and minds. Their imagination is God's playground. I once showed a copy of Rembrandt's Return of the Prodigal Son to a group of second graders without telling them what it was. They were simply to "notice" things and try to guess who the people in the picture might be. The children were drawn to the light in such a way that they noticed, not on whom the light was shining but whence it came, from the figure of the father. When I read them the corresponding passage of Scripture, one student came to love it so much that she read it every day, sometimes more than once. Another student drew a picture of Jesus, the *Ecce Homo*. She added in something I have never seen before, a handkerchief with something drawn on it. When I asked her about it, she said, "That is a handkerchief to dry his tears, and that is His mother on it, to comfort Him." She drew a battered, but peaceful Jesus with a black eye that matched the shroud or the veil of Manoppello (thought to be the veil of St. Veronica). When praying with the Scripture passage of the lost sheep during preparation for first Confession, one student drew Jesus going after the lost sheep while Mary looked after the faithful ones. Truly, "out of the mouths of infants and nurslings you have brought forth praise" (Mt. 21:16).

*U*NION

The apostolate of every Community is designed to unite its members to Jesus Christ. Our apostolate of teaching unites us in a special way with the Lord, since we are imitating the very things He did during His time of public ministry. Throughout the Gospel, Jesus is described as teaching, healing, and casting out demons. Elementary teachers not only teach their students, but also help to heal the inevitable hurts of childhood. In many ways, we also safeguard the children from the Evil One as we foster the growth of virtue within them and guide them to follow the Good Shepherd. It is rare that children remember the names of their elementary teachers or what Community a Sister belongs to, but they know and remember that they were loved. They know that they were loved, not with a merely human love, but with a supernatural love beyond what a Sister was capable of giving on her own.

In true surrender of the heart, the apostolate becomes a place of encounter and a place of union with Jesus as He works in and through the Sister for the good of the Church. All vocations, when lived authentically, follow a paschal pattern—a pattern of the passion, death, and resurrection of Jesus. Each vocation has its passion, nails, scourging, but each also has a glimmer of the resurrection and the glory that, through grace, can already be experienced, though not fully. "We are God's children now; but what we shall be has not yet been revealed. We do know that when it is revealed we shall be like him, for we shall see him as he is" (1 Jn. 3:2). So, we seek His face in the children, in our Sisters, in all those we encounter, and most of all in the Eucharist, until we behold Him with faces unveiled.

Chapter 16

They Do It All...
Post-Graduate Studies while Serving in Campus Ministry
—Sr. Miriam Holzman, O.P.

THE OFFER I COULD NOT REFUSE

My vocation to Religious Life was quite unexpected. During my childhood and teen years, the very idea of a vocation never crossed my mind, nor do I recall ever meeting any Sisters. In high school, I had big plans for my future life: get married, have children, obtain a good education, and make a reasonably good salary. Intent on making my plans a reality, I decided on a career in pharmacy and was accepted into a program when I was eighteen years old.

By the time I was twenty-two I had met some important goals: I was a licensed pharmacist earning a very good salary. I paid off my school debt within the first few months of work and began to build up a savings. Although I enjoyed my job and was blessed to be surrounded by loving friends and family, something important seemed to be missing. I was not at peace.

Gradually I came to realize that my very deepest desire was to give everything to Jesus because I loved Him. I wanted to belong completely to Him. I wanted all the moments of my life and all my gifts and talents to be completely dedicated to the Lord. I also began to realize that this desire in my heart was the Lord extending His hand to me, inviting me to the Religious Life. I was aware of my freedom to accept or to decline this invitation. Yet the "offer" seemed so beautiful that I could not imagine turning it down. Furthermore, by this time I knew that I would not have true peace unless I gave myself to God in this way.

God had made me an offer I could not refuse! In my search, I eventually came across the Dominican Sisters of Mary, Mother of the Eucharist and was struck by their joy and by their love for the Church. After visiting the Community on one of the discernment weekends, I knew that this was the Community to which the Lord was calling me. And what was the work of the Community? Teaching. How unexpected! I was going to be a teacher. I had never considered teaching as a career, but now I embraced the prospect wholeheartedly. If this was what the Lord wanted, I was happy to do it. So, at age twenty-four, I entered the convent. Although it was a difficult "leap of faith," I knew that I could trust in the Lord and in His plans for me.

The change in my goals from pharmacy and marriage to Religious Life as a Dominican Sister of Mary, Mother of the Eucharist was quite a shift. Many people had trouble understanding why I would do such a thing. Some thought I was throwing everything away by entering Religious Life. After all, I was young. I had a good job. I had *opportunity*. And why would I go to a teaching order? Some thought it would make more sense if I entered a Community where I could put my hard-earned pharmacy degree to good use.

The difficulty others had in understanding my shift towards the Religious Life was probably compounded by the fact that it was impossible for me to explain what was happening in my spiritual life. How could I put into words the experience of receiving a call from the Lord to become His bride? The Lord was communicating Himself to me in an intimate way, and the deep interior desire I had to give myself to Him was not something that could be easily expressed.

Once I embraced and embarked on the path of Religious Life, I experienced great peace. I was completely free. It might seem that Religious Life seriously *restricts* freedom. And yet, I was, in fact, freer than ever before in my life! The evangelical counsels of poverty, chastity, and obedience enabled me to be completely free to love Him. As a bonus, I soon discovered that I absolutely loved the very important apostolic work of our Community. As a chemistry teacher (I did end up putting my degree to good use), it was a privilege to get to know the students in my classes and to be a witness of the joy that comes from loving God, while teaching them about the properties of matter in our amazing universe.

FROM STUDENT TO TEACHER, AND BACK AGAIN

After four years of teaching, my journey as a Religious took an unexpected turn. I was assigned to pursue a master's degree in philosophy at the Catholic University of America in Washington, D.C.

I really could not picture it. A master's in philosophy? I have to admit, I had real qualms about this field of study. I had never taken a philosophy class in my life. Not only was it quite a departure from my current work as a chemistry teacher, it took me well out of my comfort zone in the sciences. Once again, I had to step out into the unknown!

There was no doubt in my mind that this new assignment was all part of His plan and His will. But even with this assurance, I fully expected challenges. Following Christ unreservedly does not necessarily translate to smooth sailing. After all, Christ asks us to *pick up our cross* and follow Him. Every vocation has its difficulties, and Religious Life is no exception. I knew I would find studies in philosophy difficult. The program required me to complete many units of course work, learn a second language, write a thesis, and successfully complete the comprehensive exams. No, it was not going to be smooth sailing. However, I had great peace about the future.

A HEART TRANSFORMED BY CROSSES

The reason that I experienced peace, despite the daunting project ahead of me, was because I had so consistently seen God transform crosses into something beautiful. Early in my spiritual journey, while I was studying to be a pharmacist, I experienced a period of prolonged physical suffering. This suffering deepened my spiritual life. I came to know and love God more profoundly as a direct result of the suffering. From this cross sprang my desire to give myself completely to the Lord. Once I entered into Religious Life, I could see even more clearly how every cross I encountered transformed my heart, and enabled me to love more deeply and to give myself to God more fully.

Possibly the biggest cross I encountered after entering the convent came during my fourth year as a Religious; I faced the sudden and unexpected death of my father. I felt this loss acutely, and working through the grief was a very long and painful process. I had offered my grief to the Lord on many occasions when I felt particularly sad and had asked Him to use the suffering for good. In hindsight, I can see how this cross, once again, transformed my heart. I became more compassionate and much more able to accompany people in their own joys and sorrows. In fact, in my apostolate of teaching, there were several moments when I actually thanked the Lord that I had an understanding of grief, since it enabled me more effectively to reach out to students and families when they were grieving.

Now facing the potential difficulties of a rigorous academic program, I was confident that the Lord could—and would—bring good out of any new challenges along the way. The key was to keep my eyes on Him, to ask Him to help me with everything, and to entrust myself to the care and protection of the Blessed Mother. I packed up my bags and headed to the Catholic University of America.

THE LIFE OF A SISTER GRADUATE STUDENT

Life as a Religious Sister and graduate student brought with it plenty of opportunities for growth in virtue. Perhaps one of the most frequently asked questions from students was, "Sisters, how do you do it?" Indeed, the other Sisters and I had busy schedules. By 7:30 a.m., when most students were still in bed, we had already had a Holy Hour, Mass, and breakfast. Later in the day, we would continue the contemplative aspect of our daily life by praying Vespers, the Rosary, and Compline together, and making time for spiritual reading. Besides prayers, we Sisters also had our rigorous academic responsibilities to consider. We were, after all, graduate students, with all the demands of graduate level coursework. And, in order to be present to the students, we did our best to attend residence hall programs, campus ministry events, and campus-wide celebrations. Finally, we made sure to spend some time together each day in community recreation. Our days were full, to say the least.

I am certain that, had I "jumped" into this busy schedule, I would have had great difficulty managing everything. It would have been overwhelming. Fortunately, when we enter the convent, we don't immediately "jump in" to life as a Sister in graduate studies on a college campus. There is great wisdom in the Church and in the formation process, which enables Sisters to ease into the life and grow in virtue over time. I had already had ample opportunity to practice orderliness, self-discipline, moderation, and prudence during my time in the novitiate and beyond.

But there is something beyond *human* virtue which assists us in carrying out our day-to-day affairs. This, of course, is the action of grace. Our daily reception of the Eucharist at Mass, daily Eucharistic adoration, and weekly confession all enable us to live Religious Life joyfully on a college campus and balance our various activities. I remember laughing when one student commented, "My dad looked at your horarium on the website, and he says it's not actually humanly possible for you to do all the things you're doing right now on campus." I had often had the very same thought myself. *It is not possible without the grace of God. Nothing about our life is possible without the grace of God.* Actually, I was surprised daily by God's grace and His ability to inspire me, to assist me, to make beautiful whatever I was working on or involved in. I remember being amazed at the way things would come together and the way the Lord would strengthen me to give of myself cheerfully and generously. I did my best to turn to the Lord in prayer, asking for His assistance in all the details of my life, big and small.

Lord, guide me in this talk. Inspire me for this paper. Help me to prepare for this exam. Help me to be generous with my time and my gifts. Strengthen me. Nothing was too trivial to bring to His attention. It was always evident that the Lord was helping me to fulfill the responsibilities of the Religious Life, and this realization brought me peace. The grace of God at work in my life did *not* mean that everything always went according to plan, or that there were never any difficulties. There were, in fact, many challenges along the way. But even these the Lord was able to transform into something beautiful. My job was to keep my eyes on Him, to ask Him to help me with everything, and to entrust to Him all my joys and crosses.

Sisters among the students: Becoming spiritual mothers

Without a doubt, the greatest blessing of living on the campus of Catholic University was the opportunity for spiritual motherhood. Our spiritual motherhood was carried out in ways that I could never have foreseen or imagined. The unique set-up of our role as "Religious in Residence" meant that our group of four Sisters lived right in the residence halls with the freshman girls. The inconvenience of hearing the random stereo blasting was a small price to pay for the chance to be visible, to be available and connected with the girls in our residence halls, and to be able to participate in campus activities. It was in this setting that we were frequently able to exercise our spiritual motherhood in unique and fruitful ways.

As teaching Sisters of Mary, Mother of the Eucharist, we desire to foster virtue in our students. This guidance in virtue is an important component of our spiritual mother-hood. Growth in human virtue requires perseverance, edu-cation, deliberate acts, and God's help. But it is well worth it; virtues lead to union with God and joy in leading a mor-ally good life.

In the classroom, given our roles as instructors, we are able to offer direct instruction in virtue. We teach our stu-dents to identify the good and choose it in concrete action. For example, a teacher explains to children what "patient" acts look like. She can acknowledge students who practice this virtue well and challenge those who struggle with the virtue to improve in that area.

Now that I was no longer in the role of teacher, I wondered whether we "Religious in Residence" would have an effective forum in which to foster the growth of virtue. It turned out that opportunities for instruction in virtue abounded. Sometimes it was explicit: the Sisters were invited to give a talk on virtuous living to a particular group on campus. Sometimes the opportunity was more spontaneous: a student might initiate a one–on–one conversation and candidly seek the Sisters' guidance. However, it became obvious over the course of my time at Catholic University that the Sisters' primary way of helping others grow in virtue was by doing their best to model virtuous living themselves.

LESSONS FROM THE CONVENT ON CAMPUS

Social settings on campus were opportunities for the Sisters to be models of courtesy, kindness, and respect. One student, Sarah, told me that she had struggled with shyness and that this had made meeting new people difficult. Observing the way Sisters mixed and mingled with various new students on campus, however, had given her a model of the virtue of affability, as the Sisters were easy to approach and comfortable initiating conversations with new acquaintances. Seeing the Sisters engage people in this way gave Sarah direction in her own attempts to get to know other students. Eventually, she overcame her shyness by stepping out of her comfort zone, using some of the strategies she had observed in her new friends, the Sisters.

The students also commented on the way Sisters exercise the virtue of gratitude. I have to admit, I had not always had a disposition of gratitude. I can remember my early days as a postulant in the convent and how I had been struck by the frequency with which the older Sisters said, "Thank you." They were constantly making "Thank You" cards for family and benefactors and thinking of creative ways to thank other Sisters who were serving the Community in various ways. One day when I was a postulant, I was relaxing with a group of Sisters, when suddenly another Sister came rushing in from outside to announce that help was needed in the yard. The immediate response to this message was, "Thank you, Sister," especially from the novices who were a year or two ahead of me in Religious Life. As for me, I did not say anything! I did not feel thankful about the prospect of going out to work in the yard, nor did I feel gratitude towards the messenger for relaying this news. However, I was struck by the virtuous response of gratitude from the older Sisters. Whether or not they actually *felt* like going to work outside, I do not know. But they turned it into a joyful event. They snapped into action, smiling and laughing. Their positive spirit was infectious. I soon found myself doing my best to follow their example and tried to express gratitude verbally in moments like this, even when I did not necessarily feel grateful. The beautiful outcome is that, by adopting the external practice of say-ing "thank you," my interior spirit gradually came to align with the words I was speaking. I also became more aware of people who ought to be thanked and developed a genu-ine thankful disposition of mind and heart.

Now that we were at Catholic University, the spirit of gratitude flowed very naturally; it was a habit that had been cultivated and practiced. We were truly thankful for the classes we took. Our education was possible due to the generosity of benefactors, as well to as the University's President who had initiated the "Religious in Residence" program. The Franciscan Fathers and campus ministry staff generously offered their support and assistance with what-ever we needed. Mother Assumpta, our Prioress General, had chosen our group of four Sisters for this wonderful opportunity to study. Every moment at Catholic University was a gift, and we felt tremendously thankful. We culti-vated opportunities to express our gratitude. At Christmas, we set about baking a delectable array of cookies that we distributed to professors and benefactors alike. We would invent "campus ministry appreciation" days and bestow flowers and popcorn on the staff. We put our musical tal-ent and creativity to good use by learning and singing spe-cial songs to thank the many people we encountered in our daily life. We did our best to participate in campus events, hoping to give back by contributing to school spirit. All of these actions flowed from a true disposition of gratitude and brought us great joy. We simply lived it, and our living of the virtue was instructive.

SHEPHERDING SOULS TO GOD

Another aspect of our spiritual motherhood on campus was the opportunity we had to help students know and love God. Leading people to Christ flowed very naturally from the relationships we developed with the students. Our joy was externally visible through our smiles and laughter, and as the students got to know us better, they began to recognize the source of our constant joy: Christ Himself. Here we were, living a life of evangelical poverty, chastity, and obedience, and yet we were obviously happy. We gave witness to the truth that the human heart is made for God, and that God really *can* satisfy the human heart. Our reliance on the Lord, our turning to Him, and the centrality of the Sacraments in our life, all had an impact on the students. They knew that it was the grace of the Sacraments which strengthened and sustained us. As a result of their observations, many were inspired to receive the Sacraments more frequently themselves.

Our unique arrangement of living right on campus truly enabled us to accompany students in the growth and development of their spiritual lives. For one thing, since the chapel the Sisters regularly used was located right in one of the residence halls, students were easily able to join us when we prayed the Liturgy of the Hours. It was a blessing to watch the students learn how to give praise to God by chanting the psalms and develop a more regular and disciplined prayer life. In addition, the wonderful campus ministry program offered many opportunities for students to cultivate their own spiritual lives. With several Masses each day on campus, plus adoration and Confession, the Sacraments were easily accessible. I recall that, on several occasions, I would be on my way to campus ministry's praise and worship adoration, and I would encounter one student or another on the way. The simple invitation, "Would you like to come with me to praise and worship adoration?" was most frequently met with a response such as, "Yes, I could probably really use it." We would then walk together to the chapel, visiting along the way, and, once we arrived, would kneel together in adoration. I would marvel at the fact that my chance encounter with this particular student had led to us kneeling together in adoration. What a privilege to accompany students in such a tangible way, right to the chapel, right to Jesus in the Blessed Sacrament!

On other occasions, the Sisters and I would intentionally reach out to particular students. Our close connection with our neighbors gave us an awareness of students who were struggling and students who desired to grow in their faith. To these souls we would extend a very personal invitation to join us for Mass or adoration. Overwhelmingly, the response was, "Sister, thank you so much for thinking of inviting me!" It seemed so simple to make these invitations and to bring students to Mass and adoration. And yet the ramifications were considerable. The students were always touched in some way by the grace of God when they were in His presence. The Lord Himself would reveal His Love and mercy. It was His work, not ours.

Our presence on the campus enabled us to be accessible to students who were interested in taking steps towards deepening their love for God. Often students sought out the Sisters for help and guidance. "Sister, how do I pray the Rosary? I used to know but I've forgotten," or, "Sister, what do I do during adoration?" were common questions. Students would arrange appointments with us to discuss various aspects of their lives, including growth in the spiritual life. We were able to provide resources that would help them to understand the truths of the faith. There were also those who felt the first promptings of a calling to the priesthood or Religious Life, and we were able to answer questions and offer guidance to these students as well.

One group that I particularly enjoyed spending time with was the RCIA group. These students were actively seeking to deepen their spiritual lives through the reception of the Sacraments of Baptism, Confirmation, and First Holy Communion. We had the blessing of closely accompanying one of these students as he prepared to convert to Catholicism. In the course of attending various campus ministry events, we came to know Michael very well. It was astounding to see him being led by the Lord towards Catholicism. One of his greatest desires was finally to receive the Eucharist at Mass. His excitement grew as the days to the Easter Vigil approached. In fact, we were all counting down! Being present at the Easter Vigil, watching these dear students receive Baptism, was the highlight of the year for all of us. One of the most touching moments for me was when, after Michael received the anointing of the oil in the Sacrament of Confirmation, he turned his head and smiled at the Sisters. The chapel was packed with many of his close friends and family, but at that moment he turned to look at *us*. The Sisters. And we exchanged elated smiles with him. We had accompanied him on his journey of preparation, and we were now truly sharing his joy. That was a moment when I saw, very tangibly, the special bond we had with Michael. I thanked the Lord for the privilege of being a part of his spiritual formation as a spiritual mother. Our relationship with this young man remained strong in the following year as we watched him step into faith-leadership roles on campus and as he began to contemplate the possibility of a priestly vocation.

$\mathcal{A}$ LIVING EXAMPLE OF HARMONY IN COMMUNITY

There is another aspect of the Sisters' Religious Life which had an important influence on the students: our example of communion. The umbrella of what we call "Community life" includes our times of prayer, meals, and recreation. Our Community life, even on campus, takes precedence over other activities. During our two years on campus, there were few times, if any, that a Sister was absent from our time together as a group. Each Sister is totally committed to giving our Community life the highest priority.

The document *Fraternal Life in Community* emphasizes beautifully the special calling Sisters have to give witness to life in communion and fraternal charity:

> As experts in communion, religious are, therefore, called to be an ecclesial community in the Church and in the world, witnesses and architects of the plan for unity which is the crowning point of human history in God's design... Furthermore, through the daily experience of communion of life, prayer and apostolate—the essential and distinctive elements of their form of consecrated life—they are a sign of fraternal fellowship. In fact, in a world frequently very deeply divided and before their brethren in the faith, they give witness to

the possibility of a community of goods, of fraternal love, of a programme of life and activity which is theirs because they have accepted the call to follow more closely and more freely Christ the Lord who was sent by the Father so that, firstborn among many brothers and sisters, he might establish a new fraternal fellowship in the gift of his Spirit.[1]

Authentic communion, toward which our mission at Catholic University sincerely aspired, requires commitment and charity. It entails walking with a Sister in her joys and sorrows by being compassionate, generous, solicitous, and thoughtful. It requires assuming the best intention, forgiving quickly, and solving difficulties patiently. It means interacting with each other in a positive way, even when you are feeling tired or stressed. It is expressed in helping my Sisters' gifts and talents to "shine" by encouraging them and giving them a forum to do so. Our ultimate goal, like any family, is to be of one mind and heart. Indeed, such an objective would seem incredibly daunting if not for the grace of the Sacraments and a solid foundation in a life of prayer. Through Christ, our bonds of fraternal charity are strengthened!

It was apparent that some students lacked examples of people living in joyful communion. Upon starting college life, many of the students found themselves at social gatherings that offered only a "false" sense of communion. It was for this reason that the Sisters' witness of fraternal charity was so important on campus. The students would often see us out and about as a group, talking and laughing. We would set up shop outside with our picnic basket and picnic gear and enjoy lunch together. We would meet for a walk or to play basketball or Frisbee. It was particularly special when we worked together on specific projects. For example, we participated in the campus "Battle of the Bands" as a blues band, complete with sax, trumpet, piano, and bass guitar. It delighted students to see us working together as a team and enjoying one another's company.

I soon noticed that the students not only were aware of our bond of fraternal charity but also greatly appreciated opportunities to enter into our communion. On weekends, for example, we would invite the girls to join us for a game of Ultimate Frisbee. This was an important way for us to build relationships with the girls and spend some extra time with them. In between plays, we would ask, "Tell me where you're from?" or "How are your classes going these days?" We loved the opportunity to get to know them better. I remember one student commenting on a picture taken after a Frisbee match: "It's been a long time since I've seen a picture where the people look so incredibly happy," she had said. Yes, it was true; our time together was uplifting and joyful.

One particular event stands out in my mind as a time of really beautiful communion. On Holy Thursday, we organized a group of students to wash and iron the liturgical vestments and polish all the sacred vessels gathered from the various campus chapels in preparation for the Triduum celebrations. Most of the students had gone home for Easter, but those who remained were happy to help out with the preparations. Although we referred to the event as a "polishing party," a lot of labor was necessarily involved. But, as we worked, we also basked in enjoyment of one another's company. We laughed and visited as we polished and ironed. Everyone seemed at ease because there was no need for pretense.

At the end of the year, I asked a group of girls, "So, what was the highlight of your year?" They responded, without hesitation, that our so-called "polishing party" was the highlight. I was not really surprised. Where there is communion, there is serenity, peace, joy, and belonging. I marveled at the goodness of the Lord; He had truly transformed our time with the students and made it beautiful.

Sr. Miriam: The philosopher scientist

My Sisters and I were able to influence the students on campus positively, but what about my academics? What about jumping unexpectedly into the unknown realm of philosophy from my science comfort zone? To my great surprise, I absolutely loved it. I loved the professors, the discussions, the topics covered. I could see that I was receiving a philosophical foundation which would be a huge asset, no matter where my Religious Life took me. I was not suddenly transformed into a "Philosophy Superstar." But I did my best, and at the same time I was repeatedly astonished by the assistance I received from the Lord to complete the master's degree requirements.

When I entered Religious Life, I never could have foreseen or imagined the many blessings the Lord had in store for me. I never anticipated so many moments for spiritual motherhood, the opportunities for communion with the Sisters, or the depth of peace I found in giving myself to the Lord. Catholic University of America was one stop along the way; it was an unexpected but truly grace-filled stop. There I had encountered exactly the people the Lord meant to for me to know and love. And what a privilege it was. I left Catholic University truly giving thanks to God for my time there, for the joys and challenges, and for His goodness and grace. Lord, thank you for inviting me to the Religious Life!

Simply put, the Church needs more Religious Sisters because the Church and the world need the maternal embrace of the Blessed Virgin Mary. A young woman who consecrates herself completely to Almighty God, does so, in order to embody and to bring Mary's "Fiat," her "yes," into a world that is increasingly becoming more narcissistic and self-centered. Religious women teach us what life is truly about. They have played an integral role in my vocation to the Priesthood of Jesus Christ. As a priest, I look at them as "spiritual mothers" and I call upon them often to pray and intercede for intentions that have been entrusted to me. The "yes" of one consecrated Religious Sister can change the world! I have witnessed that!
—Fr. John Paul Zeller, MFVA—Vocation Director, Franciscan Missionaries of the Eternal Word, and Director of EWTN Pilgrimages

Endnotes

[1] Congregation for Institutes of Consecrated Life and Societies of Apostolic Life. *Fraternal Life in Community*, 10. *Vatican*, February 2, 1994, http://www.vatican.va/roman_curia/congrega tions/ccscrlife/documents/rc_con_ccscrlife_doc_02021994_fraternal-life-in-communiy_en.html

Part 3: From the Heart of the Churc

Chapter 17

Come Share My Joy
–Sr. Ruth Burrows, O.C.D.

> Ruth Burrows is the pen name of Sister Rachel, O.C.D. A Carmelite nun, she lives at Quidenham in Norwich, England. We were able to obtain the gift of this original reflection through Sister's friendship with the Chaplain of the Dominican Sisters of Mary, Fr. Richard Zang, C.S.C.

"Come, beloved of my Father, enter into my joy."

All Christians are called to joy, to Jesus' joy. The sustenance of His life, Jesus tells us, His sole joy was to do the will of His Father, and He died to bring us into His joy. There can be no true and lasting joy outside the Father's will, for all He ordains is directed toward our perfect happiness. Everything our Father wills accords with our deepest truth and with our deepest desires. When the eternal Word whose whole being is from the Father, to the Father, and for the Father, became a human being, He gave as the very purpose of His incarnation: "To do your will, my God" (Ps. 40:9), to be in human nature and human life who and what He is in His eternal Being—the beloved Son of the Father.

The Catholic Church exists for the sole purpose of communicating to every human person the infinite riches of the Risen Christ, of drawing them into His life, of calling them to holiness. Our Baptism has already set us in the Promised Land that is Christ Himself; already we have received the glorious inheritance gratuitously bestowed upon us. Herein is our true joy. This is the land in which we must live, eating its choice fruits and growing into who we are—sons and daughters of God, sharing the very life–sap of our Eternal Father.

Religious are called to live this Christian vocation in a way that both manifests and actually is a living for God alone. Nothing whatsoever, not even the most praise-worthy works of charity, must be allowed to obscure the total gift of mind, heart, body offered to God alone. There is no question of claiming superiority over the secular vocation, the normal Christian vocation—rather, "humbly regard others as more important than yourselves" (Phil. 2: 3)—but of living its deepest reality and meaning in a concentrated, exemplary way. Consecrated Religious Life is one of the many ministries in the Church that is to build up the Body of Christ.

Every Religious has heard the divine invitation: "Come." She has caught, be it even for a moment, the gleam of the priceless Pearl, and has been haunted by its beauty ever since. O how important it is for God, for the Religious themselves, for the Church, and for the world that they guard that precious insight with jealous care and continue steadfastly to believe, to hope, to love, even when perhaps for long, painful periods there is no beauty, no glory to attract their gaze or their hearts, and they are tempted to turn away their eyes (see Is. 53:1-4). "Behold, I come to do your will, O God" (Heb. 10:7). Religious undertake to do all they possibly can to discern God's holy will as it unfolds for them each day and each hour of the day and, recognizing it, to accomplish it with joy. Always, always, always, the intent, the cry of their heart must be, "Not my will, dear

Lord, but Yours; let what You will be done to me and by me." If Religious would be true to their calling, this must be their very way of being.

If we reflect on what are called the evangelical counsels, we see that they represent a total handing over of the human self to God. As human beings, we are born into a fallen world, a world that has chosen self and self-will over and against God; that has refused to recognize its creaturehood and total dependency; that has rejected the God of absolute love. In St. Paul's harsh words, from our birth we are "enemies of God" and our natural orientation is to self, to what I know is good for me, to what I want over and above the needs of others. This basic selfishness is destructive of the person and of society. God is love and we are made in God's image. We are for love and become truly ourselves only when, renouncing self-interest, we go out of ourselves in love for God and for others. The very grave promise to live our whole life long in evangelical obedience, poverty, and chastity can be likened to drastic surgery that, with one cut of the knife, rids the body of a harmful tumor.

The decision to make, and the actual pronouncing of the vows is, alas, only an expression of desire and intent to be rid of self-interest and to be true to our Creator. A lifetime of effort lies before each one. A Religious, as she grows in age and experience, provided she is truly faithful, will discover over and over again the deeper meaning of what she has vowed and its searching demands. Her happiness, her fulfillment as a woman-person will lie in a constant "Yes, dear Lord," to these demands.

Holiness is the most powerful apostolate on earth. A person wholly united to Jesus secretly radiates the light and love of Jesus throughout the Church. Holiness is more powerful in itself than any outward ministry, yet it can never be a personal acquisition. Over and over again we sing: "You alone are the Holy One." We cannot have a holiness of our own that we can be aware of having and in which we can take satisfaction; yet, in practice it would seem that this is little realized. It is doubtful if any earnest seeker has wholly escaped the secret egotistic desire to feel holy; without realizing it, the person becomes more intent in fostering a "spiritual life" than living simply for Jesus, for His Kingdom. Earnest, persevering prayer for light and for the purity of heart of which Jesus speaks will surely uncover this egotism. So subtle is it that it can be renounced only bit by bit as further recesses of spiritual self-seeking come to light.

The holiness of Jesus is there for whoever would enter into it. "Narrow is the gate and straight the way" (see Mt. 7:13-14). We have to divest ourselves as much as we can of our pride and self-will and consistently train ourselves to say "no" to every selfish urge. It means disregarding ourselves as much as we possibly can: "It is You that matter, dear Lord, You and others, not I." This is a labor from which we may never take a holiday. Only God can rid us totally of our inborn selfishness and this He will do if we do all we possibly can.

St. Teresa of Avila urges her daughters to maintain a "most determined determination" never to give up no matter what the difficulties from without or within. How all-important this is! We walk by faith and not by sight. There will be hours of discouragement, of utter weariness and of self-disgust. We must cleave to Jesus, hold on to Him, and never let go of Him, not even for a few minutes. He loves us in our human weakness which, far from alienating us from Him, attracts Him to us. "I know your love will do everything for me and will never disappoint me" could well be the prayer of every consecrated woman, and this her joy in this life.

Chapter 18

Put Out into the Deep:
The Dominican Sisters of Mary, Mother of the Eucharist

RECEIVING THE HUNDREDFOLD

The founding of the Dominican Sisters of Mary, Mother of the Eucharist is a captivating love story that began twenty years ago with a challenge from Pope St. John Paul II. "Vita Consecrata", the Holy Father's 1996 apostolic Letter to Religious throughout the world, summoned Religious Communities to send out their members to begin anew in efforts to revive this vocation. This call resounded in the hearts of four professed Dominican Sisters living in a convent in the Deep South of the United States. Subsequently, they left all—for the second time—to answer the Holy Father's exhortation and God's call.

The first year of 1996–1997 found the Sisters living in a converted barn on an estate in Purchase, New York. Under the direction of John Cardinal O'Connor, then Cardinal Archbishop of New York, they prayed to the Holy Spirit, studied, and labored. In time, their love bore fruit in the Constitutions of a new Community. The Holy Father blessed the establishment of the Community and approved their Constitutions, and the Church bade the Foundresses to "go forth and multiply." Upon the invitation of Bishop Carl F. Mengeling of Lansing, Michigan, they traveled west, arriving in Ann Arbor on the evening of April 4, 1997.

Immediately, they converted a regular house provided by their friend, Mr. Thomas Monaghan, founder of Domino's Pizza, into a convent and, by year's end, they needed more cells—the monastic term for the Sisters' very small rooms. They traded beds for bunk beds as the space quickly filled again with new young women entering the Community.

By 1998 their little convent was bursting at the seams, and construction began on a Motherhouse. It would be built—due to financial constraints—in three phases, with

the assistance and generosity of Tom Monaghan. Each time a phase was finished, the Community had already outgrown its new quarters before even moving into them.

Built on the dreams and sacrifices of our first Sisters and the generosity of many benefactors, the Motherhouse is now too small for the Community's approximately 130

Sisters. All the cells are occupied, and halls, storage rooms, and kitchenettes are variously commandeered as makeshift sleeping areas when the entire Community is home. In the chapel, the Sisters perform elaborate maneuvers to reach their kneelers without bumping into one another. At table, elbow room is a long-forgotten luxury. When the Sisters dispatched around the country and to Rome come home to Michigan for Christmas and short periods of the summer, the Motherhouse is filled to overflowing. More building is being planned across the U.S. to accommodate our growing family. In this, the twentieth anniversary of the Community's history, ground will be broken in Georgetown, Texas, for another large Religious house to hold, eventually, another 115 Sisters.

What is it that attracts so many young women to this Community? Why has God blessed such humble beginnings? The simplest answer is because the Spirit moves wherever He wills. The longer answer is that love always demands a response. The foundation of this Community required a great response of love and heroic sacrifice. Early on, the Foundresses believed God's gift in this new Community would be blessed by both life and Divine love!

A EUCHARISTIC AND MARIAN SPIRITUALITY

The four original Sisters were united by a deep hunger for the Eucharist, for God-with-us and within us, and a desire that He be the heart of all they did. Consequently, from the very beginning, they combined a very active apostolate with contemplation, daily Mass, a daily Eucharistic Holy Hour, and fidelity to the Divine Office. Quite literally, they wrote their hunger for Christ's Body and Blood into the

Constitutions of the Community. The Foundresses firmly established that to be a Dominican Sister of Mary, Mother of the Eucharist, was to have the Eucharistic Heart at the center of one's being.

Perhaps no less important to these Sisters would be contemplating the face of Christ through the eyes of His mother, Mary. As one Foundress expressed it, "It is the Marian response of total self-donation that we have been called to utter, and by which we, too, like Mary, will become icons of Christ." The Foundresses wanted this self-donation to be expressed in three concrete ways. The first is the response of Mary the Virgin, the one who waits for the Spirit's coming and whose whole being becomes an empty vessel open to receive God's Word. The Sisters, too, are called to embrace this paradox of emptiness and fullness. Secondly, the Sisters reflect Mary, Spouse of the Spirit. Marian receptivity is an active response, a perpetual and never-ending "yes" to Love. Similarly, the vocation of each Sister is a single affirmation, continuously expressed in each moment of the day.

Finally, Mary's response is lived as Mother, especially as Mother of the Eucharist. In recent years, many search-ing theological minds have attempted to plumb the depths of Pope St. John Paul II's remarkable *Theology of the Body*. Mary understood and lived that theology in one single word: Motherhood. This is love that encompasses the whole person, a real and tangible love that is not afraid to reach out to the other. It sees beauty in every life, even the life still hidden in the womb. Its vision penetrates beyond appearances to the human dignity rooted in God's image, just as the adorer of the Eucharist penetrates the veils to know Christ's Real Presence. Pope Francis expressed this movingly in a meeting with sick children in Assisi in 2013:

> On the altar we adore the Flesh of Jesus; in the people we find the wounds of Jesus. Jesus hidden in the Eucharist and Jesus hidden in these wounds. But there is something else that gives us hope. Jesus is present in the Eucharist, here is the Flesh of Jesus; Jesus is present among you, it is the Flesh of Jesus.[1]

A mother's love gives and bears another's burdens as her own. She stands at the Cross, a witness to the beauty behind the gift of Christ's Blood. A mother is always faithful: Even after her child has disappeared from sight, and only the empty, bloodied Cross beams remain, a mother waits with faith and hope. The Eucharistic Mother reflects this in a very special way. In his Apostolic Letter *Salvifici Doloris*, Pope St. John Paul II reflects that, on the Cross, Christ is consumed by the intensity of His own love; but He is not alone: A mother's love stands at the heart of His consummation—and therefore at the heart of the Eucharistic mystery that represents that consummation, moment by moment, on altars throughout the world.

Such motherhood is required of a Dominican Sister of Mary, Mother of the Eucharist. These Marian elements, like the Eucharistic ones, find explicit mention and explanation in the Community's Constitutions. Not simply the desire to be Marian but the actual pursuit of its realization is incorporated into the formation of every young woman called to this way of life.

$\mathcal{I}$N THE DOMINICAN TRADITION

Tradition relates that St. Francis used to walk the streets of Europe crying, "Love is not loved, Love is not loved." St. Dominic told his brethren that it was up to them to teach the world how to return love for Love. In fact, the first Dominican novices had only just arrived when St. Dominic sent them back out into the world, fired with zeal for souls and eager to spread the Truth. Our Dominican Community of Sisters, in its turn, was endowed with the Dominican missionary zeal in two unique ways.

The first is the Sisters' charism for teaching. After Vatican II, teaching became, among charisms, the forgotten stepchild. Many Communities turned from this traditional apostolate to social work and initiatives for justice. Our Foundresses felt that the world today suffers most acutely from ignorance and spiritual hunger. Consequently, they established the Sisters as a teaching order within the Dominican family.

The second unique expression of Dominican zeal is a boldness for expansion. Knowing that Religious Life is essential to every diocese, the Foundresses would not be satisfied with a single large convent and mission houses in the surrounding area. Rather, they desired that Religious Life, faithfully renewed and animated by the Second Vatican Council, would once again be visible throughout the United States and beyond. They sought to respond to the needs of the Church in our time. In the twentieth century, as in the thirteenth, Dominican zeal for souls requires each Religious to be both a true contemplative, guarding prayer with monastic practices such as silence and the cloister, and a true apostle, engaging the culture and accompanying her Spouse into the public square.

Furthermore, the Community was founded as a unique response to Pope St. John Paul II's call for the New Evangelization, which he said would come through evangelization that was "new in its ardor, in its methods, in its expression." The Sisters cannot simply live a consecrated life; they have to be able to understand, defend, and communicate it to others in an increasingly secularized society. In short, the Foundresses had truly audacious goals that will continue to be lived out by their spiritual daughters; to be a Dominican Sister of Mary, Mother of the Eucharist, means working toward nothing less than the re-evangelization of the world.

𝒯HE CROSS

In addition to these principles, which have drawn so many young women to give their lives to God in this Community, one final essential ingredient remains. Just as the Church can never forget her founding on Calvary, this new Community cannot cease to be marked by the Cross in which it is rooted. When the Foundresses responded to God's call, they gave the Community not merely the right ideology or a solid structure but their very selves. This self-gift, faithfully learned and practiced through the years of their religious life before God's call in 1997, attains its fullest expression in the founding and continued nurturing of the Community. Their visible witness of sacrificial love is a powerful attraction to many. Young Sisters come and stay because they witness the Cross lived in love.

The Foundresses' self-offering was, and continues to be, joined by the gifts of many others: the bedridden mother who offered her sufferings; the priest who remembered the Community daily in his offering of the Holy Mass; and the white–haired man whose last years became a continual Rosary, the decades limited only by his limitless love as the beads slipped ceaselessly between his fingers. The spirit of the Cross runs through the heart of this Community and, because of that, so does joy—overflowing, abundant, radiant joy!

Send forth Your Spirit

Since the four Foundresses set out "into the deep" in 1997, the single convent has expanded to over twenty missions, with Sisters living and teaching in California, Arizona, Illinois, Ohio, Michigan, Texas, Missouri and elsewhere. One can even spot several Dominican Sisters of Mary, Mother of the Eucharist, in Rome, where they serve as librarians at the North American College. The latest chapter of this great love story includes the building of a large religious house in Texas, where many more young women will be able to respond to God's invitation of love.

In continuing fidelity to Pope St. John Paul II's call for the New Evangelization, the Community has also embraced new apostolic endeavors. Alongside their primary work of teaching, the Sisters catechize at hundreds of other sites and events throughout the year, including vacation Bible schools, conferences and retreats, youth groups, parish missions, and high school and college campus ministry events. The Community has opened its doors to secular media such as Oprah; recorded three chart–topping CDs; published their Disciple of Christ *Education in Virtue* series, along with several books; and even hosted a concert of popular Christian musicians designed to unite Christians in prayer. From the newest postulant to our busiest teaching Sister, every Dominican Sister of Mary, Mother of the Eucharist, seeks, like Mary, to bring Jesus Christ and His Gospel to the world.

Truly the Spirit moves where He wills. Even as the Foundresses toss and turn in the still hours of the night, pleading for benefactors, wondering where to house the young women waiting to join them, and prayerfully keeping vigil over the Sisters' needs and concerns, God must laugh

heartily to Himself. He knows what He is about. He is answering many prayers in this humble beginning. This is His gift and He means to bring it to fruition.

Endnotes

[1] Francis. "Address to the Sick and Disabled Children Assisted at the Seraphic Institute," Vatican, October 4, 2013, https://w2.vatican.va/content/francesco/en/speeches/2013/october/doc ments/papa-francesco_20131004_bambini-assisi.html.

[2] John Paul II. "Address to the CELAM Assembly," trans. Dominican Sisters of Mary. Vatican, 1983, http://w2.vatican.va/content/john-paul-ii/es/speeches/1983/march/documents/hf_jp-ii_spe_19830309_assemblea-celam.html.

During his pontificate, St. John Paul II repeatedly called for this New Evangelization, which aimed to proclaim the faith to "entire groups of the baptized (who) have lost a living sense of the faith, or even no longer consider themselves members of the Church, and live a life far removed from Christ and his Gospel" (*Redemptoris Missio*, 33). That is, he intended the New Evangelization to reach those who live in historically Christian countries, such as the United States.

Chapter 19

And Mary Said "Fiat"
Growing in the Spiritual Life and Suggested Prayers

"Draw near to God, and he will draw near to you."
James 4:8

PART I: GROWING IN YOUR SPIRITUAL LIFE

If you are considering a Religious vocation, you should make an effort to grow in your prayer life. In order for God to speak to your heart, you need to take time to listen to Him. Whatever your vocation is, a deeper prayer life will strengthen you to be the woman you are called to be. Women, in particular, are drawn in prayer to follow the example of Mary, who said, "Behold, I am the handmaid of the Lord. May it be done to me according to your word" (Lk. 1:38) in response to God's invitation of love.

Every baptized person is called to holiness, and to heavenly life with the Blessed Trinity. Consecrated life anticipates that union and becomes a spousal bond here on earth. If you are called to Religious Life, there is nothing better you can do than come to know Christ—your potential Spouse—better. If that is your vocation, your relationship with Him today is the beginning of your relationship with Him in the convent, the same way that the relationship between a married couple began the day they met. If prayer seems difficult, or God seems far away, remember that He is close to you, inspiring in you the very resolution to pray better.

This chapter will provide some general guidelines on prayer and building that relationship. The second part of the chapter will provide you with prayers and devotions that may be helpful as your discern your vocation.

ᵀHE BASICS

There are certain "levels" to a flourishing spiritual life. Before focusing on prayers and devotions specially directed towards helping you discern your vocation, you will want to make sure that you have all of the basic pieces in place. The Catholic Church gives us certain regulations that all Catholics are required to follow. **Church law tells us to attend Mass every Sunday and Holy Day of Obligation, to confess our serious sins at least once a year, and to receive Holy Communion at least once a year.** In her wisdom, the Church realizes that these practices are the bare necessities for the spiritual life. They provide a firm foundation for a prayer life that goes far beyond them. To fall below this minimum is a sin.

Ꮐoing A LITTLE DEEPER

Along with the practices required by the Church, there are some other spiritual practices that should be part of every Catholic's life. Incorporating these practices will support your vocational discernment.

Begin every day by offering your day to God with a morning offering. Starting your day in this way directs all of your works, prayers, sufferings, joys and sorrows to God. We want every moment of our lives to be lived in union with Christ.

End every day with an examination of conscience in which you look back over the day and try to recognize God's presence in every circumstance, thank God for the good you have done, and repent of your sins. As this daily examination becomes a habit, you can start to think about the patterns of sin you see in your life and make concrete plans to break those patterns. Pray for God's help to avoid sin and serve Him. Receive the sacrament of Confession regularly, at least every month. If you are examining your conscience every day, you will not find it difficult to confess your sins frequently.

Spend around fifteen minutes every day reading the Bible or other spiritual books and reflecting on what you have read. Read slowly and carefully. Think of the words you are reading as God speaking to you. Pause occasionally to turn to Him and ask questions or reply. Reading Scripture and other spiritual books helps us get to know the ways of God and thus hear his voice in our own lives. St. Catherine of Siena stated that "knowledge must precede love"; getting to know more about Christ—and our true selves—should lead us to love Him more.[1] Scripture and other reading can help us understand that we can be ourselves before God. For example, we see in the lives of the saints a tremendous variety of personalities and backgrounds. Within Scripture, the Psalms sometimes sing joyfully, but they also freely express tiredness, discouragement and anger, even though they always end with a prayer of trust. He doesn't want us to pretend to be pious and perfect, but honest.

Try to make a retreat every year. Many parishes and dioceses offer special opportunities to take time away from your regular schedule for God. Many Religious Communities also offer retreats. These may be retreats seeking to help you grow in your relationship with Christ more generally, or a vocation discernment opportunity to specifically ask God to help you discover His plan. Our Community provides three weekend retreat opportunities for women discerning their vocation and one weekend for married women.

Pray with your family. A loving family that attends Mass together and shares other devotions such as the Rosary or reading Scripture is one of the greatest incubators of vocations. If you are reading this book because you want to support the vocation of a daughter or friend, know that fostering a prayerful, happy, Catholic home environment provides fertile soil for the seed of Religious and priestly vocations to flourish. A young woman who has left home may find support in prayer in a young adult group, a Bible study group, or just a good group of faithful friends.

Praying through Discernment. According to the *Catechism of the Catholic Church*, prayer is an elevation of the mind and heart to God in praise of His glory.[2] Prayer can be vocal, with exterior words and actions; meditation, where the mind and heart seeks—usually using Scripture, art, or other methods—to understand more of God and what He asks; and contemplative prayer, which can be described as "a gaze of faith," fixed on Jesus, or simply "being" with the Lord.[3] While it may help to set aside times for various kinds of prayer, there is no formula for perfect prayer. Above all, humbly ask God to give you the grace to love Him more.

Fruitful Devotions. As you grow in your prayer life, here are some basic devotions that we recommend to deepen your discernment.

Attend daily Mass and receive Communion. At Mass, you bring all of your trials, fears, hopes, joys, and sufferings to offer to the Father along with Christ's sacrifice. In return, you are given the Body of Christ as the "food for the journey" of your life. If you find praying at Mass difficult, you might pick up a book explaining its meaning. A good place to start is the teaching in the *Catechism of the Catholic Church* about the liturgy. Scott Hahn's *The Lamb's Supper: The Mass as Heaven on Earth* is a good book to help you begin to appreciate the depth of the Mass.

Make a Eucharistic Holy Hour every week or even every day. The Blessed Sacrament is Jesus' Real Presence here with us. He wants to welcome us and fill us with the light of His presence. Sometimes it is good just to sit or kneel before the Blessed Sacrament, quietly basking in His love. Tell Him all of your troubles. Go through a list of all of those whom you love, asking Him for His blessings for them. Many people find that thoughtfully reading the Scriptures in front of Jesus in the Eucharist is a powerful experience, reading "the Word before the Word." A final idea regarding Eucharistic adoration comes from another Sister, who recalled choosing to go and spend time with Jesus in the dorm chapel when her roommate was spending time with her boyfriend. She thought she should give as much time to developing her relationship with Jesus as the roommate did with her future husband.

Mary is the model for every woman Religious as well as for every mother of a family. She looks on you as her daughter. She wants to help lead you along the path which Jesus has planned for your life. There are many ways to cultivate devotion to Mary. Some of these are: praying the Rosary, making a pilgrimage to a Marian shrine, and attending

Mass on Saturday in her honor. There is a tradition of praying three Hail Marys every day for the light to know your vocation and the strength to follow it.

Many Catholics deepen their relationship to Mary by consecrating themselves to her. **Marian consecration** is a way of uniting oneself more closely to Christ and is often called "consecration to Jesus through Mary." Mary is the Mother and foremost member of the Church, so consecrating yourself to her is a way of entering more fully into the family of the Church. It involves making a deeper commitment to living your baptismal vows in imitation of Mary's immaculate holiness and total availability to God. There are several books that can guide you through a Marian consecration including Fr. Michael Gaitley's *33 Days to Morning Glory*, St. Louis Marie de Montfort's *Preparation for Total Consecration*, or *Totus Tuus: A Consecration to Jesus through Mary* by Fr. Brian McMaster.

It may be helpful for you to devote some of your spiritual reading time to the history and spirituality of different Religious Communities. Choose books about saints from the Religious Communities that interest you, or about holy men and women who shared the challenges that you are experiencing. Several Sisters in our Community were drawn to Dominican life by the figure of St. Dominic. Try to meet the great Religious saints. Ask for their intercession while you read about their lives. In addition to asking Jesus what path He has in store for your life, you are also asking the founders and saints of the Religious orders to help you become a member of their families. St. Catherine of Siena realized that she had a Dominican vocation after a dream in which St. Dominic offered her the habit!

It can also be helpful to read the lives of modern women who gave their lives to Christ. For example, Mother Angelica is a recent influential figure in the Church who had to fight for independence from her mother so that she could follow God's call. She also wrote her mother some beautiful explanations of the spousal nature of Religious Life.

Making the Stations of the Cross is a beautiful way to deepen your love of Christ. Meditating on Christ's passion will give you strength to follow Him. It will help you see the value your sufferings have when they are united to His. You can make the stations with a "visual" focus, by walking around a church which has the images of the fourteen stations, spending a few moments gazing at each station. You can also use a prayer book that offers meditations to read. No Religious who has a faithful love of the passion of Christ will ever stray from her vocation.

As you come to feel connected to a Religious Community or tradition, **allow your devotion to be shaped by the charism of that Community.** If you enter a Community, you will be joining a family. Take an interest in the customs and traditions of your future family. Usually the spiritual heritage of the Community to which you are called will "match" your prior devotions in some ways, but will also give you many new treasures. Be open to these. Many Sisters had never or only very rarely prayed the Divine Office before entering our Dominican Community, but fell in love with the Dominican way of chanting the prayers. Now they can scarcely imagine life without it!

PRAYERS

As you are learning how to pray and deepening your relationship with Christ, you will often just have a conversation with Him, telling him about your desires, your joys, your struggles, and your fears. There are no wrong words in prayer. God knows your heart and the gifts that He has given you. However, the Christian tradition has also given us many "tried-and-true" prayers—including many to Mary, our Mother—that may help you establish a consistent prayer life, which will serve you well when you are distracted or can't seem to find the right words.

Prayers to the Most Holy Trinity ▬▬▬▬▬▬▬▬▬

Come Holy Spirit

Come Holy Spirit, fill the hearts of your faithful
and kindle in them the fire of your love.
Send forth Your Spirit, and they shall be created,
and You shall renew the face of the earth.
O God, who by the light of the Holy Spirit,
did instruct the hearts of the faithful,
grant that by the same Spirit,
we may be truly wise
and ever rejoice in His consolation,
through Christ our Lord. Amen.

Morning Offering

O Jesus, through the Immaculate Heart of Mary,
I offer you my prayers, works, joys, and sufferings of this day
for all the intentions of your Sacred Heart,
in union with the Holy Sacrifice of the Mass throughout the
world, in reparation for my sins, for the salvation of souls,
and the intentions of my relatives and friends,
and in particular for the intentions of the Holy Father.

Anima Christi

Soul of Christ, sanctify me.
Body of Christ, save me.
Blood of Christ, inebriate me.
Water from the side of Christ, wash me.
Passion of Christ, strengthen me.
O Good Jesus, hear me.
Within your wounds hide me.
Permit me not to be separated from you.

From the wicked foe, defend me.
At the hour of my death, call me
And bid me come to you,
That with your saints
I may praise you forever and ever. Amen.

⁓ Fatima Prayer ⁓

My God,
I believe, I adore, I hope, and I love You.
I ask pardon of You for those who do not believe,
do not adore, do not hope, and do not love You.

(The Fatima prayer was taught to the three Fatima Children by an angel. The children were told to repeat the prayer three times while kneeling with their foreheads touching the ground.)

⁓ The Divine Mercy Chaplet ⁓

1. Make the Sign of the Cross and pray one Our Father

Our Father, who art in Heaven, hallowed be Thy name. Thy Kingdom come, Thy will be done, on earth as it is in heaven. Give us this day our daily bread, and forgive us our trespasses, as we forgive those who trespass against us. And lead us not into temptation, but deliver us from evil. Amen.

2. Pray one Hail Mary

Hail Mary, full of Grace; the Lord is with thee.
Blessed art thou among women,
and blessed is the fruit of thy womb, Jesus.
Holy Mary, Mother of God,
pray for us sinners,
now and at the hour of our death. Amen.

3. Pray the Apostles' Creed

I believe in God, the Father Almighty,
Creator of heaven and earth;
and in Jesus Christ, His only Son, our Lord,
Who was conceived by the Holy Spirit,
born of the Virgin Mary;
suffered under Pontius Pilate,
was crucified, died and was buried.
He descended into hell;
the third day He rose again from the dead;
He ascended into heaven,
is seated at the right hand of God the Father Almighty;
from there He will come to judge the living and the dead.
I believe in the Holy Spirit, the Holy Catholic Church,
the communion of Saints, the forgiveness of sins,
the resurrection of the body, and life everlasting. Amen.

4. To start each decade, pray The Eternal Father

Eternal Father, I offer you the Body and Blood, Soul and
Divinity, of your dearly Beloved Son, our Lord, Jesus Christ,
in atonement for our sins, and those of the whole world.

5. On the ten small beads, pray:

For the sake of His sorrowful Passion,
have mercy on us, and on the whole world.

6. Repeat steps four and five for each decade.

After completing the fifth decade, pray three times:

Holy God, Holy Mighty One, Holy Immortal One,
have mercy on us, and on the whole world.

Prayers to Our Blessed Mother ▬▬▬▬▬▬▬▬▬▬▬▬▬▬

Vita Consecrata tells us that "A filial relationship to Mary is the royal road to fidelity to one's vocation and a most effective help for advancing in that vocation and living it fully."[4] Mary will always lead us to Jesus; she is also a model for every woman's heart. Here are some prayers to the Blessed Mother you may want to memorize, or use this book, to pray.

⊰⊱ The Rosary ⊰⊱

How to Pray the Rosary

Although different groups pray the Rosary with slight variations, here is the most common method for praying the Rosary:

1. Make the Sign of the Cross and pray the Apostles' Creed

I believe in God, the Father Almighty, Creator of heaven and earth; and in Jesus Christ, His only Son, our Lord, Who was conceived by the Holy Spirit, born of the Virgin Mary; suffered under Pontius Pilate, was crucified, died and was buried. He descended into hell; the third day He rose again from the dead; He ascended into heaven, is seated at the right hand of God the Father Almighty; from there He will come to judge the living and the dead. I believe in the Holy Spirit, the Holy Catholic Church, the communion of Saints, the forgiveness of sins, the resurrection of the body, and life everlasting. Amen.

2. Pray the Our Father

Our Father, who art in Heaven, hallowed be Thy name.
Thy Kingdom come, Thy will be done, on earth as it is in heaven.
Give us this day our daily bread, and forgive us our trespasses,
as we forgive those who trespass against us.
And lead us not into temptation, but deliver us from evil. Amen.

3. *Pray three Hail Marys*

   Hail Mary, full of Grace; the Lord is with thee.
   Blessed art thou among women,
   and blessed is the fruit of thy womb, Jesus.
   Holy Mary, Mother of God,
   pray for us sinners,
   now and at the hour of our death. Amen.

4. *Pray the Glory Be*

   Glory be to the Father, and to the Son, and to the Holy Spirit;
   as it was in the beginning, is now, and ever shall be,
   world without end. Amen.

5. *Announce the first mystery (see next page) and pray the Our Father.*

6. *Pray ten Hail Mary's (while meditating on the mystery).*

7. *Pray the Glory Be.*

8. *Announce the second mystery, and pray the Our Father.*
   (Repeat steps six and seven, and continue with the third,
   fourth, and fifth Mysteries in the same way.)

9. *After completing the fifth Mystery, pray the Salve Regina or Hail, Holy Queen.*

Hail, Holy Queen

   Hail, holy Queen, Mother of Mercy! Our life, our sweetness,
   and our hope! To thee do we cry, poor banished children of
   Eve. To thee do we send up our sighs, mourning and weeping
   in this valley of tears. Turn then, most gracious advocate,
   thine eyes of mercy toward us, and after this, our exile, show

unto us the blessed fruit of thy womb, Jesus. O clement, o loving, o sweet Virgin Mary.

Pray for us, O holy Mother of God, that we may be made worthy of the promises of Christ.

Mysteries of the Rosary

The Five Joyful Mysteries
> The Annunciation (Lk 1:26-38)
> The Visitation (Lk. 1:40-42)
> The Nativity (Lk. 2:8-7, Mt. 1)
> The Presentation (Luke 2:22-35)
> The Finding of Jesus in the Temple (Luke 2:41–52)

The Five Luminous Mysteries
> The Baptism in the Jordan (Mt. 3:13-17)
> The Wedding at Cana (Jn. 2:1-2)
> The Proclamation of the Kingdom (Lk. 7:48-49)
> The Transfiguration (Mt. 17:1-8)
> The Institution of the Eucharist (Mt. 26:26-28)

The Five Sorrowful Mysteries
> The Agony in the Garden (Lk. 22:39-46)
> The Scourging at the Pillar (Mt. 27:26)
> The Crowning with Thorns (Mk. 15:20-21)
> The Carrying of the Cross (Luke 23:26-32, John 19:16-22)
> The Crucifixion (Jn. 19:25-30)

The Five Glorious Mysteries
> The Resurrection (Jn. 20:1-9)
> The Ascension (Acts 1:9-11)
> Pentecost (Acts 1:13-14, 2:1-4)
> The Assumption (Lk. 1:46-49)
> The Coronation (Rev. 11:19-12:1)

~∾~ The Memorare ~∾~

Remember, O most gracious Virgin Mary, that never was it known that anyone who fled to thy protection, implored thy help, or sought thine intercession was left unaided. Inspired by this confidence, I fly unto thee, O Virgin of virgins, my mother; to thee do I come, before thee I stand, sinful and sorrowful. O Mother of the Word Incarnate, despise not my petitions, but in thy mercy hear and answer me. Amen.

Praying with Scripture: Lectio Divina

Lectio Divina is Latin for "sacred reading." Rather than just reading, however, it is a meditative and contemplative prayer using a text, most often Sacred Scripture. Many people start *Lectio Divina* by using the Gospel of the day's Mass; these readings can be found online.

Begin by asking the Holy Spirit to open your heart to receive the Word. *Lectio Divina* traditionally has four steps, and we've included some questions that may help you enter into the prayer.

Step 1: Reading (Lectio)

Slowly read a short Scripture passage. You might go back and read it more than once. **What does the biblical text say in itself?**

Step 2: Meditation (Meditatio)

Ponder the Scripture passage. Consider the passage from different angles. **What does the biblical text say to us? What does the Gospel passage reveal about the Person of Jesus Christ?**

Step 3: Prayer (Oratio)

Talk to God about what He is saying through the Word. Ask Him what it means for you. **What do we say to the Lord in response to His Word of mercy and love?**

Step 4: Contemplation (Contemplatio) and Action

After spending time in silence and receiving, consider how God is calling you to act. **What conversion of mind, heart, and life is He asking of me? How is my life a gift of self for others in charity?**

A Prayer for Vocations

O God, You sent Your Beloved Son, Jesus Christ, to bring eternal life to those who believe. The harvest is ready; send forth laborers, O Lord, for the salvation of souls. May Your Holy Spirit inspire men and women to do the Father's will within the heart of the Church through the priesthood, diaconate, Religious Life and lay ministry. Please, Holy Spirit, make Your will known for my life and give me the courage to live it with love and fidelity. Mary, Mother of Vocations, pray for me. Amen.

A final word: Pray as you can

When you are having difficulty praying, it might simply be a time of dryness, but you also might need to make some changes. A Benedictine Abbot, Dom Chapman, coined the phrase: "Pray as you can and do not try to pray as you can't."[5] If you are starting the beautiful adventure of a life of prayer, but can't get through a whole Rosary, pray a decade between each class or task. If you can't sit still for an entire Holy Hour, start by making quick visits at the Newman Center, or stopping in for fifteen minutes at the end of the work day. If you are struggling to just "be" with the Lord, bring a book or pray a litany slowly. God desires even your weakness.

Although God may give special graces and a burning desire for prayer, for many people, it takes a long time to build up that relationship in self–giving prayer. Trust that He loves you and desires your holiness, far more than you know.

Endnotes

1 Catherine of Siena, "A Treatise of Divine Providence," *The Dialogue of St. Catherine of Siena*, trans. Algar Thorold, 1906, accessed on line, https://www.ewtn.com/library/SOURCES/CATH DIAL.HTM.

2 *Catechism of the Catholic Church*, 2nd. ed. (Washington, DC: United States Catholic Conference, 2000), Glossary, p. 894.

3 *Catechism of the Catholic Church*, 2700–2719.

4 John Paul II, "Vita Consecrata," 28, *Vatican*, http://w2.vatican.va/content/john-paul-ii/en/apost_exhortations/documents/hf_jp-ii_exh_25031996_vita-consecrata.html.

5 Dom John Chapman, *The Spiritual Letters of Dom John Chapman, O.S.B.*, (New York: Sheed and Ward, 1935), 109.

Glossary

Apostolate: This refers to the work one does as a Religious. Apostolates are as varied as there are needs in the Church, including teaching, preaching, nursing, and, for strictly cloistered Religious, prayer.

Asceticism: All Christians are called to practice asceticism, or self-discipline through practices of self-denial. This call to asceticism is especially urgent for Religious.

Benedictines: A monastic order founded by St. Benedict of Nursia in the fifth century. St. Benedict's rule of life famously revolves around *ora et labora*, or "prayer and manual labor."

Breviary: Sometimes called an "office book," the breviary contains all of the Psalms, readings, and prayers of the Liturgy of the Hours.

Canon law for Religious: Canon law contains the juridical norms which govern the practices of the Church. Specific laws are addressed to consecrated Religious, such as the requirements for the vow of poverty and necessary spiritual practices.

Carmelites: Later reformed by St. Teresa of Avila in the 16th century, the Carmelites trace their history to a group of monks who established the eremitic life on Mount Carmel in the Holy Land around the year 1200. Carmelite Nuns and Friars claim the prophet Elijah as their spiritual father and lead a life dedicated to prayer and contemplation.

Cell: The monastic cell is the private room of a Religious, simply furnished, where he or she can pray to the Father in secret.

Chastity, vow of: By the vow of chastity, the Religious freely forgoes marriage and the goods of marriage for the sake of a deeper spousal relationship with Christ. For women Religious, this union flows into a spiritual motherhood toward those whom she serves.

Charism: Refers to a specific grace given to an individual or group for the building up of the Church. Examples include preaching, teaching, and healing.

Cloister: An area within a convent that is reserved for the sole access and use of Religious. The cloister serves as an invaluable safeguard both for the vows and for the spirit of prayer and recollection.

Common life: Also referred to as Community Life. A Religious shares her day-to-day existence with her fellow Sisters. Typically this includes common times of prayer, meals, and recreation.

Consecration: An object or person becomes consecrated when set aside for a sacred purpose. In the case of the Religious, this takes place at the moment of profession of vows.

Constitutions: The governing documents of a Religious congregation. Constitutions articulate how a particular charism is to be lived with integrity. Religious profess their vows in accordance with the Constitutions of their specific institute.

Contemplation: Deep union with God in prayer. Canon law for Religious identifies contemplation as the "first and principal duty" of all Religious (*CIC* §663).

Convent: The house where Religious reside, typically placed under the patronage of a saint or named after a title of the Blessed Virgin Mary. A Dominican convent includes a chapel, a refectory, cells, and gathering spaces.

Discernment: The process of hearing and understanding God's will in any particular instance. Above all, discernment is necessary to know and accept one's vocation.

Dominicans: Established by St. Dominic de Guzman in the thirteenth century as the Order of Preachers. Dominican Friars, Nuns, and Sisters live a life dedicated to the contemplation and preaching of divine truth.

Enclosure: Whereas all Religious houses have cloistered portions, the practice of enclosure is exclusive to contemplative Communities, whose entire convent or monastery is cloistered. A classic image of enclosure is the "grille" or grated screen which separates a Nun from guests in the parlor.

Evangelical counsels: The evangelical counsels are poverty, chastity, and obedience. These counsels are lived in imitation of Jesus Christ, who was the first to live poor, chaste, and obedient to the Father.

Extern: In Communities with the practice of enclosure, one or two Religious may be given charge of temporal affairs and interactions with the world outside the enclosure. These Religious are called Externs.

Formation: The program and process by which a Religious learns and internalizes her identity within the spirituality and charism of her specific institute.

Formation, human: The particular aspect of Religious formation aimed at developing the character of the Religious. While not imposing a mold, human formation acknowledges that "grace builds on nature," and that our fallen human nature often needs purification through guidance and experience.

Formator: The Formator is the individual Religious who holds chief responsibility for the direct formation of the young Religious entrusted to her. This term is typically applied to those working with Religious not yet perpetually professed. Examples include the Novice Mistress and Postulant Assistant.

Franciscans: Perhaps the most well-known Religious order, the Franciscans were established by St. Francis of Assisi in the thirteenth century. The sons and daughters of St. Francis live a life in imitation of the Poor Christ.

General chapter: Periodically, a Religious congregation holds a general chapter at which major superiors are chosen and significant matters of the congregation are discussed and determined. The frequency of these meetings is set by the congregation.

Great/profound silence: The practice of many Religious congregations, especially those of monastic origin, to observe absolute silence for a determined number of hours each evening. In most cases, this begins in the late evening and ends early in the morning.

Habit: The outer garment of a Religious, which reflects his or her identity as belonging solely to God. The habit's appearance differs from one Religious Community to another.

Institute, religious: Any entity in which members publically profess the vows of poverty, chastity, and obedience lived out in a common life.

Institute, diocesan: A Religious institute placed under the authority of a particular bishop, rather than the Holy Father directly.

Institute, pontifical: Religious institute placed under the direct authority of the Holy See.

Liturgical cycle: The feasts and seasons which make up the Church's prayer life. Religious especially seek to enter into the liturgical cycle through the observance of feasts and solemnities as well as the liturgical seasons of Advent, Christmas, Lent, and Easter.

Liturgy of the Hours: Also known as the Divine Office, the Liturgy of the Hours is the official prayer of the Church. Made up of hymns, psalms, readings, and intercessions, the faithful recitation of the Liturgy of the Hours is a privileged duty for all Priests and vowed Religious.

Mendicancy: Referring to the practice of begging for one's daily sustenance, the mendicant life became widespread in the thirteenth century with the birth of the Franciscan and Dominican orders.

Mission: A satellite house of any Religious congregation, apart from the Motherhouse. Mission houses are typically smaller both in size and in number of Religious in residence.

Monasticism: The monastic life originated with the desire for a life apart from the world, dedicated to God. Monasticism is accompanied by a variety of external practices, such as silent meals and custody of the eyes, aimed at fostering a greater spirit of prayer.

Motherhouse: As the name suggests, a Motherhouse may be the founding house of a Religious congregation or the official residence of the Major Superior.

New Evangelization: The call of Pope St. John Paul II for Christians to re-evangelize their own lands and nations. Many younger Religious institutes were established as a response to this call, including the Dominican Sisters of Mary, Mother of the Eucharist.

Novice: From the Latin word for "new." A novice is in the initial stages of Religious formation and is typically focused on the study of the vows and integration into the spirit of the institute.

Novice Mistress: The individual Religious who is tasked with guiding the novices.

Novitiate: The residence wherein the novice mistress resides with the novices. The novitiate may be attached to, or separate from, the Motherhouse.

Nun: The term "Nun" properly refers to enclosed, cloistered Religious but is sometimes used colloquially to describe any Religious Sister.

Obedience, vow of: By the vow of obedience, the Religious binds herself to carry out all legitimate requests of her lawful superiors, in imitation of Christ who was obedient to the Father. By this means, the Religious has the certainty of accomplishing God's will.

Perfectae Caritatis: The title of a document from the Second Vatican Council; its English title is "On the Up to Date Renewal of Religious Life." In this document, the Council Fathers invited Religious institutes to exercise a creative fidelity in returning to the original charism of their Founder or Foundress.

Postulancy: Sometimes called an aspirancy, this is the time before an individual becomes a novice. A time of transition from the world and of deeper discernment, the postulancy may last from a few months to up to a year.

Poverty, vow of: By the vow of poverty, a Religious renounces the right to dispose of material goods and possessions. All items received by the Religious are considered the goods of the Community.

Profession, vows of: The act of binding oneself to the practice of the evangelical counsels. In Religious institutes this is done as a public act, witnessed by the Church. Profession may be temporary or perpetual.

Profession, temporary: The profession of vows for a temporary and explicitly stated amount of time. The duration of temporary vows may differ by religious institute.

Profession, perpetual: The profession of the evangelical counsels in perpetuity.

Religion, virtue of: The virtue of religion is the disposition to give God what is His due. Some acts that fall under the virtue of religion include prayer and adoration, gratitude to God for His many gifts, participating in the Holy Sacrifice of the Mass, and the fulfillment of vows by those who profess them.

Rule: The founding charter and chief governing document of a Religious order. All Constitutions have their origins in the specific Rule of the Religious institute.

Scapular: A garment consisting of two long rectangular pieces of cloth attached over the shoulders. Often blessed, the scapular is a reminder of the obedience which the Religious has professed.

Superior, Local: The individual Religious invested with authority by the major superior to govern a smaller house of the institute.

Superior, Major: A Religious whose authority extends over the entirety of the institute.

Spouse of Christ: By professing the evangelical counsels, the woman Religious exchanges intimacy with a human husband for a spousal union with Christ.

Veil: The garment worn on the head by women Religious as a sign of their consecration. In many cases, a white veil indicates that the woman is a novice, while a black veil indicates she has professed her vows.

Vita Consecrata: A post-synodal exhortation promulgated in 1997 by Pope St. John Paul II after the Synod on Consecrated Life, in which Religious Life is viewed through the icon of the Transfiguration.

Vocation: From the Latin word for "call," one's vocation is the unique, loving way in which God calls the individual to achieve holiness in this life. Like the pearl of great price, one's vocation is freely given and yet hidden. A listening heart hears and responds to this call.

Vow: A Deliberate, free promise made to God regarding a higher good that is possible to attain. Once a vow is professed, its fulfillment binds according to the virtue of religion.

Acknowledgments

The writing of a book is a formidable undertaking for a busy Religious Community of professional teachers and pray-ers. Yet when I read Fr. Brett Brannen's widely popular *To Save a Thousand Souls*, I was immediately struck by the fact that women, too, need inspiration and information about possible Religious vocations. In my many years as Vocation Directress, I have often been asked for a book that might fill the same niche for young women. Priests often ask me for "pointers" for youth with questions about Religious consecration, and yet resources are rare. Yes, the Church needs such literature. Young women deserve it.

First off, I wish to thank Mother Assumpta Long, O.P., Prioress General of the Dominican Sisters of Mary, Mother of the Eucharist. Without her leadership and support, this book would not have been written. I also wish to thank the other Foundresses of our twenty-year-old Dominican Community, Sr. John Dominic Rasmussen, O.P., and Sr. Mary Samuel Handwerker, O.P. They, along with myself, heard God's call to "walk on water" and, with that first step, we were swept off our feet—and have been ever since!

The table of contents reveals the Sisters in my Community whose sacrificial efforts bore fruit in each chapter's unique perspective on our vocation. Beyond this, I wish to thank all my Sisters, because every endeavor we undertake becomes a communal intention for prayer and sacrifice. Certainly, gratitude is due to the various friends—priests, Sisters, and laity—who shared their perspective on the need for more Sisters in today's world. And to Sr. Ruth Burrows, O.C.D., our heartfelt gratitude for her addition.

A host of others deserve great thanks. Sr. Irenaeus Schluttenhofer, O.P., my remarkable assistant in the vocations office, not only keeps up with my creative ideas but surpasses me with her computer skills, her editing abilities, her goodness, and, certainly, her patience! Much appreciation also to Sr. John Dominic, O.P., Linda Kelly, and Amy Beers for behind-the-scenes layout and publishing. These three corroborate the truism that, if you want to get something done, entrust it to busy people. And of course, it is to Christ and His Mother that we must give all the glory. *Deo gratias.*

Perhaps it is fitting to end my Litany of Thanks with a quote from Fr. Brett Brannen, whom the Holy Spirit used to inspire the book you now hold in your hands:

> There is nothing more inspiring than to see a beautiful, young religious Sister walking around the parish with her habit and rosary gently blowing in the wind. Witnessing this, people instinctively experience that profound truth in their own souls: "Jesus is the answer; the only answer to which every human heart is the question" (Pope St. John Paul II). Religious Life has always been and must always be an essential part of the Catholic Faith. Because of Original Sin, there are so many things in our world that bring us down. Religious Sisters, with their beauty, holiness and joy, bring us all up!